HUMMINGBIRDS

My Tiny Treasures

HUMMINGBIRDS
My Tiny Treasures

BY ARNETTE HEIDCAMP
With drawings and photographs by the author

This edition consists of three books:
A Hummingbird in My House: The Story of Squeak
Rosie: My Rufous Hummingbird
Hummingbirds: My Winter Guests

Crown Publishers, Inc.
New York

This edition consists of three books:
A Hummingbird in My House: The Story of Squeak
  (Copyright © 1991 by Arnette Heidcamp)
Rosie: My Rufous Hummingbird
  (Copyright © 1995 by Arnette Heidcamp)
Hummingbirds: My Winter Guests
  (Copyright © 1991 by Arnette Heidcamp)

Published by Crown Publishers, Inc.,
201 East 50th Street, New York, New York 10022.
Member of the Crown Publishing Group.

Random House, Inc. New York,
Toronto, London, Sydney, Auckland
www.randomhouse.com

CROWN is a trademark and the Crown colophon is a
registered trademark of Random House, Inc.

Printed in China

Design by Jennifer Harper and Mercedes Everett
Spot illustrations by Jennifer Harper

ISBN 0-609-50245-X

10 9 8 7 6 5 4 3 2 1

First Edition

1

How It All Began

October 20, 1988—that was to be the night to finish cutting back the fuchsias; killing frost was expected and temperatures would be dipping into the twenties. The fuchsias are grown and wintered over from year to year for the hummingbirds. I've always hated cutting them back and getting them ready for their dormant period because it means discarding perfectly beautiful flowers, but it had to be done and I had decided it was definitely time.

The prior week I had done some major pruning, getting ready for the move back indoors. *Salvia greggii*, even though it still had hundreds of blossoms, had to be cut back. Likewise the flowering maple (*Abutilon* hybrid), Island snapdragon (*Galvezia speciosa*), lantana, Chinese hibiscus, Chilean

jasmine, and a *Mimulus puniceus* hybrid. Many were
to be moved to a cool place where they would
receive a winter dormancy period. Others, such as
the orchids, would be spending the winter in the
sunroom.

The majority of my plants are grown with
hummingbirds in mind. From early May through
late September, while the hummingbirds are here,
my time is spent watching, photographing, and
just enjoying them. The rest of the year is devoted
to getting plants ready for the hummingbirds when
they return the following spring—seeds are started
for annuals, cuttings are taken from some plants,
and tender perennials are cut back to begin anew.
The last bird to have left this year did so on
October 3 and as much as I wished it weren't, the
season was definitely over.

The next morning I went outdoors, as I always do, for my early-morning ritual of putting
seed in the bird feeders, changing the water in the
birdbaths, and feeding a couple of stray cats. For
some reason, my eyes drifted over to a patch of
what had been *Salvia coccinea*. There were one or
two remaining flowers behind leaves that had not
been frosted the night before. I had to look twice—I
thought I had seen a hummingbird. Then it appeared at what had been a patch of flowering
tobacco. I couldn't believe my eyes, it was October 21 and all hummingbirds should have long
been gone from this area. They generally leave

Upstate New York by late September or very early October at the latest, and the last date I've ever had one here has been October 10. I looked around and assessed the yard. The only flowers that were in a viable condition were the mums. I immediately dropped what I was doing, went into the house, prepared a nectar solution, and hung a feeder outside for the hummingbird. The bird flew into the lath house, a latticework structure used to house plants outdoors during the summer, and seemed to be looking around in the space where fuchsias had been the day before. My guess was that this was not its first visit to my yard but, since I had not seen it before, I figured that it had been here only for the one previous day.

I hung a four-flowers–type feeder filled with the nectar solution right behind the house where I was sure the bird would see it and placed a couple of flowering plants brought back outside near the feeder to entice the bird closer to it. I had no plan, I was merely concerned about the hummer having something to eat. The bird approached the feeder but obviously did not know what to do with it. It then visited the bouvardia plant and went back into the lath house looking, apparently, for the plants that had been there the day before. The poor thing must have been terribly hungry. What I noticed immediately about the bird was that it wasn't fat as they always are when they are ready to leave. This bird was not ready for migration and

The new arrival.
With all the spotting
on its throat and chin,
I knew it was a male.

the paltry amount of flowers that my garden had to offer was never going to be enough to sustain it while it fattened up and got ready to start its trip.

Certainly if the flowers in my garden were frosted, this bird would not be faring much better anyplace else. Even if a few hidden flowers here and there had made it through the frost, I wondered whether they would maintain their ability to produce nectar. Nectar production is richest under warm, sunny conditions and plant processes slow down under cool or cold conditions. I really didn't know what to do. The only thing I could think of was to try and get the bird into the house.

I've had hummingbirds in the house before, the first one during Hurricane Gloria in 1985. At that time I hung a feeder in the sunroom, opened the door, stuck a bare branch in the soil of a potted plant, and left it up to the bird to come in or not. One little female came in and spent about six hours, using the feeder and resting on the branch. As the hurricane subsided and the weather broke, other hummingbirds came around the house looking for the feeders. When she heard them outside, she would fly from window to window looking for the other birds. When one would come in, she'd chase it out. Eventually, she went outside. The next day I was afraid that she might fly into the glass on the door if she attempted to get back into the house, so I left the door open, but she never came back in again.

In 1987 we had a freak snowstorm on October 2 and while it wasn't as severe here along a strip of land on the western side of the Hudson River as it was farther away from the river, the weather was bad. While we did not have the broken branches and fallen trees that everyone else had, we did have wet snow in the morning. On that day I made a trail of flowering plants leading to the sunroom and got the last remaining hummingbird of the season to come into the house and then closed the door behind it. I kept her indoors for a couple of hours and released her when the sun came out and things warmed up and got back to normal.

I've also had young hummingbirds fly into the house, either chasing one another or alone, and land on the window screens. Some would fly in one window and out the other. Each one that has come in has reacted differently toward me. Two that came in together did absolutely nothing, they just sat in my hands; one chirped its little head off as I carried it outdoors to be released; and a third acted quite fussy, squirming all around and not wanting to be held at all.

Only 16 species of hummingbird, not counting accidentals, regularly reach the United States border. Of the 16 species that regularly visit the States, only one, the ruby-throated hummingbird (*Archilochus colubris*), visits the eastern part of the United States and Canada east of the middle of the Great Plains.

It's obvious that they gorge before they leave, a necessary part of migration. Although an occasional ruby-throat may overwinter as far north as Florida or Texas, their wintering grounds are from Mexico through Central America and they occasionally reach western Panama. They are reported to be rare winter residents in the Bahamas and Cuba and casual on some other West Indies islands. However, most cross the Gulf of Mexico, a nonstop, continuous flight of up to 500 miles, to reach their destinations. Fattening up beforehand adds the extra fuel necessary to make such a grueling trip. It has been estimated that most ruby-throats put on an additional 50 percent of their body weight in the last two to three weeks before migrating. They seem to stay until they fatten up to a certain point and then they leave. The ones who use the feeders invariably are the ones to leave first. The stragglers always seem to be the ones that don't know how to use the feeders. This little gem was obviously not fat enough to migrate and it didn't look as though he had even started to put on any extra weight at all. I was sure that he didn't know how to use feeders. By that late a time in October many should have been someplace between the mid- to southern-Atlantic states, with some having already arrived at their wintering grounds, but this one was still in Upstate New York. As a contrast to the way this bird looked, the little female who stayed in the house for the day in 1987 during the snowstorm was fat, with obvious extra weight in the breast and abdominal areas. While this little bird certainly was not scrawny, it was also obviously not ready to start a migration.

I've never had one stay overnight, however, so I was concerned. If I were able to get the bird into the house, what then? How long could I keep it? If I took a couple of hours away from it, might that work more to its detriment than its good? I wanted it to eat. I wanted to teach it how to use the feeder. I decided I would try to get it inside.

Again, I placed a trail of flowers leading from the porch to the back door and inside the sunroom the way I did with that little female the year before. I stood at the door and when the hummingbird came in, I closed the door behind it. I then set up some branches on which the bird could sit and tried to teach it how to use a feeder. This time I used a small Perky bottle, a glass gravity-type feeder with a feeding tube and bee guard, but I did not use the bee guard that came with it. Instead, I took one of the red stoppers from another feeder, placed it on the tip of the feeding tube, and held that feeder in my hand among the bouvardia flowers. The bird went from flower to flower at the bouvardia and it also visited the feeder. Needless to say, the nectar in the feeder was sweet and abundant. The bird liked it and came back repeatedly. I then attached the feeder to a wire and the hummer proceeded to use the feeder regularly for the rest of the day.

Each year when the fall migration began I would dream of how wonderful it would be if I were to have a hummingbird spend the winter in my sunroom so I might appreciate it for all twelve months of the year instead of just five. This could be a dream-come-true and, while it was what I had always dreamed of, depriving the bird of its freedom wasn't what I really wanted. I knew the bird needed more than just nectar; it also needed protein. Hummingbirds will eat 400 to 500 insects every day. Where would I get the protein? What might I add to the diet to make it complete? I certainly did not want to hurt the bird by failing to provide what it needed and I did not want to interfere with nature by preventing the bird from following its instincts; but, I also did not want the bird to die. To help make my decision, I made a few telephone calls.

I placed my first call to a local bird veterinarian and told him that I had a hummingbird in the house, that I was concerned about it being here so late in the season, and asked him about a protein supplement. He told me that, unfortunately, he had not had any experience with hummingbirds.

I then called the Cornell Lab at Ithaca and spoke with a gentleman who had a couple of suggestions for me. First, he told me, the mortality rate for hummingbirds in their first year is 60 to 80 percent and that this bird "probably was not going to make it." He suggested that I either keep the bird all winter, if I could provide suitable conditions for it, keep the bird three or four days until it fattened up and release it on a nice day, or find someone who was going south and who would be willing to take the bird along and release it somewhere between the mid-Atlantic states and Florida. Keeping it for three or four days entered my mind. I knew that I would be able to provide enough nectar for it and thought that, hopefully, it would fatten up and be in better condition to leave in a day or two. However, three or four days later would be three or four days later, and if nothing was available outside for it to eat today, there would not be anything available tomorrow either. Sending it down with someone to the mid-Atlantic states was not a feasible idea, all things considered, and I ruled that out. The only suggestion left for me was to keep the bird; I knew I certainly could provide it with suitable conditions. After all, the sunroom is 12 by 15 feet, on a separate heat zone, with three sides of glass and filled to the brim with flowering plants. But still, there was the problem of supplying protein to the bird. Without protein in its diet, the bird would die. It couldn't live on nectar alone. I'd read of someone who cared for orphaned ruby-throats by adding a drop of cow's blood to nectar for protein, but I could not imagine that such a measure would produce long-term balanced, satisfactory, or beneficial results. And, while it might be a possible emergency measure, it is doubtful that it would be suitable for long-term nourishment.

My next call was to the San Diego Zoo, which I knew to have a hummingbird aviary. The person with whom I spoke at San Diego thought it was a wonderful idea that I keep the bird. She told me that the folks there use Nektar-Plus as a complete diet for hummingbirds but thought that I might have difficulty obtaining it since it is not generally available to the public. In the meantime, she suggested that I get some fruit flies and release them in the room with the hummingbird for it to eat, which I did; but having a constant supply of several hundred on hand at all times was going to be a real problem and I was concerned. I wanted to help the bird and I wanted to give it every chance to live. I was afraid that it would die if it didn't stay here but certainly the last thing I wanted to do was contribute to its dying anyway.

If I were going to keep this bird, I would have to make some changes not only in my routine, but in the conditions that I kept for the plants as well. In other years I ran a ceiling fan in the sunroom for circulation around the plants and general heat conservation. That would be out of the question this year. I made sure that it was shut off not only at the wall switch outside the sunroom but in the sunroom at the fan itself. Insecticides would also be out. I never use any insecticides outdoors, but I had always moved plants to the garage and sprayed them each fall before bringing them inside.

If I were to keep the bird, I would have also have to be concerned about how to keep it from getting fat. After all, this is the time of year when its natural inclination is to fatten up for its trip south and it may only be retarded, not lacking, in this respect. I don't know what causes the fattening-up process. I don't know if it has to do with day length, temperature, or insect availability. Or it may be a specific hormone produced by certain birds or animals that causes them to overeat— perhaps a growth hormone. Even if that were so, some external or internal monitor would have to trigger production of that hormone. Perhaps it's all in the DNA. Of course, adult males leave by the end of August and the insects are certainly available at that time of year. Temperature varies from year to year but they do generally leave about the same time each year. The only consistency I could think of was day length. Perhaps that does have something to do with it. To combat that, in case that was the answer, I would be leaving lights on in excess of twelve hours per day in the sunroom. I know what difference this makes when growing daylight-sensitive plants, and this could be the key to keeping the bird from preparing for its migration.

My next step was to call the local pet store. Liz, the owner, very kindly contacted the manufacturer of Nektar-Plus and arranged to have some shipped UPS Next Day Air and delivered the very next day to me.

In the meantime, I had flowers for the bird, the nectar solution in the hanging feeders, and I caught some spiders to give him. I hunted through all my plants and found all the small spiders I could and held them in front of the bird by the web. With each spider held up, the bird gobbled it down and, while its mouth was opened, appeared to be smiling.

I thought over and over again that perhaps I should reconsider finding someone to take the bird south to release it there but, as the days went on, I knew that wouldn't be happening. The bird certainly seemed to be content and I was absolutely delighted. I think that deep down I knew right from the start that it would be staying until the spring.

I called the bird Squeak because of its constant squeaky chirping. With all the spotting on its throat and chin, I knew it was a male and, after a couple of days, I saw his first iridescent red spot. He had only been in my sunroom a couple of days, but already he had captured my heart and I was anticipating watching the change from young male hummer to a beautiful resplendent adult. I would do everything possible to keep him happy and healthy and I planned to release him in the spring. Of course, this too might turn out to be a problem: He might not want to leave. I hoped, of course, that he would because I wanted him to live a normal hummingbird life, but I'd probably enjoy it if he didn't. I remember when we, my two sisters and I, were young, we always found young "injured" birds to bring home to our parents. Each bird that was brought home was taken care of, primarily by my mother, and released when it was ready. But I do remember different birds, robins mostly, who had been released and would fly out one window and fly right back in another. They didn't want to leave. One robin that had been taken care of by my mother would land on her shoulder whenever she was in the yard. One day it disappeared and, presumably, migrated with the other robins. The following spring that same bird came back and landed on her shoulder again—a

year later! So it's very possible that this hummingbird might find the safety here more appealing and
not want to leave the way many other wild and
caged birds do. I thought that I would cross that
bridge when I came to it.

2

Daily Activities And Habits

The Morning

Each morning was basically the same, with variations on the theme, and although the rituals changed from time to time, he was such a little creature of habit. When the lights went on at the beginning of the day, he would waken and the first thing he would do was swallow, probably emptying his crop. His tongue would then dart in and out, he would flap his tail, shake out his wings, and then go into his stretching routine. He stretched both wings backward and then, unilaterally, first one side, then the other. The wings were stretched straight down along each side; then both wings were stretched backward again while he simultaneously fanned his tail. He took a couple of minutes each morning to bring his body temperature back up to its normal 102 to 108 degrees F.

Immediately thereafter he would eat. He would first visit the feeder at the south end of the room

At the beginning of the day the wings were stretched straight down along each side.

During his morning ritual Squeak stretched both wings backward while he simultaneously fanned his tail.

Eventually his choice sitting spot of the morning became a certain branch at the south end of the room.

and then sit for a few minutes on a certain branch near the window scratching his head and chin before returning to the feeder.

During this morning ritual he would then make visits to the various flower spikes for accumulated nectar, returning to the feeder and, finally, to his choice sitting spot of the time. The sitting spot changed from time to time. During October and most of November, it was a certain phalaenopsis spike only inches beneath the fluorescents. Later the choice spot became the rounded bottom of a wire designed to clamp to the edge of a flowerpot, but in this case inverted and used as a stake, again only inches below the fluorescents. Still later the choice morning spot became a two-inch piece of metal bar at the end of a tray frame. Eventually and finally it became a certain branch at the south end of the room.

By the time the first day of spring arrived, it was quite light outside when the lights went on at 6:00 A.M. Robins and cardinals could be heard by 5:45 A.M. On the first day of spring, March 20, Squeak began to stir before the lights went on. By March 23, he was waking and starting his routine before the lights, but Daylight Savings begins in early April and so none of this continued for very long. Daylight Savings brings lighter evenings and, although Squeak was much more active in general than he had been all winter, he seemed to be more positively affected by the extra natural light at the end of his day than at the beginning. Continued lengthening days brought increased activity and before the end of April he was again stirring and feeding before the lights went on. By the time the first week in May was over, Squeak was starting to rouse at 5:30 A.M.

Squeak also enjoyed flying around the room. This is something that was routinely done each morning and I believe it was done purely for exercise. Not all the time, but more often than not he would fly in a counterclockwise direction. I wondered if the direction of his path would reverse itself in the spring, but it didn't. Squeak spent an average of ten minutes each morning exercising this way.

The Bath

It was then time to bathe. Hummingbirds love to bathe and they do so in a number of ingenious ways and frequently. They shower in the rain or the spray from under a waterfall, bathe in pools of water on rocks or leaves, fly into wet leaves and rub on wet moss.

I bought a small plastic birdbath for Squeak right away. It is essential for a bird to keep its feathers clean and I had hoped that he would learn to use it. Instead, by his third day here, I realized he had different plans.

On most mornings I mist the plants in the sunroom, wetting the roots and leaves from a spray bottle for a little extra humidity. On the third morning, no sooner had I finished than Squeak flew over and began to slide around on the leaf of the phalaenopsis plant that I had been misting. He was obviously trying to get all of his underparts wet, his breast, under his wings, and his chin. He certainly seemed to be enjoying himself. All the

Waiting for his bath, Squeak watches while I wet the cattleya leaf.

Squeak slides around on the cattleya leaf to get his underparts wet.

Notice how wet Squeak has become.

Even the chin is cleaned; note the closed eyes.

while he was bathing, sliding around and sliding down the phalaenopsis leaf and wetting his throat, breast, and underwings, he was chirping. It was obvious that what he was doing was very, very pleasurable. After bathing for a few minutes, he would fly around the room, undoubtedly to dry his feathers. The wet wing and tail feathers produce a very sharp sound when wet. With the air passing through the feathers the way it does, the sound is like a deck of cards being shuffled. He would then return to the feeder for a drink and go back to the phalaenopsis spike, sit and wait for me to mist some more so he might bathe all over again. After hummingbirds bathe, they like to preen. Squeak really enjoyed bathing on that phalaenopsis leaf and he wanted to do it every morning.

One Saturday in early November, I bought a bromeliad on a driftwood arrangement consisting of two small tillandsias on the wood and, at the bottom, a neoreglia that holds plenty of water in its cup. I thought Squeak might use this as a place to bathe, but he didn't show any interest in it at first. He had developed the habit of using that phalaenopsis leaf and returned to it over and over again even though there were other leaves in the sunroom that were wetter than that plant's leaf.

I know that hummingbirds enjoy bathing and I've watched them in the garden approaching the spray from a hose that was deliberately left on just for that purpose. I've read about birds flying through the water over and over again, using the spray as a slide, but they haven't done it here. Anna's hummingbird apparently has done that. I don't know whether the ruby-throat will or not, but they will approach the water out of curiousity.

There have been times when I've watched one hummingbird or another during a rain. The bird would sit out on the clothesline with its head facing upward, arch its back and spread its wing and tail feathers, trying to get its entire back wet. After two or three minutes it would shake off all the water, only to start the same routine all over again.

One morning in mid-November Squeak showed some interest in the actual spraying of "his" phalaenopsis and the other plants by approaching the spray of water and hovering in front of it to check it out. When he returned to his branch I let the spray flow in his direction. Immediately, even before the water touched him, he fanned his tail in anticipation. I directed it over him lightly so several drops fell on his back. He loved it, acting the same way the others have acted while sitting on the clothesline in the rain. Afterward he rubbed his chin over the branch where he had been perching, making sure that every available drop touched him. The shower would last for several minutes. Squeak let me know when he'd had enough by backing away from the spray and flying to a branch on the other side of the room where he would sit and

Squeak loved to bathe; all the while he bathed he would chirp.

Squeak receiving his daily shower.

Finally in mid-November Squeak bathed on the bromeliad leaves.

The wings are cleaned by the bill.

preen for at least fifteen minutes. He would dry off
by shaking the water out of his wings and tail.
Then he would run his beak over the wing feathers
on one side, shake out the flight feathers again,
run his beak over the feathers on the opposite side,
and shake out again. This action was repeated over
and over again until he appeared to be satisfied
that he was dry enough. This became a daily morning ritual. Within a week he knew so well what the
spray bottle meant that he would fly to the branch
and chirp repeatedly in anticipation while going
through all the motions of his shower. All this
before feeling even one drop.

On some mornings, however, he had to make
a game of it first. He would go through all the
motions waiting for the shower. Then, the minute
I began spraying him, he would take off, straight
at my face, detour around my head at the very last
instant, fly to the other side of the room, and then
return to the branch to do it all again. This behavior would go on for several moments. Finally, after
five or six tries to get started, Squeak would settle
down for the shower.

In mid-November he bathed on the bromeliad
leaves. First he pecked at the drops of water on the
leaves and then he bathed. The edges of the leaves
of neoreglia are wavy and slightly rough or spiny.
He looked twice at the leaves, being more used to
the hard, smooth, and somewhat waxy leaves of
the phalaenopsis. He did not, however, place his

body in the cup and the bromeliad was always a second-choice bath.

My main reason for getting that bromeliad arrangement for Squeak was so that a source of water would be available to him for the whole day. Even though I wet down all the various leaves in the room, they dried off rather quickly and I wasn't always available to do this repeatedly during the day. I had hoped that he would make use of the bromeliad's cup of water during the day just as I had hoped he would do when I offered the plastic birdbath, but he hadn't. As long as there were wet leaves around, that's what he used, except, of course, for his shower. It didn't matter whether the leaves were on fuchsia plants, the flowering maple, or the gardenia, he would fly into them and rub against the leaves to get his body wet.

Eventually I stopped using the phalaenopsis leaf and switched him over to one on a cattleya plant. The benefits of using the cattleya leaf were twofold. First, its leaf is more horizontal and waxy than the phalaenopsis leaf and would therefore, hold the water longer and give him a better surface on which to bathe. Also, the worry of water sitting in the crown of the phalaenopsis was eliminated with the use of the cattleya. He accepted the switch happily. But I still hadn't found an answer to my problem of how to keep bathing water available for the whole day, and in a container that he would accept.

Feathers are fastidiously separated and the bill is drawn over them.

Wherever they can be reached, feathers are done one at a time.

Hummingbirds must resort to scratching to clean the head, neck, and throat areas.

The beak is frequently cleaned with the feet.

Then, knowing that many hummingbirds will bathe in the spray from waterfalls, I decided to make one for Squeak. I searched far and wide looking for the component parts that I would need for its construction. Finally I found a sizable piece of lava rock with which to work and was able to locate a submersible, recirculating pump for the water. What I wanted was to have the water flow from the top of the rock to two or three small, shallow pools at different levels below it. In addition, I wanted to have three or four pockets in other parts of the lava rock in which I might place small flowering plants. I began work on the waterfall early in January, chiseling out the pools, crevices, and pockets with a small chisel and hammer and, for every four or five times that I hit the chisel with the hammer, I hit my hand once. It was hard, time-consuming work, but eventually it was completed. The rock was decorated with a couple of angraecum orchids and a bromeliad in its pockets; the water was turned on, and it worked beautifully. I was happy to know that a source of water would now be available for Squeak at all times. He investigated it immediately, as he did with everything, but he didn't show any interest in using it for bathing. I hoped that eventually, as with the bromeliad, that would change, but it didn't. Perhaps if the daily bath and shower weren't provided for him, he might have taken more interest in the waterfall as a possible bathing or shower area.

Once I hooked it up he stayed near it most of the day. It became his favorite hunting area, as he could always find an insect or two there and perhaps he liked the sound of trickling water. Once the waterfall was hooked up, he seldom sat under the fluorescents except, that is, for his bath and shower. The one thing that remained most constant during his entire stay was his love of the bath and shower.

Preening

Squeak spent more of his time perching than anything else. Much of that perching time was spent preening and generally fussing over himself. Hummingbirds give their feathers a great deal of care. During preening a hummingbird touches its bill to the uropygial, or preening gland, a skin gland located near the base of its tail, to collect oil for cleaning and waterproofing its wings, tail feath-

*After each feeding
Squeak would clean
his beak on a twig.*

*At times Squeak would sunbathe, fluffing up and exposing
himself to the sun.*

*Occasionally a loose
feather would stick
to Squeak's tongue.*

*Using his foot to
remove the feather from
his tongue.*

ers, back, and abdomen, and for lubricating its bill and legs. The wings, tail, back, and abdomen are cleaned by the bill. Feathers are fastidiously separated and the bill is drawn over them. The tail is lifted and arched laterally toward the beak while the tail feathers are spread apart with the beak pulling through each tail feather. The head is also turned toward the back, enabling the bird to run its beak across the upper tail coverts. Wherever they can be reached, feathers are done one at a time, a long and painstaking process.

However, since hummingbirds cannot reach all of their feathers and do not engage in mutual preening, they must resort to scratching to clean the head, neck, and throat areas. The head is bent to place its feathers, as well as the feathers of the neck and throat, in a position to be reached by the claws. Hummingbirds scratch frequently, often without displaying any other preening behavior.

The feet and legs are cleaned with the bill by a nibbling action and the beak itself is cleaned either on a twig or branch or with the feet. After each feeding, Squeak would clean his beak on a twig.

One of the funniest things that Squeak would do was scratch while he was flying or, more correctly, scratching in midair. Usually he scratched his head, but at times it appeared that he may also have been pecking at a foot. He was probably cleaning it; I noticed that he would engage in that behavior most often after a bath or shower than at any other time. At times, however, he would raise his foot while hovering, obviously to clean his beak. While he was so occupied, this little acrobat would descend in a spiral motion toward the floor, just about managing to stay up.

Squeak spent a great deal of time preening. At times he would "sunbathe," fluffing up and exposing himself to the sun, and sitting at the window in that same position for quite a while. Afterward he would scratch the warmed areas.

Several times while Squeak was vigorously scratching himself, he fell from his branch. Each time he would immediately right himself in midair, go back to where he had been sitting, and start scratching all over again. Such an acrobat, such perfect control, no struggling, so matter-of-factly and naturally, he'd hardly miss a beat.

Squeak spent a tremendous amount of time scratching and preening during his molt—much more than usual, although that hardly seems possible. Preening, scratching, and shaking out helped him to get rid of loose feathers and pinfeather sheaths. Occasionally a loose feather would stick to his tongue. He would try two or three times to rid himself of it by drawing his tongue in and pushing it back out again, but invariably this was best accomplished when he adeptly used his foot as though it were a hand and just pulled the feather from the tongue.

Shaking out helped Squeak get rid of loose feathers and pinfeather sheaths.

Fuchsias are almost magnetic to hummingbirds.

Flowers and Food

Metabolism is the process by which food is turned into energy. Because of their size and lifestyle, hummingbirds have a very high rate of metabolism, producing a tremendous amount of needed energy. They have the greatest energy output, relatively, of any warm-blooded animal. Accordingly, they require great quantities of food.

The hummingbird's primary source of nourishment is nectar, a renewable, easily digested and quickly converted source of energy. Nectar is composed of various sugars. Of all the sugars, sucrose is the one that is preferred.

Through simultaneous evolution, hummingbirds have become most suited to extract nectar from flowers and, at the same time, many flowers have evolved to become particularly suited for pollination by hummingbirds. Hummers can frequently be seen with a dusting of pollen on their foreheads, crowns, or beaks. These "hummingbird flowers" usually have an abundant store of nectar, containing approximately 25 percent sugar; are more or less tubular in shape and somewhat open on the inflorescences; have no fragrance, since odorless flowers are unattractive to insects; pollen is quite often located outside of the flower and flowers very often have elongated anthers and no "landing platform," making the nectar less accessible to insects. Hummingbird-adapted flowers are attractive in color. Attractive means noticeable. Red flowers are the flowers of choice because they are most noticeable. However, in the shade many hummingbird flowers are of an orange color, which is more noticeable under such conditions. Hummingbird flowers are attractive primarily to hummingbirds.

Certain hummingbirds prefer certain flowers, the primary reason why so many different species can coexist in the tropics. By and large, small hummingbirds prefer small flowers and large hummingbirds prefer large flowers. The nectary in a large flower may be out of reach for a small hummingbird and there is not usually enough nectar in a small flower to make it worthwhile for a large hummingbird to expend the energy necessary to visit it. Hummingbirds with odd-shaped bills are adapted to odd-shaped flowers. The swordbill with daturas and the white-tipped sicklebill with heliconia are two good examples that may be cited.

In the United States there are many humming-bird-adapted flowers. There is even a species of cactus, the hedgehog, that is pollinated exclusively by a hummingbird. Some plants that are noted as being particularly suited to pollination by the ruby-throated hummingbird are cardinal flower (*Lobelia cardinalis*), jewelweed or touch-me-not (*Impatiens capensis*), and bee balm (*Monarda didyma*). I've grown many different flowers in my garden for humming-birds, including all those mentioned above, but from my own experience, the two favorites are tropical salvia (*Salvia coccinea*) and the red varieties of bee balm.

Knowing which flowers yield the richest stores of nectar is not something hummingbirds know from birth. They must learn which of the flowers contain nectar and they learn by trial and error. Tremendous curiosity will drive nestlings to try everything, even roses. Coupled with that curios-ity is an excellent memory. They remember, even a year later, where the "good stuff" was. One early May morning a couple of years ago I was able to witness the return of one of our regular males. He arrived in the yard, stopped momentarily on the clothesline, and then immediately turned left and went under the pine tree to where his favorite feeder had been the year before. Of course it was there again. The point is, not only was the bird

Squeak visits the flowering maple.

Squeak is very fond of the nectar that forms on parts of certain orchid plants.

All of a sudden Squeak loved the Aerangis hybrid.

Squeak loved bromeliads.

driven to the same breeding grounds as the year before, but after an absence of eight months, he remembered where to find a favorite source of food. Even after seeing such displays of memory over and over again, it still amazes me.

To what degree Squeak's association with our flowers parallels that which would occur in the wild is unknown, at least to me. Take fuchsias for instance. Flowers of the fuchsia plants are notorious hummingbird favorites. Indeed, one of the quickest ways to attract hummers to your feeders is to place the feeder in close proximity to fuchsia plants. Fuchsias are almost magnetic to hummingbirds. In the fall my fuchsias are cut back, usually in two or three steps, and then stored in a cool place until late December when they are taken out and put under the lights in the basement to start their new growth cycle. It was after the first pruning session that Squeak made his appearance in our yard and after having been cut back, flowers on the fuchsias were sparse. *Fuchsia triphylla* hybrids, such as Gartenmeister Bonstedt, are particularly attractive to hummers and will flower all winter long if given cool evenings, 60 degrees F., or below. That was one plant that was not affected by the cutting back and was made immediately available to Squeak. His interest in that plant was, surprisingly, lacking. Because of Squeak's arrival, the others were immediately put under the basement lights and began to grow again, with new flower buds visible shortly thereafter. As, one by one, they began to flower, they were moved into the sunroom. Squeak visited them but never showed the same avid interest in these flowers that had always been shown by other hummers. Why? What would make a favorite flower of the summer now become second choice—even when the total number of choices had narrowed? Perhaps fuchsias are reserved for the dominant hummingbirds on the wintering grounds. Maybe they are not producing the nectar indoors that they do outside. Is it an instinctive action to shy away from flowers that under normal and ordinary conditions would be off limits?

Sleeping hibiscus (*Malvaviscus arboreus*), so called because the flowers never fully open, is another example. Apparently *Malvaviscus arboreus* is considered the choice tubular flower in its habitat. Nectar from it is dominated by the superior resident hummers, while nectar from the less productive cup-shaped flowers is left for the subordinates who forage at such flowers. I grow *Malvaviscus arboreus*, but Squeak never seemed to show any interest in this supposedly choice flower. Although he did approach its flowers on one or two occasions, it almost seemed that he avoided the plant. Maybe it is instinctively forbidden because of the subordinate status that he would have had on his wintering grounds. There are so many questions! He did not, however, avoid the little cup-shaped flowers of

He especially loved tillandsias; here he visits T. geminiflora.

Squeak visits T. juncea.

Squeak used his beak to raise tubular, hanging flowers to a horizontal position.

Insects are captured in a variety of ways; here Squeak captures a whitefly.

flowering maple. It has been my observation that this is a plant ordinarily left for the subordinates. Here, in our garden, the dominant hummers have always claimed the fuchsias while the subordinates would sneak in while the "yard boss" wasn't looking to visit abutilon and impatiens plants, both of which have always been ignored by the dominant hummers. I suppose that I should mention here that Squeak also visited the large impatiens plant regularly. I wanted to know what his attitude was going to be toward these very same flowers when and if he became an aggressive, territorial, and, hopefully, dominant adult ruby-throated hummingbird.

Beside flowers, there are other sources of nectar available to hummingbirds, especially ruby-throats. They are notorious for visiting sapsucker holes—more frequently than any other birds, including the sapsucker woodpeckers who drilled them. In a study by Foster and Tate, it was noted that of the four hummingbird species to visit sapsucker feeding trees (ruby-throat, Anna's, broad-tailed and rufous), the ruby-throat was not only observed most frequently but was the only one to systematically collect insects in the vicinity. This sap may even offer sustenance to birds returning early in spring while flowering is still sparce.

Few orchids contain any nectar and those that do are not readily accessible to hummingbirds. Many are pollinated through mimicry, the ability of the flower to resemble and attract its pollinator.

There are a few New World orchids, however, that do depend upon hummingbirds for pollination: *Comparetta falcata, Laelia milleri,* and *Elleanthus capitatus.* Nevertheless, many orchids, such as the Cattleya alliance orchids, produce a thick and sticky nectar-like substance along the inflorescence, sometimes on the pseudobulb and on the flower stems at the base of the petals. Squeak is very fond of this nectar, as are, I'm sure, other hummingbirds, and he visits the plants several times each day looking for the accumulation. This "honey" is more copious before flowering begins and some plants just drip with it. I grow many orchids and except for the honey that is produced, they are, for the most part, useless as a food source for Squeak. Orchids in the Angraecum family are an exception. Angraecum orchids and their allies, Aerangis and Aeranthes, are Old World orchids coming from Africa, Madagascar, the Comoros and some other Indian Ocean islands. They are almost always white, some are highly fragrant, especially at night, and most have a spur, which can be extremely long, containing nectar. They are usually pollinated by moths. One in particular, a little aerangis hybrid, has white flowers about one and one-half inches across with the usual long spur and an orange column. I showed them to Squeak in an attempt to pique his interest, but I couldn't get him to pay any attention to those flowers at all—at first. Then one day he discovered the aerangis and all of a

Squeak had no problem spotting insects; here he prepares to go after one.

A specially designed feeder was chosen for Squeak.

Drawing from the reserve in his crop

Visiting Abutilon megapotamicum.

sudden he loved them. I was able to see him slide his tongue, which would be greatly extended beyond the tip of his bill, under the column and into the spur. Considering the amount of time spent on these flowers in comparison to others, it would be my guess that this plant produces copious amounts of nectar.

Another orchid that Squeak spent much time with was *Phragmipedium schlimii*, a South American terrestrial lady slipper with an exquisite roselike fragrance. Instead of attempting to get at the nectar through the slipper part, the way an insect would do, Squeak ingeniously found a way to stick his beak in through the back of the flower, behind the slipper.

Whenever possible, Squeak would perch while eating. At times he perched on one of his branches; at other times a leaf stem came in handy as a place to sit; he was frequently found perching on the edge of one flowerpot or another, stretching his neck to reach a desired flower; and, when flowers were large enough, he would perch on the petals. Squeak loved hibiscus flowers. While visiting them he would very often hold on to the edge of the flower with his claws to keep his balance while lowering his head deep within the blossom. I've frequently seen other hummingbirds do the same thing with the hibiscus relative, rose of sharon. Squeak was so fond of hibiscus that he wouldn't even wait for them to unfurl. Instead he pierced numerous holes in the petals with his beak, trying to get nectar before the flowers were ready to open.

In their native habitats, tillandsias, members of the Bromeliad family, are pollinated primarily by hummingbirds. While Squeak never visited the flowers of the neoreglia plant, he loved bromeliads, and especially tillandsias, better than everything else.

I noticed on several occasions that Squeak would use his beak to raise tubular, hanging flowers to a horizontal position. Perhaps in that way nectar that had accumulated in a particular flower would be concentrated on just one side of the tube and, therefore, more conveniently available.

To survive, hummingbirds also require a diet adequate in protein, carbohydrates, fats, vitamins, and minerals. That need is supplied by minute insects and small spiders, which are slower to digest than the sugars are. Insects and spiders are captured in a variety of ways. Some are probably occasionally taken from within the flowers incidental to drinking, but basically they are either plucked off branches, twigs, leaves, trees, flowers, and walls, or captured in flight. Many times I have watched the nightly occurrence of a hummingbird sitting on the clothesline waiting for a swarm of small insects, probably gnats, to get closer. When the swarm is near, the hummingbird dives in and flits around taking one insect after another. I've noticed

Squeak visited most available flowers; here he visits snapdragons.

this behavior more on rainy days than on sunny
ones and more in the evenings than during other
times of the day. It could be that more insects are
eaten at that time because more are available. It
might also be that nectar production in flowers is
richer during the sunny weather. It is reported that
more nectar is secreted on sunny days, increasing
with higher, dry temperatures and decreasing with
humidity or moisture. When flowers are scarce,
and most likely if nectar production is down, hummingbirds depend very heavily upon insects to
supplement their diet. Some insects are even stolen
from spiders' webs. As a matter of fact, if the
spider is small enough, it would be eaten as well.

Squeak had no problem seeing an insect from

Visiting kalanchoe.

across the room and, since I didn't use any insecticide this year, there was always an abundant supply available for him. He'd pluck them from the windows, walls, and leaves. Very often he'd sit on a branch just waiting for one to go by and grab it. When Squeak noticed an insect that he wanted, he would open his mouth wide, dip below the insect and come up, closing his beak on it and swallow. Afterward, he'd sometimes glide across the room with his mouth opened in a vertical position, almost as if to help the bug go down. I have also watched him do this after taking nectar from one or the other of the feeders. He may have been getting some sediment from the solution and was trying to get it down.

Insects form a very important part of the hummingbird's diet. For many years it was presumed that hummingbirds existed only on sugars and the estimates of their consumption of sugars in ratio to body size were grossly exaggerated. When hummingbirds kept in aviaries could not be kept alive on diets consisting only of sugar, people began to believe that it was actually the insects in the flowers to which the hummingbirds were attracted. It was soon discovered, however, that hummingbirds could no more exist on an all-protein diet than they could on an all-sugar diet. Studies conducted by Walter Scheithauer concluded that a hummingbird's diet must consist of a balance between nectar and insects and revealed much about hummingbirds' digestion in general.

Right from the start, offering a balanced diet to Squeak was my foremost concern. With this balance in mind, the diet that was suggested to and chosen by me was Nektar-Plus, made by the Nekton company. Nektar-Plus is a complete diet made specifically for hummingbirds, sunbirds, honeycreepers, and bananaquits, and containing a balanced selection of carbohydrates, protein, fat, vitamins, minerals and trace elements, all chosen to complement one another. In short, a complete and balanced diet. The protein in Nektar-Plus comes from eighteen different, pure amino acids duplicating that which has been found in hummingbirds' stomachs. Carbohydrates are in the form of glucose, fructose, and sucrose, corresponding to natural flower nectars. Nektar-Plus comes in a powdered form but is easily mixed with water. It truly took only seconds each day to prepare Squeak's food.

The only drawback to feeding Nektar-Plus is its tendency, like that of any other protein solution, to spoil over the course of a day. However, when used in conjunction with Nekton's special disinfectant, it is possible to keep the Nektar-Plus solution longer, thereby making it unnecessary to mix the formula more than once each day. The specially designed brown Plexiglas feeders offered by the Nekton people were chosen for their ability to filter light rays, thus preventing the decay of important vitamins, and for the sloping bottom of the tube, which would give Squeak access to any components not completely water-soluble. Two sets of two feeders each were used altogether; two tubes were used in the sunroom each day while the other two were soaking in the disinfectant all day long, removed to air-dry overnight and replaced daily just before Squeak wakened. No introduction to this feed was necessary; Squeak accepted and, undoubtedly, liked it from the time that he first tried it.

Two feeders were kept going at all times in case, by slim chance, one leaked or emptied during the day. One was kept on the east side of the room, the other on the south. Generally, neither location seemed to be preferred over the other.

The return of spring brought many new flowers for Squeak to try; here he visits Korean rhododendron.

However, Squeak, apparently preferring either light or warmth, would visit the feeder on the south side of the room on sunny days; on cloudy days and especially evenings, the feeder on the east side of the room and near the fluorescents was preferred. Use of the feeders was direct and without fanfare except at night—and only with the east feeder. During the last hour or so before Squeak went to sleep and every time he visited that feeder, he would take a sip and then drop down and to the right of the feeder about three to four feet. This strange action occurred after each sip. I have never been able to figure out why. Squeak visited most available flowers and caught lots of insects and spiders, but Nektar-Plus remained his staple.

Branches of flowering apricot were brought in for Squeak.

I enjoyed watching Squeak eat and I watched him at every available opportunity. When a hummingbird eats, its tongue flicks rapidly in and out of its bill. When the tongue is pushed out of the tightly closed bill, nectar from the flower which the bird is visiting is drawn into the grooves of the tongue by capillary action. The tongue is then drawn back into the slightly opened bill. Then, when the bird repeats the action of pushing its tongue out of the tightly closed bill, the collected nectar is forced into the oral cavity. This cycle takes less than one-tenth of a second. Once I learned the mechanics, I tried to glimpse one of the secrets from his tiny world—I wanted to see it for myself.

Hummingbirds feed frequently. An average of once every 10 to 15 minutes is usually given. What food is not immediately used is stored in the crop for later consumption. Two or three times between each visit to the feeder, Squeak would draw from the reserve in his crop. Swallowing action could be noted by the movement in his gorget area. After each three or four swallows, he would then open his mouth to quite a wide position. After the last series of swallows and gulp, his tongue would dart in and out, an action associated with the act of feeding, and he would then visit the feeder. He probably visited the feeder whenever he found his crop empty. However, this action took place primarily during periods of lessened activity, such as very late afternoons and evenings before going to sleep. He also swallowed in that manner frequently after capturing an insect, perhaps to bring up some nectar with which to wash the insect down.

The return of spring brought many new flowers for Squeak to try, flowers that ordinarily bloom too early in the season for the hummingbirds here. Cut branches of forsythia, Korean rhododendron and flowering apricot were brought in for Squeak. He tried them all and, apparently, liked them all. Since he visited them repeatedly, I must assume that they contained nectar, even after being cut.

In the garden most hummers can be identified by the patient observer, not only by their looks, but by their eating habits as well. One of our female regulars, for instance, can easily be recognized by the soft yellow coloration where the male's gorget would be. She has been coming here for four years as an adult and her unusual throat, different from all the other females' throats, has never changed. She always takes a certain number of sips, always uses one of the Perky gravity feeders under the pine tree, and always sits on one particular bare branch.

Even though we also know her by her looks and other habits, another female who nests here can be identified solely by the way she uses the feeder. This female has been using our feeders for three years and in all that time still has not yet learned to save energy by sitting while eating.

One other female can always be told by the chirping she does in between sips, especially after the last sip. When she leaves the feeder, she spirals up and around the pine tree trunk, chirping incessantly.

Still one other female can be spotted by the way she feeds. She was born in 1987 and always uses the Perky bottle. However, she has never learned to use it the way the others do. She has never quite been able to master the art of sticking her bill through the front of the bee guard. She always ate from the side. As an adult she eats the same way. She was gone for a whole winter and never changed.

Many, perhaps all in their own way, have an

Approaching flowering quince—note the remains of an insect on his beak.

eating routine. I've noticed that many males have a "route." Certain birds will appear at the same place at precisely the same time each day. I could always expect a certain male to appear at the monarda each day at three specific times. Another male came each night just as it was getting dark to visit the coralbells (*Heuchera sanguinea*). One male was known sight unseen. The whirring of his feathers sounded exactly like a broadtail.

They really are such individuals, with their own particular habits. So was Squeak. He always took small sips and moved to alternate sides of his feeder between the sips, and he always stretched before going to the feeder. Squeak rarely tucked his feet in against his body while hovering in front of a flower or feeder. In typical young hummer fashion, he usually allowed his feet to hang quite freely. I was anxious to see what personal behavioral habits Squeak would be adopting once released.

Sleep

Everyone who has an avid interest in hummingbirds would welcome an opportunity to see one as it sleeps. I've heard accounts of people finding them asleep in bushes only five or six feet off the ground, but surely this is rare.

Because of their small size, hummingbirds have the greatest energy output of any warm-blooded animal and they lose body heat very rapidly—a far greater amount than larger birds do. In addition, they lack the down feathers that would enable them to increase their insulation by feather-fluffing. Hummingbirds must constantly replenish food in order to stay alive. Food in a hummingbird's crop will hold it over for only a couple of hours. Since they work on such a precarious energy balance and cannot always accomplish this over long periods, many become torpid, a sort of nightly hibernation, to conserve energy during periods of cold or when their reserves are not enough to sustain them. Torpidity, a state of reduced body temperature and metabolism, is the hummingbird's greatest safeguard against burning itself out. During torpidity a bird's temperature may drop almost to the temperature of the surrounding air.

Hummingbirds do not become torpid every night; incubating and brooding females as well as nestlings do not become torpid; and hummingbirds never enter torpidity when the temperature is over 95 degrees F. When a hummingbird is in such a state, it cannot fly. It may only be able to chirp weakly. If removed from its perch, it cannot regain its grip when replaced. Being in such a condition prevents a bird from being dislodged from its sleeping place during high winds. Torpidity is like a state of suspended animation.

Some birds, once torpid, emerge from their torpor before dawn, undoubtedly by some internal clock or mechanism. I believe that is the case with ruby-throated hummingbirds. Some do not become active again until warmed by the sun. Such is the case of the Chimborazo hillstar of Ecuador, an unusual hummingbird in many ways, a species dependent upon chuquiraga flowers and of which it is the sole pollinator. The Chimborazo hillstar lives just below the permanent snow line between 13,000 and 15,000 feet on the altiplano of the Andes and the slopes of the volcano Cotopaxi in one of the most severe climates in the world. Living and nesting at 15,000 feet, higher than almost any other bird, presents very special problems. On Cotopaxi, the air is thin and cold, ice crystals form every night, and snow and freezing temperatures are a frequent occurrence. The hillstar must torpidate to stay alive. During the night its body temperature may drop to as low as one-half of its normal temperature. As well as becoming torpid, this bird shelters in caves on the lava slopes of Cotopaxi to conserve additional energy over that which is saved in the torpid state. Not only is the temperature in the caves 1 or 2 degrees F. above freezing, but the problem of freezing to death as a result of radiation into the clear sky is eliminated.

Hummingbirds arrive in our garden very early in the morning. As a matter of fact, they arrive earlier in the mornings and leave later in the evenings than any of the other birds around except sometimes the cardinals. At the summer solstice birds begin arriving at 4:45 A.M.—always before the sun. At times early in the season and then again, late in the season, nights, and especially early morning hours, can be quite chilly. It is not uncommon for temperatures to dip into the very high thirties or low forties. Many of those birds had probably been torpid on those chilly nights. I am apt to conclude, therefore, that resumption of

*Squeak slept on the
skinny branch every
night except one.*

activity in the ruby-throated hummingbird occurs
as a result of some internal rhythm and is not
temperature- or sun-related. I do, on the other
hand, remember certain young ruby-throats who
spent all day, every day here, but didn't arrive in
the mornings until the sun was shining in the yard.
I only noticed that with two birds and I believe
they were nestmates. It may be coincidence.

One of the decisions I had to make for Squeak
was how much time to allow him for sleeping.
That is, when to have the lights go on in the
morning and when to have them shut off in the
evening. Following a sunrise-to-sunset schedule here
in the north where the nights are long would not
be a good idea. In my opinion, the days would not
be long enough for the bird to get the right amount

of nourishment. I didn't want to keep summer hours either. I wanted to keep things as natural as possible under the circumstances. The closer to the equator one gets in winter, the longer the days are, so the days would, to some extent, be naturally longer than they are here. I decided, therefore, to have the lights turn on at 6:00 A.M. and go off at 8:00 P.M. This, I thought, would give Squeak ample daylight hours, actually more than he would have been getting naturally, and it would have also given long enough daylight hours to those plants affected by it with respect to flowering.

I was concerned about having all of the fluorescent lights turn off at the same time, so I had them turn off in two steps, the second half fifteen minutes after the first.

On his first night I left a light on outside the French door until he settled down. Twilight is gradual outside during the summer and I was afraid that he might be flying around and find himself suddenly and totally in the dark.

Of the several branches that I placed around for his benefit, he chose the skinniest one on which to sleep that very first night. He settled down facing the French door and slept at the very tip of that skinny branch. He went to sleep in *exactly* that same spot in *exactly* the same position each and every night thereafter except on March 1, when he decided to sleep on the branch at the north end of the room, his bird-watching branch. I could see him working himself up to that for three or four days when he was reluctant to leave that favorite branch toward the end of the evening. Once out of his system though, he returned to the regular routine that he had set for himself. While it is probably not set in stone, it may be very likely that hummingbirds retire to the same spot each evening to sleep. I have always been able to tell when it's the last drink of the day for the hummingbirds that regularly feed here—the final departure for the evening is always exactly the same pattern and direction from night to night and the flight is the same distance from the ground.

I don't know whether or not Squeak ever became torpid at night. I never touched him while he slept. It is doubtful, since his energy reserves were probably high enough that he didn't need to torpidate. Also, on several occasions, each well into the night, Squeak was observed stretching one of his wings. On one occasion I observed him scratching when he was supposed to be sound asleep. On another night he was pecking at his side—perhaps to dislodge a loose feather that had been itching or annoying him. Squeak was too active at night to have become torpid. One night I looked through the French door and, in the dim light cast by the outside porch light, could see a feather at the tip of his beak. I removed the feather, of course, but he had to have been scratching himself to dislodge that feather and have it land on his beak. However, he would puff up when getting ready to sleep. Puffing-up, or bristling the feathers, is what hummingbirds do to rapidly bring the body temperature down in preparation for torpidity by increasing the rate of dissipation of body heat. Since hummingbirds have no down feathers, puffing-up has the opposite effect of the feather-fluffing that other birds do. Perhaps there is just a slight lowering of body temperature. I can find no reference, however, to semitorpidity. An effort was made to approximate our average summer evening temperatures by maintaining a 58 to 60 degree F. range. During the daytime when sunlight filled the room, the temperature rose to about 70 or 75 degrees F. naturally. On raw or cloudy days I increased the temperature to 68 or 70 degrees F. The intention was to duplicate what I thought he would be getting in nature. Squeak had his own ideas. The hummingbirds that come to our garden are most active in the morning. Then they are next most active just prior to retiring for the evening. They feed frequently and are much more tolerant of one another at that time. Squeak was not active before retiring.

The end of the day came in three stages for Squeak. The first stage began at natural sunset. He was active all day long, flying around, visiting flowers and feeders, catching bugs, and preening. But, in spite of what I had planned, when sunset

arrived and the birds outside quieted down, so did
Squeak. At that time, he would sit quietly at his
choice spot of the time. Until February it was on a
branch stuck in a mimulus plant under the fluorescents. He apparently liked the warmth there when
the warmth from the sun was gone. He would
leave the branch periodically, albeit infrequently,
to visit a flower or a feeder and then eventually he
would move about eight inches away to a different
branch and hardly move at all. From late February
on, Squeak barely sat under the fluorescents at all.
Instead he began favoring the south end of the
sunroom. He was especially fond of branches near
the waterfall—either the one and only branch that
he would use on the Island snapdragon plant or the
branch stuck in the scarlet monkey flower (*Mimulus
cardinalis*) plant. Nevertheless, wherever he sat at
that point, he would hardly move at all. That was
the second stage. Finally, about fifteen minutes
before the lights would go off, he moved to the
branch where he would be sleeping. That was the
third stage and that's when I would pet him.

As time rolled on, and probably coincidental
to the time spring migration might have otherwise
begun, Squeak was less and less sedentary during
the evenings. Time changed and habits changed
with it. Evening activity increased tremendously
over what it had been all winter. That little plant
stake on which he had spent so many hours sitting
fell by the wayside, never to be sat upon again. Of

*The end of the day
came in three stages
for Squeak. Wherever
he sat he would hardly
move at all.*

course, lengthening days is most likely the factor
that precipitated these changes. By late January
there was a noticeable difference in the time that
he went to the skinny branch.

   The most curious habit that Squeak had is
what I call head-wagging. Each night after he settled down on that skinny branch, he spent from
several seconds up to several minutes rapidly moving his head from side to side. I'm not sure what
the significance of this action was. Perhaps it was
instinctive, whereby the hummingbird assures itself
that there are no enemies or even other hummingbirds around. I've seen other male ruby-throated
hummingbirds perform this same movement. Not
all of them, only certain ones—usually the most
dominant male around, and I've only seen this

behavior in the evening just before the particular
bird would retreat to his sleeping place. I've always
been under the impression that the bird was scan-
ning its territory, searching for intruders. I suppose
that Squeak considered the sunroom his territory
and it may be, after all, that he was giving himself
one final assurance that there were no enemies or
intruders around before falling into that vulnerable
state of sleep. If the lights were turned off while he
was engaging in head wagging, he would stop
instantly and close his eyes. Ordinarily, when he
was tired and before drifting off to sleep, he would
appear to have a little difficulty keeping his eyes
open and he slept with them closed.

During evening inspections Squeak, on numerous occasions, was found to be retrieving some
of the reserve from his crop as was evidenced by
his swallowing or "gulping."

Tidbits

Once Squeak discovered that he could sit on a branch at the north end of the sunroom and watch the birds feeding outside, he spent a great deal of time each day doing just that. For the most part he just watched, occasionally pulling his head down and flattening his body when several birds would fly overhead. There were, however, certain birds to whom Squeak responded more than others. Foremost among them, and the first bird to which Squeak reacted, was a sharp-shinned hawk.

Hummingbirds are impudent and pugnacious little birds. It is comical to watch them chase birds many times their own size around the yard so fearlessly. They carry on in their devil-may-care manner regardless of what else is around and when all other birds are frozen during the presence of a

Expelling fecal matter, a hit-and-miss sort of affair.

hawk, hummingbirds just continue their comings and goings, fearlessly oblivious to any threat of danger. They apparently are confident in their ability to escape being caught. Jays will scream and holler, sending all the other birds scurrying for cover, but the hummingbirds just continue eating in their particularly defiant way. I had no reason to expect Squeak to behave any differently here, but he did. He would stop whatever he was doing and freeze when a hawk was around. He responded to the hollering of the blue jays by crouching and becoming absolutely still, as if he were out there too. Perhaps hawks are a problem to hummingbirds in their wintering grounds, although not such a problem over the summer range. He would stay in that frozen position until either I diverted his

*Squeak had a cowlick,
noticeable here as he
visits apple blossoms.*

attention or he heard some chirping outside.

Squeak also showed interest in the mocking-birds. Perhaps it was their flashy white patches. Every once in a while Squeak would see one scur-rying across the garage roof and would attempt to chase it.

But, most of all, Squeak loved the cardinals. He would watch excitedly as the males chased one another, flying back and forth in front of and rushing right up to the windows, charging them. When he would hover in front of the windows watching the cardinals, the pitch or tone of his hovering would change. Perhaps his wings were rotating at a faster speed, for at those times he sounded like a drill.

Because Squeak showed a moderate amount of

interest in the birds outside, a mirror was set up in the sunroom for him. He seemed to dislike it, almost deliberately avoiding it.

Most hummingbirds are unable to walk or hop, depending on their wings for locomotion. When they want to move, even to change position on a perch, they put their wings into motion and, rising slightly above the perch, pivot around. They hardly ever land on the substratum. On April 27, I saw the closest thing to a hummingbird walking that I, or possibly anyone else, may ever see. Squeak landed on a shelf in pursuit of a fallen fuchsia flower. He landed about two inches from the flower and so was unable to reach it just right. He wanted to check the flower for nectar, but it was loose and each time he approached it with his beak, he actually pushed it farther away. As he continued to follow the flower, step by step, half-walking, half-sliding forward, he also continued to push it that much farther away. The movement was similar to the way a hummingbird sidles along laterally to move an inch or two on a twig, the same type of action except with a forward movement.

Hummingbirds are so small, and unless one is fine-tuned to them, they go unnoticed more often than not. People have stopped here and, while looking through the glass of the French door, have said, "How's the bird?" and not see him sitting on the skinny branch, no more than two feet directly in front of their eyes.

Expelling fecal matter is basically an involun-
tary action, a hit-and-miss sort of affair with no
mind being given to it at all. This is not the case,
however, when preparing to sleep. At that time,
Squeak would lift his back end and shoot the
droppings several feet away. Perhaps that was instinctive so as not to give away his location.

Hummingbirds can hardly be described without the liberal use of superlatives. Because most
hummers don't sing, there is only one area in
which they are ever said to be lacking, and that's
voice. This is especially true with our North American hummers. In spite of this reputation, Squeak
had quite a repertoire of vocalizations, from squeaky
metallic clinks and soft, barely audible chirps to
loud guttural chatter, and he barely did anything
without at least a chirp. He would make that metallic clink noise after every sip of nectar, chirp
while he was bathing, and respond in kind if I
chirped to him. Voice does match size and, under
ordinary circumstances, most of his adorable squeaky
little chirps would go unnoticed.

All of the feathers across Squeak's back were
sparkling emerald green and overlapping perfectly
in a mosaic pattern. All, that is, except a few
feathers dead center between the wings that crisscrossed one another and refused to lay flat. The
effect of these crisscrossed feathers was especially
noticeable by the air movement from his wings.
While Squeak was hovering, the feathers lifted up

and curved backward toward his head—Squeak had a pronounced cowlick! I have carefully examined all my photographs of other hummingbirds, as well as photographs of hummingbirds in books, and I have not seen even one other hummer with this unusual characteristic. Some day in the future, this cowlick, his trademark, may prove to be the clue to his identity.

3

Toward The Spring

The Molt

Molting is the gradual, periodic replacement of old and worn-out feathers. The molting season and the duration of the molt cycle is different in the various species of hummingbird. With some species the molt is an annual event, while others molt more than once each year. The process uses a great deal of energy and has a definite affect on metabolism. When feathers are missing, the body loses heat more rapidly than when the bird is fully feathered, thus requiring more fuel to keep the furnace going, and more power is needed when flying with missing wing or tail feathers. To compensate for this additional energy requirement, hummingbirds are often not as active during this period and some may even gain a little weight because of the inactivity.

Reference is scanty, perhaps even nonexistent, as to how often the ruby-throated hummingbird molts, and I've had to draw my own conclusion. Two, spring and fall, is a logical assumption based upon observation over the years. The spring molt precedes the breeding season and probably occurs, at least in part, prior to spring migration. At least some also molt in the fall prior to their departure for the wintering grounds. Every year we have several males in our garden that are in the process of molting. Gorgets, reportedly the last feathers to be replaced, are usually renewed toward the end of August. Birds are not sexually active in their wintering grounds and, furthermore, as migrants, they are subordinate to many other hummers. So I don't know why the gorget feathers are replaced except that they must just become worn. Young ruby-throats do not molt before leaving and we've only had one molting female here in the fall. This occurred three years in a row, including this past year, but each year it has been the same female. I don't know what the yellow-throated female does. Each year when she's finished nesting, she leaves and allows her young to have this territory for the remainder of the season. Most of the other females here do likewise. On the other hand, very many females have remained here right up to the end of the season with no signs of molting at all. Perhaps molting is sporadic, with individual birds having their own individual timetables as other birds do. For instance, you never see all the blue jays in the garden molting at the same exact time. Even among hummingbirds here, differences can be seen.

The molt is variously reported as beginning with the shedding of the first primary and finishing up with replacement of the gorget feathers, the hummingbirds' crowning glory and that which should be in the best condition for the breeding season. This is true at least as far as Anna's is concerned. The only hummingbird molting habit that has been studied in detail has been Anna's hummingbird, but there is no reason why one should not expect that the pattern would at least be similar. It has been reported that hummingbirds do not attempt to breed out of season because of the dormancy of their sex glands and it has been further suggested that until the new gorget is complete, the males don't even engage in display behavior.

Squeak's molt began in mid-January with the loss of a chest feather. On January 14, I noticed several pinfeathers on the chest and saw one chest feather fall out while he was scratching. Within a week he had pinfeathers on the throat, gorget area, breast, head, and his post-ocular spot, and was losing feathers every time he started scratching. As a matter of fact, he did an inordinate amount of scratching during that period. The loose

In early February new iridescent gorget feathers began to appear.

feathers must have either made him feel uncomfortable or itchy. Under ordinary and free circumstances, this would place the start of the molt prior to the spring migration.

Coincidentally, it was about that time that Squeak began what I perceived to be sexual behavior. It started small, with displaying in the shuttle-flight fashion, but once it started, it continued. I consider it sexual behavior because not only did he display, but he also mounted anything oval-shaped—a flower bud or even a small fuchsia leaf.

Within a few days from the time he arrived here, I noticed his one iridescent red spot, dead center at the lower part of the gorget area. It is not unusual for young male hummers to have one or more iridescent gorget feathers. Some have sev-

Squeak during his molt—notice the pinfeather sheaths on his head.

eral. I've seen them concentrated at the center of the gorget area, scattered here and there, and like a necklace across the border of the gorget and throat areas. One had such a bright band of iridescence there that I referred to him as "ring of bright feathers." The gorget is supposed to be the last area to molt, but Squeak's gorget started coming in even before he lost one primary. It began February 4 when a new iridescent red spot revealed itself. This was followed by additional iridescent gorget feathers and, before the end of February it looked as though his throat had been sprinkled with brilliant dust from rubies. The one red spot he had all winter always appeared to be very bright, but with the onset of new gorget feathers, the difference between the old and the new became very appar-

ent and incomparable. Returning male hummingbirds in the spring always look brighter than they
do toward the end of the season. Apparently the
feathers lose brilliance with the passage of time.

Squeak continued to lose and replace small
body feathers at a rapid pace and by the end of
February, I had picked up and saved lots of them.

This pace continued through March 4, when
feather loss seemed to come to a standstill. For the
next week, only one or two feathers were lost
altogether. Then, on March 12, the molt resumed
vigorously, even more rapidly than it had before.
More feathers were found in the two-week period
from March 4 through March 18 than had been
found in the almost two-month period from January 14 through March 4. Feather loss wasn't as
sporadic as it had been either. Squeak seemed to
be primarily losing feathers from the same area,
almost as if the line of feather loss was moving
down the front of him from the bottom of the
gorget area and working downward. With the two
different levels of feathers causing him to appear
sleek on top and puffy on bottom, he looked as
though he were sitting snugly in a pecan shell, or
maybe even the bottom half of an eggshell, or as if
someone had just peeled away the feathers.

Around April I began to become quite con-
cerned about the slow progression of Squeak's molt.
He had been replacing contour feathers since mid-
January and by April the smattering of iridescent

gorget feathers had begun to coalesce, appearing to all who might capture a glimpse of his radiance that he had captured light, electrified it, and shot it back. However, he had not even started to replace the primaries and was still showing the juvenile tail spots. It should be noted that these feathers appeared to be in top condition. By early April ruby-throats are well on their way to being back on their breeding grounds and other males, I am sure, had long since completed their molts.

My concern was that perhaps Squeak was deficient in a particular hormone and perhaps that same hormone is responsible for fattening up for the fall departure. If that were true, Squeak's future might possibly be in jeopardy.

With this thought gnawing away at me, I placed telephone calls to two hummingbird authorities in an attempt to find out whether this might be a problem. It was indicated that, with the exception of Anna's, very little is known about molting in hummingbirds. However, this failure to have a complete molt, especially in juveniles, is not unheard of, and that it does happen. Perhaps production of the hormone that causes the molt is the result of excessive proteins consumed on the wintering grounds—food for thought. About a year ago, I had heard of a newly returning male ruby-throat that had only a small amount of iridescent gorget feathers instead of the full gorget. Since it was much too early in the season for it to be a

He looked as though he were sitting snugly in a pecan shell.

young hummer, I had been convinced that the person had been mistaken. Although I had never noticed it during all the years I've been watching hummingbirds, and while it may not be common, apparently it does occur and apparently she had been correct.

Whether or not Squeak would be breeding this year was doubtful, not so much because of the lack of any hormone, but because of the lack of a full and attractive gorget with which to attract a female.

One point that was made was that the males are not as strict about returning to their nesting grounds as the females are. Therefore, Squeak might very well just opt to remain here in our garden rather than return to the place of his birth—which

By April the smattering of iridescent gorget feathers had begun to coalesce.

may have even been as far away as Canada. It was also indicated that juveniles have only a general idea of where to migrate to in the fall, but are pretty much left on their own to make that first trip by their own devices. Imagine, barely a few months old and having to make such a journey. If a bird is successful, it will take the same route each year thereafter. So I should not be surprised if I were to find him at my doorstep next October expecting to winter here in the sunroom.

The possibilities that existed were encouraging and exciting. The chances would be good that he might make our garden his territory. Absent that, or perhaps in addition to that, he might make our sunroom his wintering grounds. What delightful prospects.

For the better part of April, molting was non-existent and I had resigned myself to the fact that I would not be saving any tail feathers (rectrices) or wing feathers (remiges) and I would not be seeing Squeak with a full, glow-from-within gorget. Then, on May 4, it started in again. I found twenty-six feathers on the floor under the branches where he sat to scratch or preen, including five or six from the head, where pinfeathers had again begun to appear, a couple of spotted feathers from the gorget area, and one of the secondaries.

I just could not help worrying about the way he was so slow at molting as well as fattening up for migration and hoping that the two weren't related.

Growing Up

In early January, Squeak began displaying, not in the large arc commonly associated with the ruby-throated hummingbird, but in that tight oscillation of only a couple of inches and up to a couple of feet commonly called the shuttle flight. I call it buzzing because of the noise that accompanies the display. In addition to any vocalizations, a mechanical noise is made during the display. I'm not sure exactly how that noise is produced, but it sounds as though the feathers are held at such an angle so as to cause air to pass over or through them, thereby creating a vibrating type of sound. Interestingly, the display noise sounds a great deal like the sound made when Squeak flew around the

Squeak began to mount buds after displaying to them—here it is a hibiscus bud.

His little feet moved forward and backward—front view.

Rear view.

During the display, Squeak, moving from side to side, fanned his tail each time he changed direction.

room drying his wings and, possibly, tail after his
bath and shower. The first time he displayed, he
displayed twice to the metal bars under the plant
trays and once to the handle on one of the tripods.
Perhaps small horizontal objects interested him.

By mid-January, just about when his molt
started, Squeak expanded his display to include
other objects such as a leaf or flower bud (also in
the horizontal position). But, in addition to the
displaying that he had been doing, Squeak began
to mount the different buds after he displayed to
them. And, although hummingbirds reportedly do
not attempt to breed or engage in display behavior
until their new gorgets have been completed, in
my opinion Squeak was definitely showing sexual
behavior. Apparently this behavior does not hold
true for the ruby-throat, at least not this rubythroat. Actually, the only real work that has been
done, with respect to breeding out of captivity,
has been as it relates to the Anna's, a hummingbird
that breeds extremely early anyway. When Squeak
would mount a bud, his little feet moved forward
and backward, almost as if he were trying to stand
on it, and at times even pressing into the bud as if
he were trying to secure himself or hold it down.
The time spent on any individual bud was never
more than a few seconds after which he almost
seemed to slide off.

This type of behavior—displaying and then
mounting for a few seconds—continued for ap-

proximately one month. Then, around mid-February, he added a new dimension to this aspect of his personality. He began attacking the buds before he mounted them. First he would display to the unopened buds in his usual fashion and then, before mounting them, would stab at them viciously and repeatedly with his beak. This was always done as he passed from the right of the bud to the left. Consequently, there were many mangled phalaenopsis and fuchsia buds in the sunroom, each having numerous puncture marks on one side. Still, he only showed any interest in oval shaped objects in a horizontal position.

I'm not sure of what brought on each individual act of displaying but, seemingly spontaneous, it would begin with Squeak, head forward and lowered and neck sleek and outstretched, looking at something. He would then flick his tail. He appeared to get a slight muscle contraction at the base of the tail just before he would start the actual display behavior. He would then rush right up to the object of his affection and quickly begin his display, moving from side to side and fanning his tail each time he changed direction. He faced the object at all times, undoubtedly to exhibit the iridescent plumage of his gorget to its best advantage.

In addition to the dazzling aerial display flights to a female, a hummingbird may also engage in display flights as an aggressive gesture designed to show its territory, not only to members of its own

His gorget would be held in a concave position to concentrate its color.

species, but to non-hummingbirds as well. They are notoriously pugnacious during the breeding season. On a few occasions, Squeak even displayed to me. Once it wasn't just his usual shuttle display, it was an arc. A small one, but an arc nevertheless. First he sat on his branch just looking at me. Then, all of a sudden, the arc. Perhaps he was threatening me, in his own way telling me to get out, or maybe it was just a practice run.

By early March, Squeak added vocalizations to his repetoire of adult male hummingbird display behavior. The vocalizations sounded much like an extremely loud, sharp, high-pitched, and very rapid chatter and are in addition to the noise produced by the feathers when displaying. Occasionally after the above noted behavior, Squeak would perch

on one of his branches and, with his beak slightly
ajar, make a hoarse, squealing noise that sounded
like air being slowly let out of something.

While Squeak was displaying, his gorget would
be held, either voluntarily or involuntarily, I'm not
sure, in a concave position, thus forcing it to face
forward even more than it would otherwise, con-
centrating the color and making it much more
attractive to a female or threatening to an adver-
sary. This was especially noticeable when Squeak
was viewed from the side. This action may also
account for the gorget's extreme brilliance on certain occasions. We keep a clothesline up in the
yard as a place for the hummingbirds to sit. If a
male is sitting on the line and facing the house, the
beautiful ruby-colored gorget is clearly visible. However, a difference in the gorget is detected immediately if another male arrives on the scene. The
radiance then becomes so overpowering that the
glow practically obliterates the rest of the bird
from sight.

Making Friends

Each evening as Squeak perched on the skinny branch and before the lights went off, I would gently stroke his breast with one finger. He wasn't afraid and he either didn't seem to mind at all or was just tolerating it. Once, though, when I nudged him a bit, trying to get him to sit on my finger, he responded by flying over to the feeder. He was reluctant and I never pushed it.

The little female that stayed in the sunroom that snowy day in 1987 spent a considerable amount of that time sitting on my finger. At first she was somewhat cautious, but once she realized that it was somewhere to sit and that I wasn't hurting her, she was almost eager to take advantage of the perch. Later she appeared to be quite relaxed as she sat preening herself for stretches of up to ten or twelve minutes each. She did this repeatedly while she was here. She never approached my finger on her own but when I put my finger next to her and nudged, she sat willingly. Squeak, on the other hand, didn't exhibit any such signs of trust toward my hands for quite some time. Even when he finally did lose his fear of my hands, he was never willing to perch on a finger.

Right from the beginning, basically, I was able to get close to him. I was able to put my face as close to Squeak as the limit of my focusing ability would allow and it was always all right with him. He seemed to enjoy it when I would hum to him, often tilting his head and closing his eyes. At times he would just stare at me and he looked just like a bottle-nosed dolphin. He never minded my being close as long as I kept my hands away from him. If my hands were in my pockets or behind my back, everything was fine. That is, unless I was holding something that interested him. He had absolutely no qualms about being near my hands if they held something he wanted.

Hummingbirds are naturally inquisitive. Squeak was no less inquisitive here in this unnatural environment. After he had been here but a short while he became quite accustomed to my presence and grew very inquisitive about me. Within a couple of weeks he was deliberately touching me. He investigated everything, including my hair, my eyes, my cameras and tripods. He spent a great deal of time, several minutes at a clip, investigating my hair, especially at the back of my head. It may very well have been that he was merely looking for

At times he would just stare at me and he looked just like a bottle-nosed dolphin.

insects, or perhaps it was just curiosity, but he would go around behind me and investigate the hair at the back of my head. I suppose he thought that as long as he couldn't see my eyes, I didn't know that he was there. One day while investigating my eye, he stuck his tongue out and touched my lashes. He showed a remarkable amount of interest in my eyes, frequently hovering in front of them while his tongue darted in and out. Perhaps the pupil resembles the tube of a flower.

When I walked into his room wearing a floral-printed dress, he spent several minutes trying to figure out how to get nectar from the "flowers." Apparently he recognized them for what they are intended to be. I've seen him try to enter flowers that were pictures on catalog covers.

He was very interested when I talked softly to him and would cock his head, focusing in on me, and answer in barely audible chirps. Those endearing little chirps supposedly mean contentment and I like to think that they do. They are apparently age-linked, being common, for the most part, to juveniles, and I must admit that I heard them less and less often as Squeak grew up.

He was soon brave enough that he would follow me anytime I had something in my hand, floating along right beside me inspecting whatever it was that I was holding.

There were times, too, when Squeak would become angry. Primarily those times related to a change in his territory. One such time was when I moved a small-budded flowering maple that had grown too tall to fit under the fluorescents. He liked to visit that plant when he was at the stage where he sat under the lights. When he realized that it was gone, it almost seemed as if he were giving a "dirty look" to the fuchsia that had been put in its place, stretching his neck and pulling his head all the way back as if he were looking at something in sheer disbelief. He wanted that flowering maple put back where it had been and flew away and back over and over as if he expected the right one to appear upon one of his returns. Needless to say, I returned the plant to where it had been. I'm sure that he was satisfied as he immediately visited a flower and calmed down afterward.

Another time he was visibly angry when I
hung a trailing kalanchoe plant slightly above and
away from where he was to sleep. He liked the
plant very much and visited it immediately and
repeatedly when I brought it in, but didn't want it
near his sleeping branch when he was ready to
settle down for the night. He would get on the
branch, look at the plant and immediately get off
the branch again. He was waiting, I'm sure, for
that new foreign object to disappear. Finally, I
moved the plant for the night. I did that every
night for over a week. By that time he was a little
more amenable to it and I was able to leave it at
that new spot permanently.

He would also become annoyed when I tried
to clean his room. I'm sure he became angry. He
would dive at me or fly straight at my face and
then, at the very last moment, dip down to about
chest level and up and over my head. After he
would dive at me, he would go to a bare branch
and sit with his mouth slightly opened, his threat
posture, just looking at me.

When Squeak was very angry or frightened,
his feathers were held tightly against his body and
he appeared much thinner. So thin, in fact, that he
appeared skinny in the neck area. On the other
hand, when he was very relaxed, he would appear
especially puffy. Ordinarily he was somewhere in
between, slightly puffy.

I had wanted to form some sort of bond with

Squeak before I released him, not only to make sure that our garden would be his territory but to have a special relationship with him once he was on his own as well. I wanted our relationship of the winter to continue in a modified form during the spring and summer. Friendship would have to center around his needs and food, of course, would be the best bet.

I had tried several times during the winter to get Squeak interested in a small red tube that I had filled with a very sweet sugar and water solution, but I had been having poor luck with that approach. I also tried a small vial with a red ribbon tied around it, also to no avail. It wasn't that he wouldn't approach something that I was holding, because he would visit flowers as I held them up for him. I decided that I would have to offer the sugar-water solution in something more familiar to him, something like one of his feeders. That's exactly what I did. I used a Nektar-Plus feeder and made a 2-to-1 ratio solution of water and sugar and after eight or ten minutes of tempting, he tried it. He loved it and came back over and over again for more. He wouldn't leave me alone. Every time I walked into his room he would hover around me chirping and chirping, looking for a treat. I wanted the solution to be a special treat only and to serve as a bond. I didn't want him to be drinking it all the time, but he wanted it and he would poke all around me looking for it. Once, when I walked

Squeak and me.

into the room, he hovered around my face, chirping and getting closer and closer to my eyes, looking for his treat. He got so close to my eyes that I had to close them. The next thing I knew, he had inserted his beak into my nostril. He certainly made himself irresistible.

If I entered the room holding the feeder, he would spot it from across the room and would quickly and directly fly over to drink. He would then hover back and forth in front of it so rapidly and anxiously that I was barely able to turn the feeder around and switch it to my right hand. He would take one long drink and one sip. He would then fly over to the branch, sit for a few seconds, come back to the feeder, take one final short sip, and then fly to the other side of the room and sit.

He was finished. He would chirp after each sip
and everytime he sat. Of course, after every feeding, his bill was scraped, first one side and then
the other, across a twig.

Unlike most birds that beat their wings, hummingbirds rotate their relatively long wings at the
shoulder with little flexing at the wrist or elbow
and receive power on both the up and down strokes.
During hovering the wings move horizontally in a
figure-eight pattern and cycle about eighty times
per second. The air movement created by his hovering wings was so strong that when I fed him
about level with my neck, it felt as though there
were a fan right next to my feet. Not only is the
down draft strong, but the air movement would
even set plants swaying several feet away laterally.

If I entered the room without the feeder, he
would actually follow me around, chirping, until I
left to get the feeder. It was quite difficult for me
to resist when he begged for the sugar-water. I
wanted the solution to be particularly sweet, especially later when I, hopefully, would be feeding
him outdoors, but I knew that the 2-to-1 ratio was
much too sweet, so I began to gradually increase
the solution of water and sugar to 3-to-1.

Until that time, a turning point, Squeak appeared to be oblivious to the door, seemingly un-
concerned about what was on the other side. All of
a sudden he began watching for me on the other
side and upon seeing me, would fly right up to the

door, hovering all around and looking for his treat. It's unbelievable how quickly he learned and it only took one taste of that sugar-water. All of a sudden he began sitting on that skinny branch at all different times. After all, it's a perfect place to sit for a good view of approaching nectar. When he saw me approaching the door, he would drop down to the door handle and hover there waiting for me to come into the room. He quickly made the association of either the sight or sound of the handle turning with the receipt of his treat. It was noticeable that he was especially active about bug-catching once he started having that solution. Perhaps it is instinctive for him to keep his diet balanced. At any rate, I believe it certainly was best that I had to leave him most of the day while I went to work. This kept him using the balanced Nektar-Plus for the major part of the day.

The only time that he would not take the offered solution was the time I walked into his room wearing a T-shirt with a picture of two broad-billed hummingbirds and a castilleja plant. He fanned his tail, hovering from side to side, and then flew over to a branch on the other side of the room. It was apparent that he didn't like what he saw on that shirt. I changed the shirt and when I went back into the room he was back to his usual behavior. That wasn't the first article of clothing at which he had shown disapproval. He wasn't very fond of the sweat shirt with the picture of a cat with large eyes on it either.

Squeak was especially active about bug-catching toward the end of the day, just as the other hummingbirds appear to be in the garden, and there were certain places where he hunted more than others. One of those places, of course, was the waterfall, a natural magnet for little gnats and aphids. Squeak would also rush into certain plants to stir up the whiteflies, with the scarlet monkey flower plant always yielding generous numbers for him to catch.

The weather had warmed up nicely and by mid-April I decided to move the mimulus plant outside to the lath house. Actually, I was happy to get rid of some of the whiteflies. Squeak, however, missed the plant almost immediately. When he would rush in the way he did to stir them up, his efforts were unproductive. Failing to find any insects in a place where they had been available before, Squeak moved to the branch at the north window and tried the same action toward some of the other plants.

In an attempt to help him out, I disturbed some whiteflies from the undersides of a particular fuchsia. To my surprise, Squeak flew over immediately to where my hand was and started catching and eating one whitefly after another in a feeding-frenzy manner. He showed absolutely no uneasiness about being so close to my hand whatsoever and took complete advantage of my help for as long as I was willing to give it. After helping him only two or three times, Squeak learned that all he had to do if he wanted my assistance was to go to that fuchsia plant, hover and chirp to get my attention. All during fall and winter Squeak had taken care of his own protein needs with no interference from me and had done very well for himself at that. But, as winter turned to spring, building a bond between us became more and more important to me and becoming involved in what he liked was the way to do it. In no time at all, Squeak and I became an effective hunting team.

He always knew what he wanted and always knew exactly how to get it. He begged and pestered me for sugary treats by hovering around my head, chirping and dancing back and forth in front of my eyes or hovering all around my hands (of all places) looking for the feeder. Sometimes he would chirp softly while circling my head and then hovering back and forth in front of and so close to my eyes that I could no longer focus in on him. He would watch for me through the door and greet me the minute I entered the room. The very last thing I did each night before Squeak went to sleep was to bring the feeder of sugar-water in to him and hold it while he sat on the skinny branch lazily sipping one last time. When he was ready for his shower and bath, he would wait for me to enter the room, fly over to the bathing area and, while sitting on the branch under the fluorescents,

Squeak having a sugary treat.

chirp and look at the cattleya leaf, waiting for my
compliance. And, when he wanted some hunting
help, he managed to get that across to me as well.
He'd sit on the branch, look at the fuchsia where
we hunted the whiteflies, look at me, look at the
fuchsia again, and chirp. Or he would go to that
fuchsia and hover over it, doing nothing else,
waiting for me to come over and do my part. I was
supposed to know what he wanted and I did. I've
always thought that a vacuum cleaner would be an
effective way to control whiteflies but Squeak worked
without electricity. I think he rather liked having
me around and would hover around my head just
looking at me for no apparent reason. No matter
what I may have been doing, Squeak would dart
over to investigate. Eventually it got to the point

that anything that I held in my hand was regarded as a possible food source and was promptly investigated. And, if he wasn't hovering around my face or flying as closely as possible to me, he'd fly over to wherever I was and sit near me. He liked sitting right behind me best; of all the branches in the sunroom on which he could sit, he always chose the one closest to me.

Once the turning point had been reached, Squeak became more responsive to me than he had ever been and even though I like to think otherwise, I'm sure that he consented to be my friend because he, like most other animals, is such a little opportunist. Nevertheless, by late April I felt that we had really and finally become friends and my only hope was that it might carry over to the outdoors.

The Release

Spring rolled around far too quickly in 1989. It seems as though it was just yesterday that I discovered Squeak in the garden. He had been my ray of sunshine for the whole winter, but I knew all along that eventually I would have to start thinking about releasing him and I knew that it would be difficult. Never before in my life had I wished it were still January when May rolled around, but this year has proven to have been different.

As the inevitable drew near, it became increasingly difficult for me to accept, and not nearly as clear that releasing him was the best and right thing to do. Of course my rationale had become biased by my innermost desires. I envisioned many different scenarios, all of which had Squeak wanting to stay. I wanted to keep him here, protected from the sometimes harsh world of nature, and it wasn't as though he had been chomping at the bit to get out. He had accepted his entire stay here very matter-of-factly, but this is not where he belongs. All I had to do was look at him and it brought a smile to my face and my heart. I'd watch him do all the little things he did and as I watched, I'd beam. How was I ever going to be able to do it? He had been doing the same things here all winter that he would have been doing outdoors: visiting flowers, hunting for insects, bathing, preening, loafing, and sleeping. He had never known the hardship of fighting elements to arrive at some foreign destination, of being chased away from a flower that some other hummingbird had claimed for its own.

It is so hard to let go of something you've

treasured as much as I'd treasured Squeak, even
when you know it's the right thing to do. This
would turn out to be one of the toughest decisions
that I had ever had to make and stick with. Whether
or not to release him was thought out very carefully and with very mixed emotions. All the pros
and cons were weighed diligently. If Squeak were
to stay in, a regular source of food, plenty of
flowers and insects would always be available to
him, longevity would virtually be assured, and sleeping in the rain (and as much as they like rain, I'm
sure they don't like it when it's cold and constant),
pesticides, spiders' webs, and other such perils would
be unknown to him. But, if he were to be released,
he would have interaction with other hummingbirds. The longer he stayed here, the further removed from nature he might become. It could
become ten to twelve years of living in one room
and that would not be fair.

     I don't know where this bird had come from
originally—it may have been twenty, thirty or fifty
miles away—nor did I know whether or not he
would be going back. My greatest fear was that
when I opened the door he would just take off and
I'd never see him again, and I knew if that were to
happen, it would break my heart.

     Initially the plan was to release Squeak during
the first week in May, hopefully a day or two
before any other hummers returned. Being the first
one here might give Squeak an edge on becoming

yard boss. I wanted him to make our garden his
territory so his progress could be monitored. It had
been suggested to me by more than one person
that I have someone band Squeak. As with everything else, banding has its pros and cons. After
consideration of all the factors, I decided against it
as being unnecessary, possibly undesirable, and of
no benefit to Squeak, only to a person who might
find him.

The first week in May, however, was unusu-
ally cold and rainy, certainly too cold, I thought,
to expose Squeak to the elements. It was decided
to postpone his release for several days. On May
10 it was pouring and I couldn't help wondering
where Squeak would have been sleeping had he
been released. I began to reevaluate my decision.
Perhaps I should scrap the release plan altogether.

But then, after the first week of May when
other hummers began to return, everything changed,
and my thoughts changed too. Although he had
not been chomping at the bit to get out, it was
quite another story when he spotted other hummers outside. He became very excited, chattering
and flying rapidly back and forth. Or he would
hover in front of the window, watching them.
Somehow they always knew he was there also. I
walked in one day to see Squeak and another male
hovering beak to beak with the window in between them. I knew what had to be done. May 14
would be the day that he would be released. The

weather was back to normal and, besides, it was
Mother's Day.

The morning of the release went about as
usual, eating, preening, a bath and shower, preening, begging for treats, preening, hanging around
loafing and begging for treats. About 10:30 A.M., I
finally got up the nerve to make a move. I opened
the back door for the first time since last fall and
stood there with his treat in my hand. He came
over periodically for a sip and each time I stood
farther outside. Three times he came out, took a
sip, and flew back inside. The fourth time I stood
a couple of feet out of the door. After almost
one-half hour of coaxing, he finally came all the
way out. After a drink he flew over and inspected
the buds on a fuchsia hanging under the porch's
overhang, along with the windows and the latticework of the overhang. He then lifted up and over
the roof of the porch toward the front of the house
and that was it. That was the last I saw of him.

I must admit, tears welled up in my eyes and
for an instant, just a split second, I was sorry for
what I had done. Not so much sorry that I let him
go, just sorry that he didn't stay. Words simply
cannot express the heartache that I felt when he
failed to come right back. Maybe hummingbirds
are just free spirits that don't form any attach-
ments. They do lack the typical avian social
structure.

He's a free bird now. Although it was not what I had been expecting, I had hoped that he would hang around, eagerly accepting our human handouts. As hard as it might be, I knew that I'd have to be willing to say good-bye.

I look for him everywhere, even now. I keep the screen off one window in the sunroom hoping that one day he'll fly in to beg for his sugary treat or shower, or that one night he'll decide that he wants to sleep on the skinny branch. I've even replaced one of the regular feeders with a Nektar-Plus feeder; it should make an excellent training feeder for new hummers but, mainly, I want Squeak to find a familiar sight should he decide to return. I know I'd feel much better if he'd make that one appearance that would tell me that he's making out just fine on his own. It rained his first night away.

It seems like only yesterday that I worried so about whether he would make it through the winter all right. Now, in retrospect, it all seems so easy and natural. I suppose that being rescued and making it unscathed through a winter that would have otherwise brought about his demise is happy ending enough for me.

As far as looks are concerned, right now I'd recognize him. When he gets a full gorget, he will no longer look the same. When I do see him, if he acts the way "old Squeak" acted, I shall surely recognize him. Until then, every time I see a male

Parting shot—the last photo taken of Squeak, May 14, 1989.

sitting around looking in the direction of the house,
I'll take an extra good look—and each time I'll
hope.

   The pleasure of his company was fleeting, as
are so many of the best things in life. I often think
about what I was told that I might expect. Perhaps
the sunroom will be his imprinted wintering grounds.
Perhaps when the fall arrives, we will again have a
winter guest, a living jewel among the flowers.

part II

ROSIE
My Rufous Hummingbird

First, for Rosie,
a beautiful bird and endearing personality
who has brought much happiness to my life

Next, for my husband, George,
and my family

and, finally,
in memory of Rupert

Introduction

In the fall of 1988 a young male ruby-throated hummingbird who had failed to migrate appeared in my garden. To save that bird from a certain unnecessary death, I lured him into my sunroom to spend the winter until it became safe to release him the following spring. That bird is the subject of my earlier book, *A Hummingbird in My House: The Story of Squeak*. Having Squeak as a winter guest had been a wonderful experience, one that I shall never forget and one that I never expected to experience again—unless Squeak himself returned, ready to spend another winter. This book is the story of another hummingbird, a species that is exceptionally unusual for my area, who paid me a visit one autumn and then refused to leave—the story of an off-course rufous hummingbird who spent the winter of 1993–1994 as yet another guest in my sunroom.

Since the first book was released I've received many cards, letters, and telephone calls from people who read Squeak's story, asking whether he had returned. I'm sorry to report that he didn't, and I think it would be appropriate here to tell a little about the conclusions I've reached with respect to that question and why.

All who have read Squeak's story know how it

broke my heart when I released him, but another experience has given me some insight into the rubythroat's
powerful territorial instincts and has offered a plausible
answer about what may have happened with Squeak. In
May 1991 a woman turned over to me the care of an
adult male ruby-throated hummingbird that five days
before had been captured by a cat. The attack caused
extensive soft-tissue damage to the muscle that elevates
the bird's wing and left it totally incapacitated and in
need of constant hand-feeding and related care. The
bird hailed from an area about twelve miles away and
was delivered to me at my office, ten miles in the other
direction. For the first week and a half, Charlie, as I
called him, traveled with me to and from work, where
he would sit in an open basket on my desk to be handfed at regular intervals. After that he was able to
maneuver well enough in his basket to reach the feeder on his own. With steady improvement, eventually
he was able to generate the lift necessary to get himself
out of the basket and that was followed not too long
afterward by gliding, very short flights, regular flying,
and, finally, hovering. In less than one month after
Charlie's episode with the cat, he was flying and hovering and vigorously exploring his surroundings. The
only problem Charlie seemed to have was a deformity
of one foot that was probably preexisting. Once hovering was perfected and other signs of progress were
evident, Charlie began to exhibit an avid interest in the
world beyond the sunroom. It soon became apparent
that he was close to being ready to be on his own.

Charlie was released on June 26, six weeks after the encounter with the cat. Like Squeak before him, he stopped and checked out the fuchsia under the back porch overhang and then took off. Territorial instincts, as they relate to returning in the spring, are well known. I had been wondering whether he would be following those instincts and whether he would attempt to return to his original breeding territory. His rapid departure answered my question. Much may be said for the rubythroats' territorial instincts and much may be said for their sense of direction as well. After having been taken several miles away from his territory, and after having been driven ten miles each way to work and back every day for more than a week, Charlie still found his regular stomping grounds. Members of the family of the woman who had brought him to me spotted him in their garden. They had been able to positively identify him by his deformed right foot. Charlie was a lucky bird, as the rate of successful rehabilitation and release attempts of songbirds is notoriously low. And that brings us to another lucky hummingbird, Squeak. On the basis of what happened with Charlie, I would speculate that Squeak returned to wherever he had been before he appeared in this garden. Of course, one can merely theorize about what happened ultimately to any of them. You do your best to change the courses of their misfortunes and hope that things turn out positively.

There may be those out there who feel that nature should take its course, thus assuring that only "good" genes are passed on for the benefit of the species, but I just can't agree. This bird is an individual first, a species second. The bottom line is that there are two choices: to let nature take its course, or to intervene. At times hard choices must be made when one encounters these situations, but at other times conditions exist that soften those choices. Fortunately, most people readily agree with the concept that distressed wildlife should be aided. We must be responsible trustees of our natural world and its inhabitants. To me, that means helping when one can. The ability to blend a scientific mind with a compassionate heart allows one to experience the best of both worlds.

It seems that an unprecedented number of rufous hummingbirds appeared in the East in 1993. Apparently two rufous or Allen's type hummers appeared four days before Thanksgiving at the perennial garden of the Wave Hill Conservancy on the Hudson River. These birds either succumbed to the cold the night before Thanksgiving or moved on early Thanksgiving morning; temperatures on Thanksgiving eve were around 15° F., all the flowers in the garden froze, and the birds were not seen again. A different rufous had appeared at a hummingbird feeder in Flushing (Queens County, New York City) in mid-November, and there were four reports for Maryland and one for New Jersey at about the same time. This inordinate number of Northeastern sightings in one season suggests to me that an external force was at play—some common denominator physical in nature, such as a weather or pressure system, and not "bad" genes. Perhaps El Niño was a factor.

Apparently this bird is a species on the move. According to Paul Johnsgard,[1] the rufous has only recently invaded Alaska—so recently, in fact, that flowers adapted for hummingbird pollination have not kept up, and the rufous frequently pollinates flowers more suitable for bees. Many years from now, if we are fortunate enough to still have hummingbirds, those that have been able to expand their ranges will be the ones that survive. The rufous hummingbird is essentially a mountain bird, and the Rocky Mountains mark the eastern edge of its migratory route. Perhaps one day its range may include the mountains of the Eastern states as well.

This is the story of one bird's adventure far from home, and is the chronicle of what will probably be the first confirmed sighting of a rufous hummingbird—a very unusual winter visitor—in New York State. I realize that of all North American hummers, the one most likely to be seen out of its normal range is the rufous. But there has yet to be a confirmed sighting in New York State, and I consider her visit to be an exciting and noteworthy event in the bird world.

Because there was such a sharp, natural division in events, the story is broken into three seasons—autumn,

1. Paul A. Johnsgard, Foundation Professor of Life Sciences at the University of Nebraska at Lincoln, is the author of *The Hummingbirds of North America* (Washington, D.C.: Smithsonian Institution Press, 1983).

winter, and spring—each beginning with a brief synopsis of what Rosie would be doing under normal circumstances and then what she was doing here. Autumn represents her arrival here and her adjustment period once she was taken in; winter details her daily routine, the time that she would ordinarily spend between migrations, her period of rejuvenation; and spring describes changes that precede a migration, a winddown toward her release.

First and foremost, I have derived great pleasure and personal satisfaction from being able to offer help to this bird, as well as from sharing my experience with others. My greatest hope is that this written account will contribute in some way to an increased knowledge of this species.

When I was young, I was told to put butter on a burn. I didn't listen; I had that "gut feeling" that water would be better. Likewise, when I was told to take down my hummingbird feeders by Labor Day, I had the feeling that the opposite would be better. I know that the hummingbirds that use the feeders are the first to leave in the fall, but feeders available later will be a welcome haven to stragglers while they accumulate extra weight in preparation for migration. These darling little stragglers are the bonus birds of the hummingbird season. And this year's straggler was the biggest bonus of them all.

AUTUMN

Autumn, for our purposes and irrespective of the dates on the calendar, is the time between the end of nesting and the arrival of hummingbirds on their wintering grounds, and consists primarily of the migration.

The rufous hummingbird migrates earlier than is typical for north temperate hummers such as the ruby-throated (*Archilochus colubris*), broad-tailed (*Selasphorus platycercus*), calliope (*Stellula calliope*), and black-chinned (*Archilochus alexandri*). Males tend to precede females, and adults the juveniles. William Calder reports that adult males are first to migrate, arriving at the Rocky

Mountain Biological Laboratory at Gothic, Colorado, as early as the end of June or early July.[2] Females, who follow the southbound males, migrate an average of six days later, and their numbers gradually increase at Gothic until they become more abundant than males. Later, juveniles, making their maiden migrations, start to arrive. The average time between the influx of males and juveniles is two weeks. Transients can usually be found in California through late August.

On the southbound journey, the rufous migrates along one of two major flyways flanking the Great Basin Desert: the Coast Ranges and the crest of the Sierra Nevadas or the Rocky Mountain Cordillera, where they may be found foraging among wildflowers in montane meadows. One such important wildflower is skyrocket, or scarlet gilia (*Ipomopsis [Gilia] aggregata*). The rufous hummingbird is the primary pollinator of skyrocket, which commences flowering by early July, just in time to provide nectar for the migrants. In the early summer, during the beginning of the skyrocket flowering season, broad-tailed hummingbirds, still in their breeding season, and the early migrating rufous hummingbirds descend on large patches of this attractive red flower. The rufous dominates the broadtail on the best territories, which contain not only skyrocket

2. William A. Calder, Ph.D., is professor of evolutionary biology at the University of Arizona at Tucson and the author of "The Rufous Hummingbird," *The Birds of North America*, Life Histories for the 21st Century, no. 53, 1993, and "Migration of Rufous Hummingbirds," *WildBird* 7, no. 5 (May 1993): 43–45.

but penstemon and paintbrushes as well. The adult
male rufous vigorously defends his feeding territory
(temporarily established for southbound refueling)
from both juveniles of his own species and broadtail
competition. Populations remain steady through July,
but by early September all hummingbirds are gone and
the skyrocket begins production of lighter-colored
flowers. The rufous continues south along the central
and southern Rockies and the Sierra Madre Oriental in
eastern Mexico, and then proceeds westward along the
transvolcanic range to its wintering range in Mexico.

An Unusual Visitor

Vagrant birds often stray far from their usual migration routes. Of all the hummingbirds, the rufous (*Selasphorus rufus*) is particularly far-ranging, and particularly so during its fall migration.

I'm not sure just when that hummingbird first appeared in my garden. I do remember, however, that once, while I was trying to take a mental tally of the season's young hummers, I thought, "Oh, yes, and there's that one with the cluster of iridescent gorget feathers that I saw the other day." After I observed a little more of that bird and determined that it was probably a rufous, I began to refer to her as "the little wanderer," which eventually led to "Rosie" from the song "The Wanderer" by Dion.

Perhaps it was the result of El Niño, but 1993's weather was quite the flip-flop from the norm, with West Coast rains ending a drought there that had persisted for several years and many parts of the East experiencing an almost totally rainless summer. The drought was so severe in this part of the Hudson Valley that the average backyard looked more like chaparral than the lush green we ordinarily get in a humid Eastern summer.

That year's weather may also have had an effect on local hummingbirds. Because of the drought, natural food was not plentiful and hummingbirds reportedly flocked to feeders in record numbers. Perhaps more important, albeit less noticeable, with reduced moisture it appears that less insect food was available to feed the young, resulting in fewer subsequent nestings. The number of hummingbirds dropped sharply in early September. Individual birds departed daily, and by the first day of autumn, only three or four hummingbirds could be counted. Because my garden is planned around hummingbirds, there are always birds here late in the season. Until none have been seen for several weeks, the feeders are cleaned and refilled every other day. Because of the garden's attractiveness to hummingbirds, even after the usual residents leave, new birds stop by for a few days to fatten up for their southward migrations, so it's not unusual to have new birds here as late as early to mid-October.

On September 22 I heard a new hummingbird at a feeder just outside the kitchen window. This new bird was very vocal, very loud, and its voice was particularly chirpy. I made a mental note of the obvious *chip-chip-chip*, but each time I attempted to peek at the bird through the window, it would fly off. When I did finally get a glimpse of the new hummer, something else struck me as different: it didn't appear to be of the same proportions as the other hummers. It was not out of proportion, but different. The head seemed larger in relation to the body, and the body shorter and more tapered than usual—a stockier bird. But then I detected what might be the start of a gorget in a loose, horse-shoe-shaped cluster, smack dab in the middle of the throat. This immediately reminded me of a *Selasphorus* species, but that would be virtually impossible in this area. Still, this bird was different and I wanted to get a better look.

Fortunately, after three or four days of only a glimpse here and there, I managed to get that better look. What I saw was exciting. This bird, with a somewhat different green coloring than the rubythroat and with different light green iridescent spotting at the sides of the throat, also displayed a remarkable amount of rufous coloration on the sides, flanks, and tail. That was the coup de grâce—I had to get close to that bird. It might easily have gone unnoticed as just another greenish hummingbird, but now every glimpse I was able to get revealed a little something different. This was not an ordinary rubythroat migrant; this, I was sure, was a rufous hummingbird many, many miles east of its usual migratory route.

I sat hidden in the garden, with field glasses in hand, to observe the bird without frightening it. To my surprise and excitement I could tell that the new hummer was a vagrant member of the genus *Selasphorus*. Although the females and immatures of rufous and Allen's hummingbirds are extremely similar in appearance, I eliminated Allen's (*Selasphorus sasin*) for the most obvious reason—geographic distribution and migratory habits. I was unsure, however, whether I was looking at an adult female rufous or an immature. It certainly looked like a female, but since immatures with no prior migratory experience to draw from are the usual wan-

The tail is the most reliable feature by which to distinguish female rufous from Allen's hummingbird.

derers, I reasoned that this probably was an immature rufous. This was important and exciting. I would have to get photographs and turn them over to someone more qualified than I for a positive identification.

The preeminent authority on the rufous hummingbird is Dr. William A. Calder, professor of evolutionary biology at the University of Arizona at Tucson. He agreed to examine my photographic material and give his opinion. A couple of days later, he called with the news. What I had was indeed *Selasphorus rufus* and the bird was a young adult female. That determination was based on the following: (1) the white tail spots of typical width for a female; (2) no streaking radiating from the chin, which is present on immatures—this bird had a clear throat, indicating an adult female; (3) under a hand lens, the bill appeared smooth, with no ridges or wrinkles common to an immature's bill; and (4) only a few red feathers on the throat (the number increases with age).

The photos also revealed that the bird had molted or otherwise lost two wing feathers. But additional photos—far superior to those I sent to Dr. Calder—were taken one week later and showed even more. The bird was in an active state of replacing the feathers on both wings and new growth was visible. There is a difference in the rectrices, or tail feathers, between the female rufous and Allen's. In the female rufous, the outer rectrices are wider than the female Allen's. The new photos clearly showed the tail to be that of the rufous. This positive identification, documented by photographs, should make this the first confirmed and unquestioned record for *Selasphorus rufus* in New York State.

There have been other Eastern reports for the rufous and several sightings in southern states, including wintering over, but no confirmed record for New York State. While there have been some prior recorded sightings in New York, no photographs were taken and none of these sightings as of this date have been accepted, although a report of a *Selasphorus* species has been accepted.

According to one expert on recorded sightings of birds in New York State, in twenty years there has been one report of a rufous, but within the last fourteen months, there have been three. However promising this may sound, the sightings may reflect the results of a six-year drought in the West. Or they may be due to the increased popularity of hummingbirds, with more people noticing them. Being a typical birder, each time I read of a Western species sighted east of the Rockies, I fantasize about it happening in my yard, though the chances of one of these off-course migrants finding my spot is hardly imaginable. The realization that it did is utterly astonishing.

That the bird was attracted to my yard is no surprise. The large number of other hummers and the many feeders undoubtedly would have gotten its attention, but surely the abundance of flowers clinched the attraction. But what in the world would take this bird so far off its course in the first place? The rufous is the champion migrant of the hummingbird world, making a 2,000-plus-mile trip from its wintering grounds primarily in western Mexico to breeding grounds in western North America from southeastern Alaska and southern Yukon, as far north as 61° N., south to the western Canadian Provinces and northwestern United States. It has an oval migratory route, with its spring movement northward up the Pacific Coast over a variety of habitats at lower elevations and its fall southward trip at higher elevations via the two major flyways that flank the Great Basin, and follow the Sierra Nevada and Coast Ranges or the Rocky Mountains. Because of its oval migratory route—as opposed to a retracing, or backtracking of prior steps—there is a natural tendency to move eastward for the southbound journey. By mid- to late September, female and immature rufous hummingbirds can be found in Arizona and New Mexico; in Texas, migratory rufous hummingbirds are present from July until late September, with a few persisting into October.

Recaptures of banded rufous hummingbirds suggest that there is loyalty to the wintering grounds and the successful migratory routes to reach them. As an adult, my visiting rufous obviously had at least one successful migration, so why would she be so wrong now? Storms might throw a migrant off course, the prevailing westerlies could have helped carry it, and recent magnetic storms on the sun might have interfered with the bird's ability to navigate. The old string-on-the-globe trick showed me that the distance from southeastern Alaska to my area is about the same as to a normal wintering ground. While some say that these errant migrants can right their mistakes in subsequent journeys, others feel that the birds will maintain some alternative form of north-south migration, perhaps faithfully traveling up and down the East Coast. Perhaps she's made this trip before?

The rufous spent the entire day in the yard except to sleep, and I do not know where that was. However,

she retired earlier in the evening and arrived later in
the morning in relation to available light than did the
rubythroats. In Dr. Calder's superb treatment of the
rufous for *The Birds of North America*, a copy of which he
very kindly provided, he points out that, when on the
wintering ground, the rufous's average use of an 11.4-
hour solar day is 10.5 to 10.9 hours. This is consistent
with the daylight activity I observed.

Somewhat fickle about her choice of feeder, Rosie
first used the Perky four-flower type at the kitchen
window exclusively (out of sight from those used by
the rubythroats). Then, as the rubythroats departed,
she branched out and tried them all. Of all the feeder
types, however, the small Perky bottle with the tube
and bee guard seemed her favorite. Feeding was at
intervals of fifteen to twenty minutes, with no increase
in frequency at the beginning or end of day, also unlike
the rubythroat.

Before and after each feeding, she spent approximately one minute at her perch loudly announcing her
presence—*chip-chip-chip*. A very limited amount of time
was spent foraging at the flowers. Of the available
flowers, she visited the salvia, skyrocket, four o'clocks,
honeysuckle, fuchsias, and jewelweed. According to
the DesGranges studies, nectar production is best
under hot and sunny conditions.[3] Perhaps the feeders
are just plain convenient, but since our weather

3. Jean-Luc DesGranges, and P. R. Grant, "Organization of a Tropical
   Nectar Feeding Bird Guild in a Variable Environment," *Living Bird*
   17:199–236.

changed abruptly from hot and sunny to cool and damp, the lack of foraging may well have meant that available natural nectar was insufficient to make hovering in front of the flowers worthwhile.

During the few times I've had the opportunity to observe rufous hummingbirds under natural conditions, I've been struck by how much more pugnacious they are than the rubythroat. They are reported to be the most aggressive of North American hummingbirds, defending their feeding territories during migration as well as on the breeding ground. However, I did not observe any belligerence on the part of this rufous toward the resident or transient rubythroats. I have even seen the bird perching three to four feet away from and in full view of a juvenile rubythroat on one of the bare, arching branches at the top of the weeping cherry tree. The rubythroat was preparing for its migration and had fattened up, but the rufous, obviously already in migration and in spite of the need for extra fat for the southbound journey, showed no such plumpness. The rufous occupies a variety of habitats during its migration, and will spend several days to two weeks at one location before continuing on. Dr. Calder indicated that the expected daily weight gain in a premigratory (or, I would presume, refueling) rufous is .25 to .50 gram. This may seem negligible, but relative to the whole, it is significant; it's a gain of as much as 72 percent. Thus for a 3.5-gram bird, when all reserves have been depleted, it can take from five to ten days to be ready to resume a journey.

In comparing species, scientists measure intelligence by relative resourcefulness, proficiency or the ability to adapt. It is evident that hummingbirds are quite intelligent, particularly when you consider the size of the brain, but it may also be that certain species are smarter than others. I do not know where the rufous fits in relative intelligence among hummingbirds, but I was very impressed by my hummer's ability to master the different feeders in an extremely short time—noticeably faster than the rubythroat.

The rufous hummingbird's stay here filled me with many questions. In particular, her behavior toward the rubythroats seemed atypical for the species; perhaps her body was telling her that she was on her wintering ground, where her status is only of intermediate dominance. Might there be something in the genetic makeup that tells a bird how far to go during its migration, or when to stop? If so, she would reach a point when her physiological need to put on weight would cease. Only time would tell.

The Decision

After those first pictures, I had hoped that the rufous hummingbird would stay long enough for me to get some better photos—at least until the next weekend, when I would be able to take my camera outside again. The first thing I did upon returning home from work each afternoon was to check whether Rosie was still there. When Saturday arrived and Rosie was there, I became determined to get shots good enough to unquestionably distinguish her from a female Allen's. After that weekend, I continued to check each day when I arrived home, half hoping for her own good that Rosie would have taken off for warmer parts, but knowing also that I would be disappointed and undoubtedly worried not to see her there. She always was there.

Eventually I became concerned about Rosie. She had made no obvious weight gain and seemed to show no inclination to leave. She had settled in and developed a routine centered in this new territory that she was apparently considering her winter home. I felt sorry for her, so far away from home, all alone and with such an uncertain future.

Each day more summer birds disappeared to be replaced by winter birds. The yellows, golds, oranges, and reds of autumn were all around me and I knew that by Halloween the leaves would have fallen. The mornings were frosty and the nights were getting colder, and less food was available for her foraging. In spite of drastic overnight changes, Rosie appeared at the feeders at the same time each morning, even when temperatures were in the twenties. The rufous is probably a hardier hummingbird than is the ruby-throat; but it wasn't only the cold that concerned me. According to DesGranges, optimum nectar production is achieved at warm temperatures under sunny skies. While his may have been a study under conditions in Mexico, I could relate the information to this area, since hummingbirds here appear to do less foraging under cool and wet conditions, sticking at these times to feeders and catching more insects. Even if and when the flowers are available, frost is not only a genuine threat but nectar stores may be naturally low. The sugar solution in the feeders would continue to give Rosie energy, but what about protein? As she began restricting herself more or less to the feeders, it was obvious that her diet would suffer. And what about the feeders? Could I reasonably expect to keep them from freezing all winter? Life or death for Rosie was entirely in the hands of the weather, and we were on borrowed time.

This area's climate, as that of most of the Northeast, is one of cold, frequently wet winters with ice,
snow, and bitterly cold temperatures often accompanied by strong winds, interspersed with occasional
milder spells (the "January thaw"). Severe weather can
and frequently does endure for days and sometimes
weeks on end. I thought about the March 1993 bliz-
zard, which had dropped seventeen inches of snow on
our area. And I thought about other winter sightings, in
particular a letter to the editor that appeared in the
October 1990 issue of *WildBird* magazine.[4] The writer
related the problems in keeping feeders from freezing
during an out-of-season visit by a rufous in Tennessee
around Thanksgiving, presumably 1989. The area had
experienced a cold wave around mid-December, with
temperatures dropping to below zero most nights until
late December. For several days, the feeders were
changed every twenty to thirty minutes so that the
nectar would not freeze. Eventually a heat lamp was
installed to help keep the nectar liquid. At that point,
the rufous stayed all day near the feeder. The writer
speculated that the bird ultimately succumbed to the
sustained cold. I also thought about a conversation I
had with Jack from The Nature Conservancy's Ramsey
Canyon in southeast Arizona. We discussed two blue-
throated hummingbirds (*Lampornis clemenciae*), who a few
years back were still at the preserve in mid-January.
After an overnight temperature drop to about 14° F.,

4. *WildBird* 4, no.10 (October 1990): 3.

Jack found that one of the birds had succumbed to the cold. Here, we consider it a relatively mild winter if nighttime temperatures don't go below 14°.

Who really knows just how many of these out-of-season wanderers die because they have strayed too far, often on their maiden migrations. A hummingbird is able to withstand subfreezing temperatures for a few days, and may even enter a state of torpor for extended periods, but sustained cold as we experience here is a different story altogether. If I had taken all the feeders down, would that have caused her to leave? I doubt it. There were still flowers around—the same flowers that may have attracted her in the first place. Eventually the flowers would not have been enough to nourish her, and she would have perished from starvation or succumbed to the cold, as the Tennessee bird had. Even if there were no flowers, removing the feeders is the most inappropriate alternative and would have invited a certain agonizing death by starvation.

I recently had a call from a woman in Chicago. She told me of a juvenile male rufous that appeared in her garden last November and remained. As the bird stayed longer, the woman became more alarmed and began telephoning zoos and other organizations for advice on how to handle the situation. Unfortunately, she was ill-advised to take down her feeders to force the bird to migrate, because the bird had already migrated to her yard and had no plans to move on. For the next three days, the bird remained, sans feeders. The woman and her husband then decided to go against the advice, but by that time the bird had succumbed, having exhausted his energy reserves.

So many thoughts passed through my mind. One might expect to see them during July or August, but late September? And what about shelter for Rosie? How much good would an incandescent lamp do? Would she sleep near it? What is a safe drop in temperature? There has to be a point beyond which she could not emerge from torpor.

I worried about when the icy winter winds would cut right through this area, situated at 42° N. To be on the safe side, I dug up a plant of *Salvia coccinea*—just in case everything else was killed off by a hard frost. In a pot and protected in the garage, I would have no trouble finding something to offer her once all the other perennials had turned black. I decided to play it by ear. I would give Rosie every opportunity before I would take action. Each weekend I listened to the extended forecast, thinking, "Well, she can make it through this week. If she's still here next weekend, I'll lure her in." I thought again about the struggle of the Tennessee rufous and the bluethroats at Ramsey Canyon. The thought of finding that frozen little body is a sad one and I didn't want it to happen here. I knew what had to be done.

The night before Christmas was cold and snowy. Christmas Day never made it above freezing, with a little more snow and no sun. The day after it was cold— 10° F. in the morning and never out of the teens for the rest of the day. And it was extremely windy—so cold

and windy that even all bundled up, I could not be outdoors for the ten minutes it takes to feed the birds.
That night went below zero. We were only a couple of
days into winter, with the worst yet to come.

There's no need to give a blow-by-blow descrip-
tion of the entire winter—suffice it to say that the first
week of January saw snow and bitter cold on six days
out of seven, and snow, ice, or freezing rain on almost
half the other days in the month—some with a wind
chill factor of 40 to 50° below zero. Day after day of 10
to 15° F. below zero at night and only 10 to 15° F.
above during the day. January temperatures were below
normal (one early-morning temperature was −24° F.,
the coldest since the 1970s) while precipitation was
above normal. In fact, January 1994 turned out to be
the coldest, most brutal one on record. I couldn't help
wondering about other hummers sighted in the Northeast late in the season. When I looked at the clouds of
snow ferociously blowing across the open and now
barren backyard, I knew that I had made not only the
right but the only choice.

Bringing Her In

Rosie obviously wasn't planning to travel any farther than she had. For the most part, once the competition had departed, the loud *chip-chip-chip* that announced her claim to this territory stopped as well. In her mind she was where she belonged. One night in early October, the majority of flowers were frosted. There was a complete change in the outdoor picture, with a drastic reduction in available nectar. Providing for her outdoors would become increasingly difficult and ultimately impossible. She couldn't possibly make it through winter, irrespective of help. However hardy she might otherwise be, she was just ill-equipped for the rigors of a Northeast winter.

I had a suitable area to offer Rosie and had successfully housed a hummingbird before, so I was less scared this time around. The sunroom had proven itself to be an excellent hummingbird haven for a lengthy stay. Flowers grow there all winter. Squeak had spent a very nonfrustrating several months in that sunroom, relaxed and content, while he reached maturity in preparation for his release the following spring. Rosie had been given every opportunity to continue her migration; as long as there was a chance, no matter how remote, that she might depart on her own, I waited. But she had passed the point of no return. As November approached, I decided to bring her in. I gathered my thoughts, carefully weighing the options. I needed a plan. Rosie was different from the other hummers. She was a skittish bird and she would have to be coaxed. I didn't want to do anything that had the potential of hurting her, so nets were out. I would have to arrange for there to be no other alternative.

Rosie's favorite place in the garden was the circle, an area where sun-loving hummingbird flowers grow in abundance. It is the highest and driest spot in the yard, and the southern half receives sun all day long. In the center of the circle is an overgrown privet with many branches and twigs, and hundreds of places for little hummingbirds to hide. On the shady, north side of the privet, four o'clocks and *Saponaria* flourish, while on its south, tall red cannas form a background for such fall favorites as *Salvia coccinea, Zauschneria californica,* and stands of *Ipomopsis rubra*.

Among the flowers is a tall branch stuck in a pipe in the ground, a place where the hummingbirds may rest, and a NektarPlus feeder filled with sugar-water. Rosie spent much time there, but it was just too far away from the house. She was totally out of reach; I'd have to get her closer. I'd have to narrow down the number of places to visit and draw her closer to the door of the sunroom by creating more abundance where I wanted her to be. I could do nothing—nor would I—about the flowers. I'd have to work strictly with the feeders. The first thing I did was remove some feeders. The next thing I did was move the remaining feeders closer to the house. One feeder that she was particularly fond of was the Perky gravity-type bottle under the spruce tree. That feeder remained, as it was the one that drew her closest. Other feeders were hung under the overhang just outside the sunroom, and were moved gradually closer and closer to the door, thus forcing her feeding activity to gravitate more toward the house.

Next, I stood near the Perky feeder under the spruce tree in an effort to force her to use the feeders near the sunroom door. Eventually, she began to use the target feeders. Once she automatically returned to the feeders near the door, I opened it, hoping that she would notice the flowers inside and go in but she didn't. Finally I moved one of the feeders inside, just beyond the door and I waited. Two cold hours later and without any fanfare, she nonchalantly entered the sunroom and I shut the door behind her. That was the start of our winter together.

WINTER

Although small numbers of rufous hummingbirds regularly winter from Texas eastward along the Gulf coast to western Florida, and occasionally to southern and coastal Georgia, its primary wintering area, as for so many other hummingbirds that breed in north temperate regions, is Mexico. Dr. Calder indicates the birds like shrubby, woodland habitats.

In his paper on the co-existence of resident and migrant hummingbirds in an area of western Mexico, DesGranges describes four selected habitats determined by altitude and running from the semi-arid lowlands at sea level to higher and wetter areas. All four habitats experience a dry winter season from November to June, as is typical of western Mexico, with a major flowering period from December to February. DesGranges indicates that the rufous hummingbird inhabits three of the four habitats along this altitudinal gradient.

The arid-thorn forest, found at the lowest elevations, is an open area of thick undergrowth and thorny vines, containing cacti and flowering trees, most of which are leguminous. The forest is deciduous and flowering occurs primarily in the dry season. The rufous arrives in early January, and its status is territorial (early January might indicate that the rufous's arrival may be the first leg of the spring migration).

The rufous is a "traplining" hummingbird on the open, dry forests of tall pines and medium-size oaks on the arid pine-oak habitat; that is, they follow a regular feeding route between patches of flowers, as opposed to a specific territory. In the arid pine-oak habitat at elevations between 4,920 and 8,200 feet, flowers are the most abundant of all four habitats, with *Salvia, Leonotis, Stachys, Calliandra,* and *Lobelia* blooming during the dry season. *Malvaviscus arboreus* and *Fuchsia parviflora* bloom year-round, but peak in the spring and again in autumn.

The rufous arrives in late November on the humid pine-oak habitat at loftier elevations of over 8,200 feet. This habitat has a wetter and denser forest of oaks with mosses. Except for the white-eared hummingbird

(*Hylocharis leucotis*), inhabitants of this cooler area exhibit daily movements in altitude, going uphill between 7:00 and 8:00 A.M. and then back down to the lowlands for the evening. DesGranges indicates that the green violet-ear (*Colibri thalassinus*), broad-tailed (*Selasphorus platycercus*), and rufous hummingbirds concentrate their foraging on blossoms of *Cestrum terminale, Ribes ciliatum, Buddleia cordata,* and *Senecio angulifolius,* as well as garden plants such as *Jacaranda* and *Musa,* and that they all have territories that they reestablish each morning, with the best going to the "aggressive" rufous. It appears that migrant hummingbirds generally have a status of low domination except the rufous.

Winter was Rosie's period of rest and rejuvenation. It consisted of sleeping, visiting flowers, eating, bathing, preening and scratching, and finishing the molt that had started in September or earlier. It was a relatively quiet period with short days.

Night and Day

When you come right down to it, Rosie wouldn't really be doing anything much different indoors than she would be outside, sitting around, eating, bathing. But it seemed such a monumental change for her, from the complete and unequivocal freedom of moving clear across the country to confinement, no matter what size sunroom. I felt very sympathetic. I knew I had done the best thing, but did she? I also knew that there would be some adjustment to the changes thrust upon her, and I was afraid it would be quite a challenge to get her to come around. For me, it wasn't at all difficult to fall back on having a hummingbird guest for the winter.

Squeak was a last-minute addition to the sunroom, but Rosie was anticipated and that allowed for a little advanced planning. So once it became evident that she would be my winter guest, I got the room ready.

Sleep—To start with, Rosie would be needing a place to sleep, something similar to the skinny branch

Squeak had used. I had discarded that branch and now had to find something suitable for Rosie. I settled on a tall branch with many small, skinny twigs, and this became her "tree." Rosie's "tree" was tall enough so that when placed in the pot of *Salvia coccinea* that had been brought in from the garden, it practically reached the ceiling and branched out across the southeast corner of the room. Eventually the tree became the core of the majority of her activity, with particular branches reserved for very definite actions.

Turning off the fluorescents her first night in the sunroom proved to be somewhat of a problem. I wanted them to turn off around 8:00 P.M., but was afraid to have them operate from the timer lest she be flying around and left suddenly in the dark. It seemed that the only answer was to shut them off manually once she settled down. While she was outside, darkness fell gradually and there was ample time for her to settle in during twilight and ready herself to roost for the night. The situation would be different indoors because, while it appears dark inside, light enters from outside, not only from the twilight but from the street light, porch light and, frequently, moonlight as well. Turning off the back porch light made it seem darker inside, thus the outside light became even more obvious. This undoubtedly was confusing Rosie, and she headed toward more light, hovering right up against the window. Then she landed first on the door lite and then on the windowsill, where she kept her little body pressed against the glass. Since there was little I could do about the ambient light, and I would never be able to make it totally dark outside, I'd have to add a little light inside. I decided to use a night light to balance the intensity between inside and outside, creating a dusky atmosphere that seemed to put her at ease and set the pattern for the remainder of her stay.

In order to survive an energy emergency, the rufous, as do other hummingbirds, may enter a state of torpor. During torpidity all processes slow down as a way of conserving energy. Many hummers would not survive were it not for this state of suspended animation. The onset of torpor, at least for the rufous, relates to energy reserves; that is, they pace themselves according to how much reserve remains. Indeed, Rosie's sleep seemed to deepen, with less nocturnal activity as the night wore on.

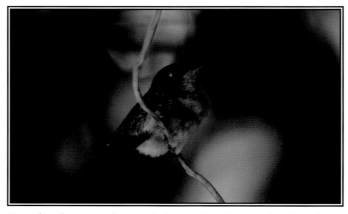

Rosie found a new and unusual place to sleep, the root of an Aerides *orchid—it is the perfect size for little hummingbird feet.*

Arousal from torpor is fixed to daybreak. With ample food and overnight temperatures set between 56 and 62° F., I did not expect that Rosie would become torpid overnight. Neither Squeak nor Charlie had and, although Rosie generally consumed less toward evening, the rufous seemed to be the naturally hardier

Sleeping among the Cestrum *leaves, Rosie was difficult to find—just a shiny little green object, smaller than the leaf itself.*

of the two species. As a matter of fact, Rosie seemed to be somewhat of a light sleeper. Not only did she occasionally peck at her wings when she gave all other appearances of being asleep, but she even turned around on a couple of occasions.

For the first two weeks Rosie used a different branch each night, probably looking for just the right one. Since one of her feeders was hung from a branch on her tree, I found it difficult to change the feeders in the morning. The tree would move slightly in the pot

At dawn, Rosie's silhouette as she sleeps at the top of the shrimp plant.

and that movement disturbed her. But then, thankfully, Rosie found a new and unusual place to sleep. She settled on a root of an *Aerides* orchid plant. An orchid root is nothing like an ordinary plant root. Most orchids are epiphytes—that is, they attach themselves to and grow upon something else, usually tree trunks or branches. Consequently the roots, wandering either along the bark of the host tree or branching out into the air, are thick and firm, some pencil-thick, and covered with a white spongy layer of velamin that absorbs water and nutrients. They are the perfect size for little hummingbird feet.

The *Aerides* has several long roots between twenty-four and thirty-six inches that meander through the air under the skylight. Rosie slept on the same root at the same spot each night after that until mid-December.

Then one night Rosie abandoned the root and decided to sleep near the end of one of the branches on the *Cestrum* plant, less than three feet above the floor. I had to wonder what went on in that little mind when all of a sudden she decided to do something different. There was no apparent reason for the sudden change and there was no building up, the way Squeak had done when he "strayed" that one night and slept on another branch instead of the skinny one. She just changed, period, and that was that. Hidden among the *Cestrum* leaves, she was difficult to find, just a shiny little green object no larger—actually smaller—than the leaves themselves. At times she approached a similar-looking branch when ready to retire, but soon realized it was not the right one. She would then fly back and forth across the room a couple of times before landing on the exact spot of the right branch. It's almost as if one of the ways she remembered where to sleep was by repeating her previous steps, or flights, until it "felt right."

Many of the plants offered to Rosie were grown under lights in my basement and brought up to the sunroom once blooming began. One of the shrimp plants (*Beloperone guttata*) began to flower late in February and when the blossoms started opening, I brought it up to the sunroom. At about that time, when Rosie was ready to roost for the evening, she would fly back and forth across the length of the sunroom, flitting from flower to flower, including the blossoms on the shrimp plant. She'd linger only a split second at each one, and then land on one high branch or petiole after another, as though she were looking for another new place to sleep. When the branch or petiole swayed or if her landing wasn't just right, she'd immediately retreat to her regular sleeping branch on the *Cestrum,* sit for a few seconds, then run through the process all over again. Rosie paid particular attention to the uppermost part of the shrimp plant. Evidently something about that plant appealed to her. Finally on March 3, she landed at the top of the plant and stayed longer than she had at other times. She stayed for perhaps an hour before she got up for her final sip. After her nightcap, she returned to the shrimp plant and spent the night in yet another new spot.

All day long, and especially in the morning, Rosie was a live wire, bathing, preening, flitting from flower to flower, hunting, exploring, and flying all over the room, but as the solar day came to a close, Rosie turned quiet and would leave her perch only sporadically for an occasional sip. The interim branch changed when Rosie's sleeping place changed, so she could face the sleeping spot for five or ten minutes before she retired. She seemed to have a sense of timing, an internal clock. However, if she were to see me during those last few minutes before the lights went out, she would leave her sleeping perch and follow me around for a nightcap.

Such was the case for her second night on the shrimp plant. Unfortunately, on that night the lights went out before she could get back to the branch where she wanted to sleep. She attempted to make her way back in the perpetual twilight that had been created for her, but she missed her mark. On the branch where she landed, she had to grasp the little upright twig sideways. I couldn't imagine that she might be comfortable in that position for the night, so I turned the timer manually until the lights went back on, figuring that when she became comfortable, I'd shut them off again. It went well; she returned, and I quietly passed by her and manually turned the lights off. It worked like the proverbial charm—until I knocked one of the tripods over on my way out. That sent her scurrying and I quickly got the lights back on again before she hurt herself. This time she decided to sleep on the old *Cestrum* branch. After that, I saw to it that she had her nightcap in ample time to return to her sleeping perch. It left me wondering again about what went on in her mind and how and why she made the decision to switch. The following night she retired to the shrimp plant as if she had been sleeping there for months.

If I were standing near her branch when she was ready to retire, she would fly back and forth across the room or circle around me. In fact, it became a nightly ritual to fly around my legs when she wanted to go to her branch, or she would fly in large circles until I moved away from the branch where she watned to be. Every once in a while, after her last drink, she'd fly about four feet away and then come back for another sip, repeating that "here and gone" motion five or six times.

Occasionally Rosie would do something similar to head-wagging before retiring to her branch. Head-wagging with the rubythroat seems to be a territorial matter, with only the most aggressive males displaying such behavior. So I was surprised to see that Rosie also engaged in head-wagging. This was not done from the actual roosting place but from the branch where she would sit after her nightcap. Every once in a while she would swiftly "spin" around on her branch, first facing forward and then backward in a semicircle, tracing and retracing the pattern several times before finally retiring once and for all.

Morning Routine—Rosie's mornings were busy but relatively constant. She awakened immediately when the fluorescent lights turned on. But later the timer had to be adjusted to correspond with earlier sunrises. As soon as the sun rose by 6:30, Rosie awakened each morning a minute or two earlier, and by late February, I had to push the timer ahead daily to accommodate her. On February 25, I was in the sunroom before the lights turned on, when all of a sudden, at 6:18, I heard the purr of her wings, hovering next to me. She was looking for the treat feeder that I held. She sipped and then retreated to her branch. Within a minute, the lights turned on and she started her regular morning chirping. By the first day of spring, 5:45 A.M. was Rosie's time to awaken.

When the lights went on, Rosie would open her eyes and just sit there for almost a minute, looking

Rosie sat quietly in the morning until the sun came up.

from side to side. As she sat a bit longer, her tail would pulsate up and down and her tongue would flick in and out; sometimes she'd empty her crop. She would then stretch her wings back twice while stretching her tail to alternate sides. Frequently while she stretched, I could see that she also stretched her claws. She would then fly directly to the feeder for the first sip of the day.

Her behavior after the initial feeding changed from time to time, although it basically consisted of the same variables arranged in different order or for different lengths of time. When she first arrived, she would sit on one of the high branches of the tree and do some minor preening before moving to the lower branches and getting ready to bathe. But later, once she became totally relaxed, she would leisurely stretch, scratch, preen, peck at her wings, clean her bill, do lots of scratching and shaking her wings while repeatedly fanning her tail in and out. After feeding, Rosie would have a morning bath, dry off, and do some preening. Then she would explore, foraging among the various flowers, and peck at the Spanish moss, at roots and stems, and at windows and walls, presumably hunting for insects.

Keeping Beautiful

When the sun streamed down on Rosie from the skylight above, she shimmered and glowed like a bit of
amber. She was a beautiful bird and she was so diligent
about staying that way. Not a day went by that Rosie

A shower substituted quite well for a gentle rain.

didn't fuss over her feathers, and one of her favorite ways was with water. It is a great deal of fun to watch hummingbirds take a shower in the rain. They lift and spread their tails, flutter their wings, and bare their throats to absorb every drop. They are adorable. Of course, when the rain is heavy, hummingbirds are quick to take shelter. Not only do hummingbirds love to shower in the rain but they also take delight in bathing in the puddles that collect on leaves. In fact, they seem to play in the water, splashing, pecking, and chirping.

In captivity, a shower substituted quite well for that gentle rain and the waterfall for that puddle. The waterfall is a three-level structure chiseled out of a large chunk of black lava. The water spills from a top pool and courses down into another pool, a grotto of sorts, then to a lower pool before emptying into a large, plastic tray that the rock sits in, to recirculate.

Sitting at the edge of the grotto.

Flying over to the top pool.

Once in the water, she splashed and chirped.

The waterfall was made for Squeak so he would have bath water available at all times, but although he developed an interest in its surroundings, he never took advantage of this source of water. The sound of trickling water is pleasant and soothing, lending a tropical air to the sunroom. For this reason it became a permanent fixture after Squeak left.

Rosie took her first bath in the waterfall her second day here. No checking it out, inspecting beforehand, or testing—she just went to the waterfall as if well versed in the procedure. She hovered in front of the grotto for a second or two, and then sat on its edge and proceeded to bathe. When she visited the waterfall for a bath, she would spread her tail, splash water by fluttering her wings, chirp, and peck at the water. She stayed four or five seconds, retreated to the *Aerides* root, and then repeated the procedure. She might be in the middle of preening or just sitting there, facing the other way and then she would spin around and make a beeline to the waterfall just as though she had been thinking about it. She did not confine herself to bathing in the mornings; even on snowy, dismal days in March, I watched her go to the waterfall and take prolonged baths late in the afternoon.

In early April, Rosie flew past the waterfall and deliberately skimmed her undersides across the top pool. The next day she sat on its edge. By and by she discovered that the upper level was a delightful alternative to the grotto, and she would fly over and sit right in the one-half-inch-deep pool, fluttering her wings and splashing around to get wet. Frequently she would stop at the edge first and peck at the water a couple of times before getting in. Who knows what made her decide when to go to the pool? Four, five, or six times each day she would head to the waterfall, sit on its edge, and flap, chirp, dip, and dunk. It may have helped to dislodge loose feathers, for I would find them floating on the surface while Rosie was molting. If she got a bit of spider web on her feet or her beak was sticky, she'd take a couple of pecks at her feet or run her beak once or twice across a twig, and then immediately go to the waterfall for the easiest cleaning.

When she was finished at the waterfall, Rosie would be soaking wet and need to dry off. She looked comical, trying to shake out her wings while flying from one perch to another. To dry her wings, Rosie would run her beak across alternating sides two or three times each and then "ruffle" them by taking off from her perch but simultaneously clasping it with her feet so she didn't go anywhere. At times she would spin her wings so fast they became just a blur. Other times she'd just shake them out.

I had a distinct advantage this time around. I knew what Rosie should like and what to expect from her. I felt like an old hand at this hummingbird thing. After allowing her the first couple of days to adjust a bit, it was time to introduce Rosie to the delights of a shower. I started by allowing a very gentle mist to fall over her while she was sitting on one of the lower branches of her tree. She instinctively fluttered her wings. I sprayed again, this time allowing a bit more lukewarm water to reach her. She fluttered her wings again. As I sprayed some more, she pulled her head back and fanned her tail. Her pleasure was evident. After the first shower

Rosie braces herself with her tail during a shower on the Cestrum *leaves.*

she knew what to expect, and within a matter of days, she made the association between seeing the spray bottle and a shower. Indeed, the spray bottle made an annoying noise when I squeezed the trigger; when Rosie heard that noise, she would fly to the shower branch and flutter her wings in anxious anticipation.

Hummingbirds don't play, but Rosie almost seemed to make a game of the shower. On some days she'd chirp while practically jumping from branch to branch, perhaps peck at a couple of drops, hop away to a different branch, come back for another spray, and chirp, chirp, chirp as she repeated all of this over and over. The routine was that I would approach with the spray bottle and she would go to the shower branch and flutter her wings or squirm around on the leaf. After one or two sprays, she'd move to a dry branch. I'd spray in the vicinity of where she had been and she'd come back, repeating this until she decided that she had played long enough and then it would be solid spraying. And I would continue to spray until she was finished. I easily emptied half the spray bottle of water during each session. One morning I emptied the entire 32-ounce bottle and she still wasn't satisfied. When I returned from the kitchen with a refill, Rosie was sloshing around on a wet leaf. Howling winds and the frigid weather of winter made no difference to Rosie. She got all the pleasure from her morning shower that she would have had it been a hot day in July.

During her shower, Rosie would flutter her wings and spin around, then, with her wings back and arched up over her back and her tail lifted and spread, she would turn her head from side to side and chirp. Then she would rub her head and beak on the twig. Occasionally, she would turn completely around so I could spray her back. On one occasion, either as a result of curiosity or because she wanted to be closer to the water source, she approached the spray bottle and hovered to the side of the stream of water and then crossed repeatedly from one side to the other.

Once the shower was over, I faced the task of soaking up the water from the slate floor. Rosie, being very interested in my activity, would hover above me with head cocked to the side.

Squeak made such a ritual out of drying off while Rosie would simply shake out her wings, sit under the lights and drip dry. She spent little to no time flying around afterward to dry off. When she was finished shaking out, the wet feather sound led directly to the lights, where she'd sit until dry. After drying off, Rosie would do some minor preening. She would run her wing edge through her beak and then shake out the wings. Whatever she did to one side, she repeated on the other—exactly. Even if she scratched her head twice and pulled her foot once over her bill, she repeated it, action for action on the other side. After her bath, she liked to sit on the branch near a tiny, perpendicular twig for beak cleaning. Shaking out her wings was a major part of each preening session. In a typical session she would peck and poke under her wings, shake the wings, preen her tail on one side, shake, preen the other side, shake, run her foot over beak, shake again, peck and poke here and there and then shake out her wings some more.

Rosie watched with great interest the dripping water from freshly watered orchids. She'd dart right over and attempt to peck at the falling drops and then inspect the leaf where a drop had landed. One day she discovered that a soft leaf from the *Cestrum* plant draped over part of the branch was an even more desirable place to shower because of the additional room. This time when she fanned her tail it was more than just spreading the feathers to get them wet. Now she braced herself to stop from falling off the leaf. She tried to stay put by bracing herself with her tail, but still she slid off. I think she especially liked to bathe on the leaves because she liked having something on which to rub her face.

In the winter, when the sun was low in the sky and its warmth streamed through the windows, Rosie would sit in front of the south windows to absorb the rays. Later, when the sun was higher, she sat on the *Duranta* or on another plant in the well of the skylight. She would stretch, and with tail spread would tilt and stretch her neck, baring it so the skin showed in between her feathers and allowed the sun to warm the skin. She obviously enjoyed sunbathing but didn't engage in that activity as much as Squeak did.

Rosie's Winter Garden

The backbone of Rosie's nourishment was NektarPlus, the water-soluble diet of carbohydrates, vitamins, minerals, and proteins formulated specifically for hummingbirds and sunbirds. Still, Rosie had an instinctive need to forage. Perhaps because she was so far off course and I felt sorry for her, I felt a strong need to provide familiar flowers for Rosie to enjoy.

To start with, Rosie had bright red flowers from the *Salvia coccinea* that I had dug up and brought in. It continued to bloom sporadically during the entire winter and spring, and Rosie enjoyed the flowers whenever they were available. The impatiens was also available throughout her stay. Next were the ever-popular fuchsias, always a hit with the hummers, especially the *Fuchsia triphylla* hybrids. Fuchsias were a standby for Rosie—she visited them regularly—but as we shall later see, they were not her favorite.

The initial impression that one might get of a hummingbird working a flower patch is that they are oppor-

Fuchsia triphylla *hybrids are especially attractive to humming-birds.*

tunists who try everything. While this may be true to some degree, especially when the birds are young and learning about the world around them, adult hummers have learned and show definite preferences. *Salvia coccinea* is a rubythroat favorite, as is bee balm (*Monarda spp.*), but the hummers will all but ignore the bee balm in favor of the salvia in almost every instance. Since most of my flowers are grown with hummingbirds in mind, I had plenty to offer Rosie—the gorgeous scarlet bouvardia, or trompetilla (*Bouvardia ternifolia*) of the Southwest, with its two-inch-long, tubular, scarlet flowers; the monkey flowers (*Mimulus* and *Diplacus spp.* and hybrids) of the West Coast; fuchsias and shrimp plants (*Beloperone guttata*), scarlet bush (*Hamelia patens*), and fairy dusters (*Calliandra spp.*). But I wanted something different for Rosie. I wanted to offer her flowers familiar to her—rufous preferences. I wanted her to feel at home. The most logical and easiest solution was to acquire some West Coast natives that the rufous is known to work; chuparosa (*Beloperone [Justicia] californica*), currants (*Ribes spp.*), and manzanitas (*Arctostaphylos spp.*) would bloom in winter, others not until spring.

All species of *Ribes* are important to hummingbirds because they provide nectar during winter and early

Inspecting Alstroemeria *flowers.*

spring. Blooming from October to March is the beautiful, pink, chaparral currant (*R. malvaceum*); both pink-flowered currant (*R. sanguineum*) and white-flowered currant (*R. indecorum*) bloom from January to March; fuchsia-flowered gooseberry (*R. speciosum*) blooms from January to May; hillside gooseberry (*R. californicum*) blooms from February to March; golden currant (*R. aureum*) from April to

Ribes malvaceum *was the first of the currants to bloom.*

It was followed by Ribes indecorum.

May; and pink Sierra currant (*R. nevadense*) from April
to July. Farther north, where seasons are later, these
plants flower somewhat later. I wanted to offer a
good variety that would bloom over an extended

By Christmas, Mimulus cardinalis *was in bloom.*

period so *R. malvaceum, R. indecorum, R. nevadense,* and
R. speciosum were selected.

The West Coast native scarlet monkey flower
(*Mimulus cardinalis*) is a perennial that may grow to
three feet and will prosper under a variety of conditions from sun to shade, but it loves regular watering.
The showy, two-inch scarlet flowers appear most of
the year and are important hummingbird flowers in
the wild. Squeak loved it and Rosie did, too. By mid-
December there was evidence of bud formation and to
Rosie's delight, by Christmas the first of the *Mimulus*
plants had blossoms. Rosie's fancy for these flowers

was evident by the frequency of her visits; the unmistakable yellow *V* stamped on her forehead and crown revealed her actions. As a matter of fact, I could walk into the sunroom, look at the pollen on her head, and

New Diplacus puniceus *began flowering in mid-January.*

know exactly where she had been: a fluorescent pale yellow *V* meant *Mimulus*, yellowish-orange, the honeysuckle, and so on.

Related to *Mimulus* is *Diplacus*. The *D. puniceus* hybrids that Squeak had relished so began its flowering in mid-January and offered rather longish, slender, red tubular flowers. Azalea-flowered diplacus (*Diplacus bifidus*), as its name suggests, looks a bit like a yellowish-orange azalea. Rosie kept a watchful eye on the first buds as they matured in the sunroom and checked repeatedly, waiting for them to open. When they did, she treated the plant with much less enthusiasm than she had led me to believe she would.

Visiting Turk's cap.

Chuparosa is a member of the mainly tropical Acanthus family, many species of which are attractive to
hummingbirds. The flowers offer winter sustenance to
Anna's (*Calypte anna*) and other hummingbirds. It is a difficult plant to grow indoors, as it requires a very arid
atmosphere and abundant sun. The plant grew quite
well, I thought, but flowering was somewhat sparse.
When it did develop some flowers, Rosie was so anxious
to get to the nectar that she wouldn't even wait for them
to open completely, forcing her beak into unopened
buds and ruining most of them. She was obviously
familiar with chuparosa and poked around at the buds
when they were just beginning to show some color.

Orchids are beautiful flowers. Some are big, bold,
and colorful, and some are soft and delicate. All are
delightful, but most are passed up by hummingbirds.
Species in the genera *Aerangis, Angraecum*, etc., all mem-

bers of the Orchidaceae, hold copious amounts of nectar in their spurs—some of which are as long as one foot. Most will recall learning about Darwin, who theorized that a moth must exist with a proboscis at least as long as the spur on a certain flower in order to attract the moth and thus pollinate the flower. The flower to which he referred is an *Angraecum* orchid. Just as Squeak had, Rosie loved the *Aerangis rhodosticta* hybrid

Rosie showed only moderate interest in fiery spike.

when it was in flower, as she did other Angracoids. She would return over and over to the same flower, pushing her beak in as far as it would go to get the nectar. Her tongue is essentially as long as her bill, yet her tongue was not long enough for the length of the spurs on some of the *Angraecum* and *Aerangis* hybrids. Still, she managed to get enough to satisfy herself and she came back again and again almost as if she knew that she hadn't gotten it all. She knew where all the developing orchid buds were and periodically during the day she would visit each one to remove the sweet, viscous liquid that they produce. She also managed to find that same nectar-like substance produced on stems of *Laelia albida* just as Squeak had done. I was delighted to see that she was comfortable enough to explore. Unlike Squeak, however, she continued to visit the *Laelia* flowers after they opened, indicating that there was a supply of nectar accessible to her. Blooming in late November and December and coinciding with the start of the dry season in its native habitat, *L. albida* flowers at elevations of over 6,000 feet, at a time and in areas where rufous hummingbirds may be found

Late winter offered Martha Washington geraniums.

Rosie would find only one flower on a plant—here it is Hamelia cuprea.

wintering over. *Rodriguezia venusta* is a lovely, white, botanical orchid from South America and was her favorite of the orchids. Once discovered, it was never left alone. As a matter of fact, Rosie liked it so much that when I held her feeder about eight inches away from those flowers, she "hemmed and hawed," moving back and forth and turning from side to side, as if trying to decide which to choose.

Members of the Acanthus family, *Ruellia* is a genus of attractive, if not spectacular, brightly colored, funnel-shaped flowers. Most varieties grow in Brazil. Three that are grown here are *Ruellia macrantha*, *R. makoyana*, and *R. graecizans*. *R. macrantha* is a full six feet tall and bears clusters of large, beautiful, deeply textured, rosy-pink trumpet-shaped flowers. Rosie visited the flowers of this striking plant, but definitely preferred the other two small and more suitable *Ruellia*s.

Rosie showed only a passing interest in two important Mexican flowers from the DesGranges list: sleeping hibiscus (*Malvaviscus arboreus*) and the two *Calliandra* species that I grow. Turk's cap (*Malvaviscus arboreus var. drummondii*) is an important hummingbird flower on its native habitat from the southern Edwards Plateau to the Rio Grande Plains and along the Gulf coast from Florida to Mexico. Rosie loved Turk's cap, a smaller, somewhat squat version of sleeping hibiscus, but showed absolutely no interest in its relative. Because *Calliandra* (fairy duster, powder puff) is one of the cited winter flowers on the arid pine-oak habitat, I was anxious for the flowering to start on the two from that genus that grow here. To my surprise, Rosie showed only a limited interest in either of these flowers. Even after trying them, she rarely went back for seconds.

Interaction

In his discussion of hummingbird memory and social behavior, Johnsgard recounts the remarkable story of one Mr. Fitzpatrick and his relationship with a particular rufous hummingbird. Fitzpatrick spent several months watching a rufous that had taken possession of a feeder the man had hung outside his bedroom window at a California sanitarium. When the man eventually ventured outdoors, the hummer greeted him by hovering in front of his eyes and flying about his head. About one year later, when Fitzpatrick returned to his home about eight miles away, the rufous followed him and took up residence near his house. The bird is reported to have accompanied Fitzpatrick on his daily walks, warning him of dangers and calling his attention to animals that Fitzpatrick otherwise might not have seen, and is also reported to have ridden on a piece of rawhide rifle sling. When Fitzpatrick again returned to his home after a one-month absence, he was greeted within moments by the rufous, who again flew around his head and hovered in front of his eyes. The story is the most amazing account of hummingbird and human interaction that I have read yet.

At first Rosie was quite skittish and would fly around in the well of the skylight whenever she saw someone. But that behavior soon subsided, becoming reserved for times when I was right in the room. Before long, Rosie felt confident enough to just leisurely retreat to the opposite side of the room from me and eventually she'd even stay on the same side if I didn't get too close. She relaxed and basically ignored me. It didn't take very long to get her turned around after that, and what made her relax around me the most was receiving a shower. After breaking that barrier, it was time to make friends. I knew that Rosie could overcome any remaining apprehension, and a relationship could develop. But I also knew I'd have to work at it. One can hardly expect a bird that would not even bond with another bird to bond with a human much beyond taking what is given, but I was extremely optimistic. Once the initial adjustment phase passed and she became more relaxed in my presence, we could get down to the business of making friends.

The way to any animal's heart is first to encourage it to feel relaxed around you, best accomplished by quiet behavior, slow and steady movements, and only moderate eye contact initially. Next is to offer it something special and desirable to eat. I wanted to give Rosie the ideal diet that NektarPlus provides, but I had to break the barrier and a sweet treat was the way.

Since I planned to start offering Rosie a treat early in her stay—and I knew that it would be sustained over several months—a 3:1 ratio of water and sugar would be a good minimum starting point. Rosie had a definite curiosity about me that indicated she was ready. The first time she fed from my hand in mid-November, it took at least half an hour of tempting and coaxing, and her effort consisted of darting movements and rapid flicks of the tongue in and out at the feeder tube versus the long, lazy sips when she drank alone at the feeder. She liked it very much. When she made the association between the hand-held feeder and something sweet, and she wanted the feeder that was being held, the ratio was increased to 3.5:1 and finally 4:1, the best ratio. At that point, I felt comfortable about the occasional deviation from her perfect diet. As her confidence in me increased, short sips turned into long drinks and the darting movements gave way to relaxation.

Once that plateau was reached, Rosie became brazen enough to let *me* know when she wanted a treat. Whereas Squeak would follow me about the sunroom and dance around my head, openly soliciting, even insisting, upon a treat, Rosie's approach was to retire to what she had categorized as the spot to be handfed and to excitedly chirp alternating with a flick of her tongue in and out. When she saw me entering the room holding the feeder, she immediately went under the lights and waited.

And that's the way it was for quite some time. Then one day she discovered that I could be elsewhere in the

*After taking a sip, she moved backward about two inches
and flicked her tongue in and out.*

*Before Rosie left her branch for a treat, she would stretch
her wings, fan her tail, and squeal.*

room and still feed her. Once she stopped associating her treat with that one particular spot and associated it instead with me, she changed her behavior and would hover inches away from my face, waiting. As she really settled in, she redesigned the scenario and the southeast corner became her headquarters. She then preferred that everything emanate from that area, including being handfed. I knew she really trusted me when she would hover inches away from the hand that held the treat feeder and look out the window with her back to my hands! Each time I'd handfeed her, I'd say, "sip, sip."

Eventually it reached the point where if I said those words, she'd dash to where I was standing. After taking a sip she would move back about two inches, flick her tongue in and out five or six times so just the tip showed, chirp, and then come back for another sip. She would then retire to a branch and chirp—not the loud *chip-chip-chip*, but a soft and sometimes very soft chirp. Once she felt comfortable around me she seemed to take particular delight in flying right up to my face and then whizzing by my head, only centimeters away.

In many ways, Rosie was a creature of habit, designating certain places for specific activities. In the beginning when she wanted a treat, she would fly over to the *s*-hook under the lights, where I had first gotten her to use a hand-held feeder. Later when she wanted something, Rosie would charge at me. She'd sail right across the room so quickly that she could barely be seen moving and then she would hang there in midair in front of my face, just looking at me with her tail fanned and slightly curved, appearing completely motionless except for her wings and flicking tongue. If I didn't respond, she chirped—always louder than usual.

When truly relaxed, Rosie settled down snugly on top of her feet.

Likewise, when she was ready for her shower, she'd alight on the "shower branch" of her tree and shake her wings out, perhaps peck at them a bit, and chirp, going through the motions she associated with what she wanted in order to get the idea across. She was communicating with me. Most often, when I would call her, she'd turn her head and look at me. If I were holding the feeder, she'd come over immediately. Each time I would imitate the soft *t-chip* noise she made after drinking, she'd lift her wings a tad as if she were planning to fly off.

Rosie had taken to following me around. One day

she daringly followed me into the potting closet, a four-by-six-foot area with sliding louvre doors off the sunroom. She stayed, hovering, for only a second or two and then departed. She is just a little humming-bird, no different in many respects from any other hummingbird, but she had become very special to me.

She'd fly right up to my face, emit one chirp, and leave.

Rosie accepted my presence very nicely and as time went on, she seemed to enjoy having me nearby—and even developed a curiosity about everything I did. When I talked softly to her she would shake out her wings while sitting, looking at me, just as she did when having a shower. When I sang softly to her, she would cock her head and listen to me. At these times she seemed partic-ularly relaxed. When Rosie would settle down snugly on top of her feet and become puffed up and flat-looking at her bottom, she was the epitome of relaxation.

I really wanted her to sit on my finger. One ruby-throat who had spent an October day with me in 1987 during an early freak snow and ice storm needed only to be nudged to move to my finger to sit and preen; she even allowed me to walk around with her on my finger. Oh, how I wanted to hold Rosie. I knew I could have just gone over and scooped her up from behind while she was on her sleeping branch, but I couldn't bring myself to betray her confidence in me. It would have to be done in a straightforward manner or not at all. Sometimes, particularly when I would talk to her, she'd fly right up to my face, two or three inches away, emit one chirp and go back to her branch. I'm not sure if that was positive or negative, but it's the same chirp as the one she emitted after drinking.

Eventually Rosie became brazen and feisty enough that, if I were doing something with the plants in a place where she wanted to be, she would hover above my head and, in effect, holler at me until I departed.

Rosie liked a nightcap and was given her very last drink of the evening while she sat at her sleeping spot, but prior to retiring she would fly over to the tree to wait for a treat, shoot across the room the minute she saw me and then take her very longest drink of the entire day, really fueling up for the night. Most often Rosie kept her feet tucked in while feeding at flowers, but one thing I noticed as she stopped in front of the hand-held feeder was that her feet would go through motions similar to treading water. They seemed to be paddling, alternating one foot in front of the other. I wonder if that helped her stop. For her nightcap, Rosie took very long drinks, pushing her beak almost all the way into the feeder and ingesting so much that she caused a bubble to float up to the top while she was drinking. She would then fan her tail and, keeping the tail spread, move up a little to inspect the bubble to make sure it was no threat to her. For her last sip she would sometimes take one sip; fly five or six feet away, low toward the floor; stop; hang there and look at me for a second or so; and then come right back for more, repeating these actions four or five times.

One evening she took her last sip of the day, after which she proceeded to hover all around my legs about eight to ten inches off the floor, around and around, back and forth. Then I realized what else she wanted— I was standing too close to the *Cestrum* branch where she wanted to settle in. As soon as I moved, she positioned herself in her then-regular spot. On other nights she refused to settle in until after I left the room. One afternoon as darkness began to fall, I do believe Rosie was chasing me from her territory. Each time my back was turned she'd fly after me chirping or warning loudly and then, when I'd turn around, she'd fly back and forth and then return to her branch. When I finally left the room, she immediately retired to her sleeping branch. But flying around my legs didn't always signify a desire for her to settle in for the evening. There were other times when she would fearlessly fly around my legs, about one foot above the floor, weaving in and out, hunting bugs.

I wanted to photograph Rosie, not only for this book but for my memories, for I knew one day she'd be gone. But she bordered on being downright and deliberately uncooperative. While I'd spend half an hour sitting, camera and flashes poised and ready she, instead of visiting bougainvillea, for instance, or the waterfall, would inspect the reddish-orange "ready light" on the flashes. Then, if I left the room for a minute, I'd return to find her at the bougainvillea or just leaving the waterfall, soaking wet. While I would stand in position, six inches away from the camera, she would decide that she wanted a treat instead, and would fly back and forth in the five-inch space between my eyes and the viewfinder. On one occasion as I sat poised and ready to get some shots at the waterfall, she decided instead to investigate every red snowflake on the arms of my pajamas. In fact, Rosie investigated me any time she felt something warranted inspection—a solid red dot that was part of the logo on a t-shirt, my lipstick, a colorful hairpiece. Eventually the tripods became something to fly around, or under, when she had someplace to go. Rosie immediately investigated everything in her room; therefore, the best picture-taking opportunities came just after a flowering plant was brought in.

I've read that it's the feeders hummingbirds recognize, not the people, but I do not believe this to be so in Rosie's case. One day my husband asked if he could come in to handfeed her a treat. She came over to the feeder immediately but she was reluctant to drink. She knew the person was different. And it was more than just *seeing* the feeder. One early March morning the light of dawn brightened the sunroom just before the fluorescents turned on. Rosie sat with her back to me. I said, "Good morning, Rosie," and she immediately turned around and came over to the feeder without going through her stretching routine. So it's obvious that she both recognized me as an individual and associated at least my voice with a treat. Association is apparently more than just visual. When she heard that annoying, raspy squeak of the spray bottle, she immediately went to her shower branch. When I called her name, followed by the words, "sip, sip," she immediately came over to look in my hand for the feeder. To test her, I frequently did this with my back turned. The stimulus was the sound.

She clearly knows the difference between people—at least between me and others. When my daughter came in to help with some photos of Rosie being handfed, Rosie investigated her over and over, flying right up to her face, approaching from both sides of the camera, from under the camera, in between the legs of the tripod, from behind Terry's head. She knew that this was not me.

And she knew where I kept the feeder. She would shoot over there and hang in midair, waiting for me to turn around and pick it up. When she saw me moving the feeder, she'd move that foot or two to meet it. She understood that I had to go to that spot to pick up the feeder before I could give her some. At times Rosie couldn't decide whether she wanted a flower or the feeder so, on her way over for the treat, would take a poke at a flower or two. At times I wondered if she knew what she wanted at all. She'd go to the shower branch and flutter as if to say, "I want a shower," then she'd fly right up to my face and hover there with tail fanned, chirping as if to say, "I want a treat." In a whimsical manner, she'd repeat her behavior over and over as though she were playing a game. With the abundance of flowers, there were times when she behaved quite independently, refusing the treat in favor of flowers, especially during the spring when she had so many to choose from. Deep down inside, I knew that was best.

To a creature as small as a hummingbird, the sunroom must seem like a jungle with all of the plants inside but Rosie knew her way around in every nook and cranny, under and between pots, cork bark and other mounts, stems, roots, and branches—she always seemed to know exactly where she was going and the only thing I ever noticed her brush against was my hair.

Plumage

When first hatched, the rufous is about the size of a honeybee and naked except for two slight tracts of grayish natal down along the back. The natal down grows longer each day. Pinfeathers begin to show on the sixth and seventh days, and the chicks are soon feathered in juvenile plumage. The juvenile plumage in both sexes is similar to that of the adult female, with some minor differences such as more streaking at the throat. Except for a metallic greenish-bronze head, and occasionally on the back, the adult male rufous is primarily a noniridescent, cinnamon-rufous bird with a brilliant scarlet gorget. It has the distinction of being the only north temperate hummingbird that has evolved from iridescent to pigmented coloring; there is hardly any mistaking the identity of this bird. And as attractive as the male rufous is, the female is as beautiful. The adult female is an iridescent green to bronzy-green bird with white underparts and rufous coloring at the sides and flanks. Her throat is white, speckled with scarlet red centrally and greenish laterally and her tail flashes rufous.

Hummingbird feathers are both beautiful and efficient, but like everything else, they wear out. Molting is the periodic replacement of those old and worn-out feathers. The process is a gradual one and, at least for most U.S. hummingbirds, occurs primarily in winter. Especially because Calder had indicated that the molting cycle and chronology for the rufous are undescribed, I tried to monitor feather loss and replacement.

For the rufous hummingbird, flight feathers are reportedly replaced in January, with males ahead of

Molt of the contour feathers started at the throat and they were lost in bunches.

females. The entire molting period appears to run normally from mid-December until late March. However, as the initial photographs revealed, Rosie's flight feathers were obviously being replaced at least by the second half of September.

By the first week of November, when Rosie began her stay in the sunroom, she was molting at the edges of her throat. I would find her feathers on leaves when plants were removed to be watered, discover them on the floor, or see them floating in the air. Within a week she had a dark half-moon below the gorget area where feathers had fallen out. The loss was rapid compared to Squeak's. It started at the left side of the throat line and as each group was replaced, the next bunch would fall out, thus working the molt across to the right side of the throat.

Rosie lost contour feathers in bunches. What I didn't realize is that occasionally a cluster of feathers falls out together. On December 4, one bunch of eight

Rosie scratched constantly.

The number of iridescent gorget feathers increased from a loose horseshoe shape to a striking central patch.

to ten feathers fell out or were scratched out at once, stuck together at the tips of the quills. Loose feathers obviously annoyed Rosie and probably made her feel itchy. She scratched constantly, frequently in midair, and took more baths per day, with several visits to the waterfall. Rosie would scratch and then shake to dislodge loose feathers, watching them as they softly and slowly floated down to the floor. Occasionally she would meet one halfway down to inspect it. The iridescent contour feathers started to molt in mid-December.

Just as Dr. Calder had suggested, the number of iridescent feathers in the gorget area increased and what had previously been a loose horseshoe became a striking central patch of iridescence as, by late December, new iridescent scarlet feathers formed in a cluster on

her throat. By January 1, pinfeather sheaths were showing above her right eye and on her forehead. On January 4, feather replacement was taking place under her
tail at the side as well as over her head and dorsal areas.
On January 8, pinfeather sheaths were visible on her
forehead; by January 10, they were visible under her
right wing and lesser underwing coverts; and on January 15, pinfeather sheaths were visible on the breast
and abdomen.

Through December 31, 110 contour feathers were
found, including the cluster. Of that total, twenty or 18
percent had iridescent tips. In the two-week period of
January 1 through January 14, forty-eight feathers were
found, 50 percent of which showed some iridescence.
In the next two-week period, January 14 through January 31, twenty-seven contour feathers were found, all
of which showed either iridescence or rufous coloration. In the month of February, two contour feathers
were found, one with and one without iridescence, and
in March only one plain feather was found (March 3).

Although 188 contour feathers were found, many
had not been replaced. Replacement of Rosie's contour
feathers was concurrent with flight feathers, took
place over the entire length of flight-feather replacement, and were lost in a pattern. The pattern seems to
be that feathers were lost at intervals of about seven
days, were lost for two or three days in a row and then
none were lost for about four or five days. There was a
cycle of approximately one week for feather loss, rest,
and replacement.

I can relate only what I actually found, and although I made a diligent effort to find them all, they are all very small and many undoubtedly found their way into inaccessible places. Because of their larger size and small number, primaries were easiest to monitor. The pattern was from the base to tip of the wing except that the ninth primary was skipped, the tenth was molted after the eighth, and then the ninth after the tenth. On November 24 and November 25, Rosie lost the sixth primary on each side. One was found on the floor, the other in the waterfall. Then on December 18, approximately three weeks later, Rosie was acting as though she were extremely agitated, fluffing and shaking her wings and tail, and chirping, loudly and incessantly. The next thing I knew, the seventh primary was lying on the floor beneath her. A search of the surrounding area found its counterpart, which would have had to have fallen out that day or the one before.

On December 23, Rosie's behavior was again very agitated. She hovered around three times in a small counterclockwise circle no larger than four inches in diameter and sat back down. Then, as she lifted from her branch, the eighth primary, left side, fell out. She then proceeded to peck at her left wing repeatedly in the same spot. The next day Rosie came over for a treat when all of a sudden she buzzed and returned to her branch as the eighth primary, right side, fell out. On December 26, Rosie was flying back and forth, again in an agitated manner, and sounding much like a sputtering motor—I could see a dark area on the usu-

Replacement of Rosie's contour feathers was concurrent with flight feathers—as Rosie visits Ribes malvaceum, *different areas of molt are obvious.*

Molting and replacing flight feathers.

ally transparent wing, where one feather overlapped another as it made its way forward; this, too, must have been uncomfortable.

Molting and replacing flight feathers.

Several areas of molt.

By the end of the month, the sound had returned to much more of a soft purr, but on December 30, the soft purr of the morning turned dull by 5:00 P.M. I could hear the difference in the wing sound immediately, and when I searched, I found the slightly curved and thinner tenth primary from both the right and left wing. Finally, on January 8, Rosie held her right wing straight out and was pecking at it when she suddenly got up and flew in one three-foot-diameter circle, counterclockwise, and the ninth primary fell out. The tip was worn. Then, within half an hour while she was hunting, the ninth primary on the opposite side fell out. The tip was unworn. As far as primaries one to five are concerned, I am assuming that they were replaced during the six-week period she spent in the garden before moving into the sunroom.

By January 15, the new tenth primaries were visible. On January 22, the ninth primaries started coming in while pinfeather sheaths for the tenth were still visible and the tenth was about 75 percent complete. The white pinfeather sheaths stood out even while Rosie was hovering, but by January 29 they were gone and her wings sounded normal.

In his paper, Calder indicates that at times rectrices number three to five (the outer three) are not molted by the female, who arrives on her breeding ground with color-marked or worn outer tail feathers. Rosie apparently had started her molt at least in September, by the end of January had stopped and much had been replaced with the exception of her entire tail. Every once in a while she'd hover and vibrate her tail as if she were trying to get rid of something—maybe one of the tail feathers. The noise was loud, but the feathers stayed in. There were times when she'd sit and rattle her tail feathers as if trying to dislodge one, but it was a fruitless attempt as the feathers remained intact.

SPRING

Rufous hummingbirds start their northward spring migration very early in the year, with some departing their winter haunts as early as January. Much of their year is spent traveling. Although stragglers may still be found on the wintering grounds in Mexico, some individuals arrive as early as late February to their breeding areas in the state of Washington. With males preceding females, the bulk of the migrants move through central California in April, for an ultimate mid-April to early May arrival in the Pacific Northwest and southern Alaska, where they inhabit forest openings and brushy places.

Quite simply, the rufous hummingbird has an elliptical migratory route more or less around the deserts: up the coast in spring and down the Western mountains in fall. The pattern coincides with advantageous weather conditions and the onset of blooming of such preferred species as the tubular red to yellow flowers of chuparosa, which is native to semi-arid areas of California, Arizona, and New Mexico; the many species of currant that flower in succession from fall to spring; as well as ocotillo, salvia, penstemon, and delphinium.

One has only to look at the fundamental nature of the West Coast climate to see how a successful migration can take place so early and how the birds can be so far north compared to the Northeast migration. The coast is mild year-round, with a late fall and winter rainy season, and a dry summer. Spring on the West Coast is an early affair. By December, Anna's hummingbirds are beginning to nest in California. By January, the manzanitas are starting to bloom in many areas of coastal California, while lupines, larkspur, paintbrushes, and other wildflowers bloom along roadsides in southern California. By February, fruit trees are in bloom along the coast and up through the Central Valley. Many slopes just south of San Francisco are covered with the blossoms of peaches, apricots, cherries, and nut trees. In contrast, spring in the Northeast lags far behind. In January, when many rufous hummingbirds begin to migrate, we are having snow and cold. In

February, when fruit trees start to bloom on the coast and hummers begin arriving on their breeding grounds, we are having more snow and cold. In the sunroom, however, Rosie flitted around the tropical habitat that had been provided for her, oblivious to the horrendous conditions out of doors.

Spring is a time of new beginnings everywhere. The sunroom was exciting with new buds peeking out on an entirely different array of plants for Rosie to savor—a smorgasbord of flowers. It's the time of year when she should have been on the move, but she wasn't. I felt badly about being the one who had stopped her, and I did all I could to make it up to her.

Out of necessity, Rosie would, unfortunately, be off her normal schedule. But in spite of that, her behavioral changes appeared consistent with what would have occurred naturally, had she gone to Mexico, and all her natural changes occurred in order.

In her annual cycle, winter ended and spring began with the completion of her molt at the end of January and, if I may be presumptuous, her natural increased intake of insects. This would be just prior to the start of her regular northward migration. The sun changed and days got longer, only slightly noticeable in January but the tempo picked up in February. Rosie exhibited a definite change in behavior, with activities that seemed to parallel normal rufous behavior, and it all seemed to be falling into place. Her behavior took on more of a skittish aspect, particularly with others, and she would repeatedly fly to the north side of the room. Whereas January revealed an increase in protein consumption, the desire waned somewhat in February as her "movements" began. By late March, when her movements stopped, Rosie showed an interest in nesting materials.

Spring Behavior

Hunting—Nectar is a rich, renewable resource imparting quick energy, but it is an incomplete food source. The need for protein has been well established, and NektarPlus has proved itself for a well-balanced diet in captivity. Yet there is, apparently, a time or times during the year when protein needs are greater than usual. DesGranges indicates that migrant hummingbirds spend 61 percent of their foraging time before spring departures feeding on insects, as compared to only 1 percent in mid-winter.

For Rosie, insects were a regular supplement to her diet. But birds and animals seem to know what they need and when they need it, and Rosie's desire for insects reached a peak around the start of the year. Too much should probably not be read into this, but it coincides perfectly with completion of the molt and the start of migration, when insects normally form a greater proportion of the total diet. This might be

instinctive behavior, and further may coincide with or
in some way initiate the start of certain glandular activity that helps the bird get ready for breeding. This very
noticeable change indicates that increased consumption of insects occurs, not as a result of increased avail-

*The screen of the skylight was an excellent spot for finding little flying
insects.*

ability or lack of suitable floral nectars, but as a necessary part of the cycle.

One might wonder just what Rosie could possibly
do all day. Much time was spent foraging among the
flowers, of course, but Rosie would also bathe, sunbathe, preen, just hang around, and hunt. As we got
closer to spring, Rosie did more and became more
active. At first she spent a small portion of the day
hunting. She would visit different places looking for
insects, but primarily it was incidental to some other
activity. However, around the start of the year I

noticed that Rosie was spending much more time hunting. At first I became concerned. But as she began
hunting relentlessly, I realized that Rosie just wanted
more. She looked everywhere, up and down walls and
under leaves. She thoroughly investigated the Spanish
moss; every speck of dust, every blemish, and every
dried-up raindrop on the window was checked out,
too. She captured some insects in midair and plucked
others off the windows, leaves, and every other place
imaginable. The screen of the skylight was an excellent
spot for finding little flying insects.

Rosie was a much more aggressive hunter than
Squeak had been and would take off like a little chee-
tah and, with her mouth open to an angle of approximately 45°, would capture an insect with a snap. One
whitefly had the misfortune to land right on her bill.
She whipped her head around to dislodge it, opened
her mouth wide, and devoured it. I think that the preferred manner of insect collecting is capturing on the
fly. When stationary, the insects at times get stuck on
the tongue.

Rosie had a different place to sleep, bathe, rest, and
hunt. Her favorite hunting branch was a low branch on
the *Cestrum*, about one foot above the floor, where she
would sit and watch until she spotted something
appealing. She would also hover close to the floor,
looking for her prey. I really shouldn't say "hover,"
because that implies that there is no forward movement. This vertical flight was somewhat choppy; she
would sputter no more than 2 inches above the floor

and check out the entire sunroom for insects, looking under everything. And she would look up and down my legs, during which time I was afraid to move lest I step on her. One day early in January when the temperature was in the low 40s, she was flying up and down at the window while a small moth-type insect did likewise in unison with her outside the window.

Rosie spent her time at one or the other of her favorite spots at the south end of the room. That is, except when she was hunting. While Rosie looked for insects, she explored every available spot, including that portion of the sunroom which lies between the floor and the underside of the loveseat—a six-inch space more or less—and, with forward vertical movement, would float along underneath, looking for spiders.

Once, while I was feeding Rosie, she spotted a spider crawling across a large *Pachystachys* leaf and went to investigate. When the spider became aware of Rosie's presence, it scurried to the underside of the leaf and Rosie attempted to capture its silhouette. At other times, she would be drinking from the feeder that I was holding when she would stop abruptly. She would then dash across the room at a right angle and capture an insect, and immediately return to the feeder to resume taking nectar. Amazingly, she saw that bug across the room while she was feeding!

Rosie's new voracious appetite prompted me to have some extra protein for her, but for some unfortunate reason, I wasn't plagued—or blessed, as the case may be— with as many whiteflies as I've had in other years, and

Rosie would spot a dangling spider, dart over, open her beak, and devour it.

the supply in the sunroom didn't seem adequate. I'd have to bring her some from elsewhere, and the richest place for insect collecting is the basement growing area. There I was able to find some whiteflies on the undersides of the fuchsia leaves and little spiders that I carried back upstairs, dangling from their webs. Rosie, with her excellent eyesight, would immediately spot the dangling spider and dart over, open her beak, and devour it. When she ate a spider from my hand she displayed her soft, orangish gape. In an attempt to satisfy her, I would then trek back downstairs to repeat the process. It was evident that the spider supply too was being exhausted.

A local radio gardening show had a listener call in to have a small insect found near some plants and windowsills identified. The specimens collected and sent to Cornell for analysis turned out to be an unknown member of the order Diptera, which contains many

small-winged fly-type insects such as fruit flies, common near rotting vegetation. My New Zealand tree fern
had a number of these insects, and they were a good
snack for Rosie. The little guys weren't too difficult to
catch once I got the hang of it. I learned to pull my
cupped hand forward and close it to catch one. I'd then
carry it up to Rosie, still imprisoned in my clenched
hand. When I opened my hand, the insect flew off but
Rosie was incredibly fast. What took me five minutes to
catch, she captured and devoured in two seconds. After
two trips into the sunroom with a clenched fist, Rosie
knew what I would be offering and started looking for it
before it was released. On one occasion she even
plucked one off my finger.

Rosie's request for insects came so frequently that I
had to figure out another way to get them quicker than
one or two at a time. My idea was to use a small,
battery-operated hand vacuum to suck in several at
once. It was wonderful: I could bring in a dozen whiteflies and several slightly larger Diptera and twist the
vacuum in half, releasing the little treasures for Rosie at
once. She would flit from one to another, capturing
each in turn. When one landed in my hair, Rosie flew
over and plucked it out with absolutely no fear. She
quickly learned what the vacuum represented and
would fly over to meet me any time I carried it into the
room. Eventually, even the supply of Diptera was
depleted. I started thinking about how I might import
some insects when, around the first week in February,
her appetite began to wane a bit.

On the Move—Once Rosie's desire for protein returned to its normal level, her attention turned to new spring behavior. Beginning in February, Rosie was on the move. She knew the boundaries of her room and would fly across its length at breakneck speed, do a little dip before she got to the other side, and turn around about two inches from the glass. She knew what she was doing, but because glass is an invisible barrier, she scared me when she did it. I had to do something.

Sheer curtains were the answer. Most light would be transmitted, while making her limitations more visible to Rosie. I took her in, therefore it was my responsibility to see to it that she made it through the winter unscathed. The sheers were tacked over the window frame and pulled taut. Now, if she were to inadvertently fly into the curtain, there would be some resilience there, something to bounce off. Since the south side of the room—specifically the southeast corner—was where she took off from when flying across the room, I covered the north windows and part of the east.

Since her movements seemed to parallel the time of normal migration, I had to entertain the possibility that they were significant and satisfied an instinct. The movements occurred primarily on sunny days, which may indicate that migrations occur or at least are initiated on pleasant days and not during inclement weather. Her February movements were always to the north-northeast area of the sunroom. I thought nothing of that until, after a slowdown about the second week in March, her flying shifted to the west side of the room. There are no windows on the west—only a wall—so I looked for some explanation or relevance. Perhaps the direction has something to do with the route she should have taken. By late March, the flying slowed to a trickle. Rosie's movements pretty much ended by late March, coinciding with the likely conclusion of migration.

Thinking About a Nest—Beginning much earlier than nesting time itself, perhaps initiated by increasing day length, the gonads swell and signal the start of breeding. Since Rosie's instinctive behavior had not been altered by artificial light, she followed a natural pattern.

On its regular breeding grounds, the rufous nests farther north than any other hummingbird—from about 61° N. in Alaska and southern Yukon, south to Oregon and southwestern Montana. Nests are built on blackberry vines, on dry roots, in conifers, and in other trees and bushes. The nests are commonly built on top of old nests. Most nests are no higher than fifteen feet, with earlier nests lower to the ground. Bent reports colonies of up to twenty nests within yards of one another in second-growth vegetation.[5]

Most hummingbird nests are beautiful little structures, with mere size alone one of their most charming characteristics. The cup-shaped nest of a rufous hummingbird is less than two inches across on the outside, less than one inch on the inside, and approximately

5. Arthur Cleveland Bent, *Histories of North American Cuckoos, Goatsuckers, Hummingbirds and their Allies* (New York: Dover, 1989).

one and one-half inches high with less than one inch of interior depth. Nests are lined with soft, pale buff, cottony plant materials and moss. They are decorated on the outside with bits of bark, bud scales, moss, and lichen, and are held in place by spiders' webs. Nest construction starts in late March and April, and may take as little as one day or as much as one week to complete, if the nests of similar hummers are any indication. The white, elliptical-oval eggs, measuring approximately 13 by 8 millimeters (approximately ½ by ⅓ inch), are laid from April to July. A nesting bird usually lays two eggs, which are incubated for fifteen to seventeen days, entirely by the female.

Many of my orchids are potted in a shredded coconut-husk fiber medium and are grown in slatted cedar baskets; consequently, little strands of the fiber stick out here and there. On several occasions I noticed Rosie pulling pieces of coconut husk out of an orchid basket. She didn't do anything with them, and at first I assumed she was looking for spiders.

There are cotton sheets covering the chairs in the sunroom. They are the hospital type—more a cross between a cotton sheet and a terrycloth towel. Rosie investigated the covering and grabbed the knap in her beak and tugged on it. When she did, the covering would lift about three inches away from the chair itself. She was pulling the entire piece of material up by a thread. I wasn't sure whether she was hunting or perhaps looking for nesting material.

I began to wonder whether Rosie might be thinking about a nest. I was curious about what her reaction would be to one of a rubythroat, and was quite surprised at the result. When the nest was brought in to her, she responded differently than to any other object that I had held. I got the distinct impression she knew exactly what it was; furthermore, although definitely interested, she was quite apprehensive about it. She immediately came over to investigate and while she was checking it out, she chirped repeatedly while circling it with tail fanned and facing the nest at all times, threateningly moving from the back side of the hand that held the nest, around in a circle to the front side of my hand. I interpreted her reaction to be basically a negative one. Her posture was equivalent to a female rubythroat's threat posture, and I presume that it conveyed a similar message here. I also interpreted her loud chirp as a threatening announcement that the sunroom is her territory. And so I removed the nest.

On the last Sunday in March, when I entered the sunroom, Rosie was just leaving the southwest corner. I wondered what she might be doing, when my eyes focused on an orchid mounted on wood sparsely covered with bits of lichen. She appeared to be pecking at the lichen. Again I wondered whether Rosie was taking stock of potential nesting materials. My friend Vickie has a second home in Scottsdale. This year she brought me some pictures of two baby hummingbirds in a nest just outside one of her windows. The most unusual and surprising part was this female's choice of nesting site: an artificial outdoor sheffelera plant. If that female

Rosie gathers dryer lint for a nest.

found that site suitable, then I could see no reason why
Rosie might not build hers right here in the sunroom.

I save dryer lint to offer the outdoor birds some
nesting material. All-natural, undyed and unbleached
cotton flannel pajamas produced the softest, purest lint
I could find. I had put it aside for hummingbirds
months before, but I took it out now and offered it to
Rosie, placing a handful of the cottony material in
between some of the lower branches on the honeysuckle plant. I couldn't help notice how warm the material became when I held it. Practically within seconds,
she started gathering bits of the fluff. She flew down
and, while bracing herself with her little feet, clasped a
piece of the lint in her beak and yanked it away from
the rest. Instead of taking off with it, she proceeded to
gather more, holding on with her feet, taking additional pieces and fitting more and more in her beak

Rosie with fluff.

until the bunch of cotton was larger than her head; and then she took off. Most of the material fell to the floor as she flew up to a branch, and she dropped what was left while she sat there. She visited the lint at least a couple of times that first day. I felt sure that Rosie knew what this plant down equivalent was for.

I didn't know whether Rosie would attempt to complete a nest, but in case she did, I wanted to provide whatever materials she would need. Spider's web and cobwebs are available in the sunroom, and she could find all the moss she could possibly want on several of the mounted orchids. Although there was some lichen here and there, my husband brought in a fallen maple branch that was covered with soft, greenish lichen. We placed the log in an area where Rosie could help herself to the pieces of decoration.

On Easter Sunday, Rosie went to the fluff periodi-

cally to take a piece. Again, she didn't do anything with
it, but she did do something else. Rosie had a long
piece of spider's web dangling from her foot. I watched
as she weaved her beak over and under the branch,
back to front, as if sharpening a knife. I couldn't be sure
whether she was starting a nest or just trying to remove
the web. But after most of it was on the branch, she had
the task of removing what remained on her foot. After
a couple of fruitless attempts, she immediately went to
the waterfall, chirping, fluttering, and pecking for a full
two minutes. What remained of the web probably
stuck to the roughish surface of the lava rock. She
really kept me wondering about her nest and at that
point I added some bud scales from a camellia plant to
Rosie's collection of nesting material, piling them on
top of the lichen-covered maple log. Each evening

*Rosie weaves her beak over and under the branch when she gathers
spider's web for a nest.*

after returning from work I looked around to see if a nest had been started. Although I didn't find anything, Rosie did move large pieces of the lint from time to time especially late in April when finding bits of the fluff was practically an everyday occurrence.

Also, the rufous is reported to forage for midges on sandy ground early in the breeding season. On April 20, in addition to finding pieces of the fluff around, I noticed Rosie fly over to the pot of blue curls, pick up grains of sand with her beak, and literally toss them!

Spring Flowers

Rufous hummingbirds are common spring migrants in the southern California foothills and valleys, with the males preceding the females and arriving in early March just as the currants, particularly crimson-flowered currant, come into bloom. The bulk of the spring migration through central California occurs in April, where aggressive migrant rufous hummingbirds visit flowers of chuparosa, ocotillo (*Fouquieria splendens*), mints (e.g., *Stachys coccinea, Salvia spp., Satureja mimuloides*), penstemon, delphinium, tree tobacco (*Nicotiana glauca*), and other currants. Other West Coast favorites are columbine (*Aquilegia spp.*), madroña tree (*Arbutus menziesii*), paintbrushes (*Castilleja spp.*), salmonberry (*Rubus spectabilis*), and honeysuckle (*Lonicera spp.*).

I knew I couldn't duplicate all that Rosie would find in a normal spring journey northward, but I was determined to give it the best shot possible. This seemed so much more important for her spring season because she appeared to be carrying on all her normal activities.

Aquilegia formosa *is a West Coast favorite for the rufous hummingbird.*

I had wanted to offer Rosie as much as possible of what she might have encountered naturally, and a good stock of California plants proved to be the answer. Many of the California natives I had acquired for Rosie

Rosie spent much time visiting another West Coast favorite, delphinium.

during the winter came into bloom in spring. The very
beautiful romero or woolly blue curls (*Trichostema lana-
tum*), a stunning plant with fragrant foliage and deep
bluish, woolly flowers; western columbine (*Aquilegia formosa*); and the monkey flowers, *Mimulus* and *Diplacus*,
that had been so popular over the winter continued to
flower through the spring, as did the *Ribes*.

*The very
beautiful
woolly blue
curls is a
stunning plant
favored by
Rosie.*

Ribes flowers at first glance might seem unlikely
candidates for hummingbirds because the blossoms are
so small, and one might reasonably expect a hummingbird to be most attracted to flowers similar in size to its
beak. Rosie loved all the *Ribes* species offered, returning
again and again to drink their nectar. Other flowers
you might never expect to be attractive to hummingbirds are the manzanitas (*Arctostaphylos spp.*), with an
unbelievable number of cultivars and tiny, creamy-
white, dangling, urn-shaped flowers. Rosie would cling

Rosie preferred small flowers such as the manzanitas.

Rosie and a small mint, Stachys bullata.

to the twiggy branches of this plant, at times almost
upside down, to get at the nectar in the flowers, and
she made numerous trips to the plant each day. One of
the biggest surprises was the size of individual blos-

The small Brazilian sky flower.

One of the smallest was bumble bee plant—nothing special, just tiny.

soms most favored. She consistently preferred the smallest flowers such as the many tillandsias, *Stachys bullata*, scarlet bush (*Hamelia patens*), bumble bee plant (*Scrophularia atrata*), and Brazilian sky flower (*Duranta stenostachya*), in addition to the *Ribes* and *Arctostaphylos* already mentioned, with the single notable exception of *Passiflora*, which she loved. One of the smallest, bumble bee plant, with its one-quarter-inch green and yellowish flowers, is listed as attractive to bees. It is nothing special or outstanding as far as I can see; it was just tiny, but Rosie loved it and it brought to mind Johnsgard's comments that in Alaska, the rufous hummingbird frequently pollinates flowers more suitable for pollination by bees.

Rosie was much more attracted to Hamelia patens *than are the rubythroats*

Over the years that I've grown scarlet bush, I've noticed that although the rubythroat visits its small, tubular, orange flowers it is never with the zeal that other flowers, elicit. I've always felt that this is because of the size of each blossom, concluding that it held less nectar and must be most suitable for the smallest hum-

*Mints are
popular with
hummingbirds
and Rosie
visited them
frequently—
here she visits*
Satureja
mimuloides.

Salvia microphylla,
a spring mint.

Salvia officinalis,
another spring mint.

From time to time Rosie would make use of the dahlias.

The spring bloom of Calliandra *presents a new picture.*

mers such as the bee hummingbird (*Mellisuga helenae*) of Cuba and the Isle of Pines. Scarlet bush is one of those tropical plants that, like one of the California paint-brushes, hosts mites that move from flower cluster to flower cluster and plant to plant as passengers on the

Abelia grandiflora *was a pleasant spring surprise.*

Tillandsias were her favorite.

bills of hummingbirds, even taking shelter in their nostrils. The flowers open shortly after midnight, allowing time for the mites to move in before the hummingbirds become active at dawn. Clusters of the flowers form above the leaves at the ends of the branches and are

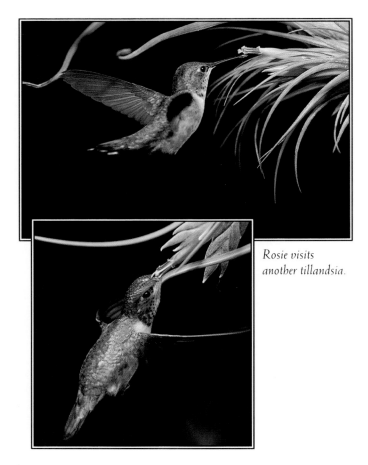

*Rosie visits
another tillandsia.*

usually at various stages of development from buds to mature tubes. Rosie found the single, first mature flower on this plant within minutes of waking up, and she wouldn't leave it alone for the rest of the day. Obviously, Rosie loved *Hamelia* flowers; again, the smallish size of a particular flower was no deterrent.

Mints such as *Salvia, Stachys,* and *Satureja* are popular with hummingbirds. Rosie had flowers on *Salvia coccinea* sporadically all winter. For spring, it was joined by *S. officinalis* and *S. microphylla.* Two other spring mints, *Satureja mimuloides* and *Stachys bullata,* were in bloom and

Rosie visits Squeak's favorite, Tillandsia geminiflora.

Rosie visited them both frequently.

Squeak loved the big, bold hibiscus flowers so much he couldn't wait for them to open. Once they did open, he'd get lost in them. But Rosie acted as though they frightened her. She would approach the opened flowers to about two inches and hang there looking for a second or two, but then fly off elsewhere. I can't very well say she didn't like them; she just refused to try. Similarly, Squeak loved flowering maple (*Abu-*

tilon), but Rosie would visit it only after she had gone to everything else. But remember how Rosie showed only a passing interest in *Calliandra* during its winter bloom? The spring bloom of the *Calliandra* plants presented an entirely different picture. This time around she loved them so much that she wouldn't leave them alone, even attempting to extract nectar from the fallen flowers.

There were both disappointments and pleasant surprises in the sunroom this year. Glossy abelia (*Abelia grandiflora*), with its dainty, white, hanging bells, is a garden plant that does well under rhododendron conditions but is only marginally hardy in this area. Accordingly, abelia as a potted plant has always been wintered over in an unheated porch. This year, however, it was kept in the sunroom. The early bloom was a complete surprise and Rosie loved the blossoms visiting them frequently to drain their nectar. For quite a while, visits to abelia alternated with visits to all other flowers.

Tillandsias are interesting and attractive, make great companion plants for orchids, and are pollinated in the wild almost exclusively by hummingbirds. Of all the flowers in the sunroom, it was the tillandsias that Rosie would follow me around to get at while I was holding them. It was also the only flower she would leave the hand-held feeder for, alternating from feeder to flower, feeder to flower. Tillandsia nectar must be very special. She would find the flowers even if they were in an out-of-the-way spot.

For years I've wanted to get a photograph of one of

Each blossom of passion flower was greeted with enthusiasm.

the hummingbirds at the passion flower (*Passiflora vitifo-lia*), but could not synchronize my camera with their visits. Since it is cut back each winter, the vine, with its grapelike leaves and profuse, dramatic red blossoms, usually blooms during the summer and fall. Because of my busy schedule the past winter, I neglected to give it the usual trim and was excited to see that the plant would be in flower much earlier this year. When the first flower opened, I thought Rosie was in ecstasy, visiting that initial blossom repeatedly and chirping up a storm. *Passiflora*'s only negative quality is that the flowers stay only one day, from just prior to sunrise to just after sunset. They are most beautiful as they first open and just before they close; during the bright part of the day the petals are somewhat reflexed. Neverthe-less, Rosie greeted each succeeding blossom with the same enthusiasm. She would even visit passion flowers

Shrimp plant was a spring favorite.

the day after, when the buds are just about closed but there's still some nectar at the base of the petals and even in the bracts.

Rosie made her rounds among all the flowers, but when something was new, or when particular flowers first began to open, they would get special attention.

Penstemons are always popular with hummingbirds (P. spectabilis).

Once something was no longer brand-new, it became part of the route, even though fresh individual blossoms would open on the plant.

Some of the other spring flowers that Rosie enjoyed are the shrimp plant, penstemon species (*P. utahensis* being a possible favorite), columbine (*Aquilegia formosa*

Penstemon utahensis, *Rosie's favorite.*

winning hands down over the garden hybrids), and trumpet honeysuckle (*Lonicera sempervirens*). Common kalanchoe (*Kalanchoe* hybrids) was okay, but she loved trailing kalanchoe (*Kalanchoe uniflora*) and she didn't lift the blossoms as Squeak had to drain the nectar.

I was anxious to get Rosie's reaction to Mexican orchids, such as the very beautiful *Cuitlauzinia pendula*, which grows at lofty elevations of the dry oak forests of western Mexico. When the flower spike was forming, Rosie systematically removed the "nectar." When the blossoms opened, she ignored them, preferring to

*Western columbine
(Aquilegia
formosa) won
hands down . . .*

*. . . over garden
hybrids*

take the drops of nectar from behind the flowers where
they joined the spike. Spring also offered other orchids
with long flower spikes, such as *Aerides* and *Dendrobium*
and Rosie continued to find these orchid spikes to "de-
nectarize." She would hover in front of or behind them
at times, but mostly she'd hang on to something else

Trumpet honeysuckle never turned as dark indoors, but Rosie loved it anyway.

She loved trailing kalanchoe but didn't lift the blossoms to drain the nectar

Zauschneria *ordinarily blooms in late summer and early fall.*

Rosie bears down on lantana.

and stretch her neck to reach them. Typically, the orchid flowers themselves didn't appeal to Rosie.

I was able to get a few flowers on the old growth of hummingbird or California fuchsia (*Zauschneria latifolia* 'Johnstonii'), which ordinarily blooms during late sum-

Penstemon barbatus.

Rosie visits bleeding heart (note how her tail is held high).

mer and fall, and Rosie, of course, made use of them. However, she preferred western columbine to the *Zauschneria*. That really surprised me—and perhaps it is that columbine is truly a spring flower as compared to *Zauschneria*, which is noted for its importance to hum-

Rosie loved scarlet bouvardia just as much in spring as she had earlier in her stay.

mingbirds because of its late flowering; or western columbine could be a flower to which she has had more natural exposure, a "learned" flower.

Knowing which flowers to use is a learning process in hummingbirds. Young hummers try everything in the beginning; it is not something known from birth. If

Rosie was most beautiful when set against the soft lavender-blue of delphinium.

Rosie visits
Dianthus.

this is so, and columbine is a familiar flower to Rosie, it
might indicate that her first migration was correct and
that the very best thing I had done for Rosie was to buy
her familiar native plants. The fact that Squeak visited
several flowers that held no interest for Rosie might be

*What would a
garden be for a rufous
hummingbird without*
Ribes sanguineum?

because he, as an immature bird, was still learning and, therefore, willing to try more than Rosie was.

When the lantana (*L. montevidensis*) came into bloom, Rosie was in heaven—another small-flowered plant with hundreds of individual blossoms. With such a bountiful crop of flowers on one plant, I was able to observe her method of foraging. It appears that her pattern was completely indiscriminate, although she started at basically the same place on the plant regardless of where she was sitting beforehand. She would move in either a clockwise or counterclockwise, up or down, direction, not necessarily the same way twice in a row. However, she was consistent in not draining every blossom in the cluster—usually only two or three flowers per cluster were drained per visit. And when the lantana did start blooming, Rosie had a field day. As far as she was concerned, I am sure, this was what foraging was all about, flitting from lantana to fuchsia, columbine, scarlet bush, jasmine, honeysuckle, *Mimulus*, impatiens, one after another. There is no doubt that she preferred small flowers. While I can't very well say that it's conclusive about all rufous hummingbirds, it certainly was about Rosie. When given a choice between a beautiful red fuchsia with abundant flowers and the lavender lantana, she chose the tiny lantana blossoms. Her most favorite flowers of what was offered here were manzanitas, currants, and tillandsias. The only large flowers that she especially liked were passion flower, delphinium, and the beak-sized trumpet honeysuckle.

Once spring came, I went shopping at the garden center on a weekly basis. If anything was being offered for planting that I thought would be attractive, I bought it for her: delphinium, *Penstemon barbatus*, bleeding heart (*Dicentra*), as well as a new flowering quince and *Dianthus*. Flowering quince branches were also brought in from the garden. From an aesthetic point of view, Rosie looked most beautiful when set against the soft lavender-blue delphinium, probably because it brought out her rufous coloring so well. Since the ones she had in the fall weren't in flower yet, new scarlet bouvardia plants were purchased for Rosie, and she loved them every bit as much in spring as she had in the fall and early winter.

And finally, what would a garden for a rufous hummingbird be without *Ribes sanguineum*? This is the plant so timed with the return of the rufous to the West Coast. I had been unable to purchase this plant during the winter when I purchased the other *Ribes*, but found a supply for the spring and bought a four-foot pink one for Rosie. Needless to say, she wouldn't leave it alone. As with several of the other West Coast plants that were purchased, *R. sanguineum* would be planted in the garden once Rosie was released, where it would, I hoped, serve the local hummers in subsequent springs.

Odds and Ends

One of the strangest things that Rosie occasionally did was to approach a branch and while chirping incessantly, behave as though she were being stopped or held back by an invisible barrier or as if in a wind tunnel, struggling to reach the branch. After one or two seconds, she would alight in the normal manner.

A bluejay warning outside would result in an immediate halt to whatever Rosie was doing inside. She would then freeze in position with her beak held upward at an angle of approximately 45°. Occasionally I would enter her room and she'd be on a twig or on her root, frozen in place. Invariably the birds outside would be similarly frozen and patiently waiting for a hawk to leave. When she was afraid of something, such as the scraping of a snow shovel or people moving about outside, she retreated to a very low branch, six to eight inches off the floor, to hide. She seemed to be apprehensive about any overhead noise or shadows. When Rosie detected a shadow overhead, seen via the skylight, she would fly right down to about one foot above the floor, under some leaves and hide.

When she was frightened, she favored low branches and if she sensed danger, such as when the bluejays would announce the presence of a hawk, the sound of a helicopter overhead or even when my husband cleaned snow off the roof, she would cling sideways to one particular very low, but quite upright, branch. Noise must be partially to blame for her fright when a helicopter was overhead. She liked to be the loudest thing around, except for the waterfall, which she had become so accustomed to hearing that she became upset when it wasn't babbling. Although she did not like overhead sounds, rain did not produce the same reaction.

Rosie moved in and out, between and among branches and under leaves, to hide, hunt, or forage at flowers, but she never bumped into anything. She seemed to have a sense about just how much room she had and would contort her little body so she could fit into the space available.

One day Rosie was searching up and down the trunk of the sleeping hibiscus for either sap or insects. As she got near the lower portion, a dried-up leaf lying on the floor was pushed along by the breeze she had created while hovering. As she lowered herself to inspect the moving leaf, it moved some more and she followed after it. It was comical to watch Rosie follow fallen objects, such as one of her molted feathers or a fallen blossom.

A hummingbird's iris is dark brown. Their eyes are capable of both monocular and binocular vision, and

One of the few times that Rosie was willing to sit while feeding was at a tillandsia.

their eyes have two areas of sharp vision. If behavior is any indication, they appear to have excellent eyesight, not only for close focusing on flowers and insects but for distance as well, being quite capable of spotting another hummingbird, even when it is perched, at least a hundred feet away. But what's most surprising is that they may be capable of either simultaneous execution of both types of focusing or rapidly alternating between the two, as was frequently demonstrated by Rosie. While drinking from the hand-held feeder, she would spot an insect flying off to the side, and would immediately leave the feeder, capture the insect, and

Rosie would approach certain flowers and hover in front of them . . .

. . . and then would spin around and fly away without taking any nectar.

then return to the feeder. So while she was looking forward, guiding her beak in and out—binocular vision—she also appeared to be capable of focusing on what was happening to her side.

The skylight was one of Rosie's favorite places where she might sunbathe or hunt, but when the first snow fell the week before Christmas and temporarily covered the skylight, Rosie flew up there and looked at it over and over. Something was different, and she was quick to spot the change. Once some of the snow slid off the sloping skylight and Rosie was able to see new, heavy, wet snowflakes falling anew, she tried to catch them.

Rosie had many opportunities to sit while she was drinking to conserve energy, but she rarely took advantage of them. She did, however, repeatedly cling to the upright branches of *Arctostaphylos* to achieve a more advantageous position for reaching the flowers. The only other times she was willing to sit were when she was either drinking from the tillandsia or lantana flowers or taking that sweet, sticky coating from the orchid buds and spikes, at which times she'd sit on roots, plop down on stiff leaves, or hang almost upside down on wire and crane her neck to reach the desired spot.

Just as she would occasionally hover in front of a feeder as if there were an invisible barrier to stop her from approaching it completely, she would approach certain flowers and hover in front of them in a similar manner. But then she would spin around without taking any nectar and fly away. She even did this with flowers that she generally enjoyed.

Pollination of flowers that only Rosie could have had contact with is the prima facie evidence of her floral foraging. I think it's absolutely adorable when I look around at plants and find fruits forming on the currants, green berries on the *Arctostaphylos*, a large round seed on the Turk's cap, or being blinded by threads of seed falling all over me from the tillandsias.

Comparison

There are differences in all manner of natural beings except clones. Differences in individual behavior are common in the rubythroat, and one has only to watch identifiable individuals to see that certain ones are aggressive, certain ones subordinate, some more cautious, and some braver. The differences are even more noticeable among the very young.

But what makes individuals so *individual?* Squeak was such a laid-back soul, whereas Rosie was a fickle, feisty, sometimes capricious, little live wire. Squeak was the consummate creature of habit for his entire stay here. Rosie, on the other hand, was true to her habits only while they lasted. I can speculate, but I really have no idea which differences may be attributed to genera or species, which are gender-related, and which are individual behavioral characteristics. For instance, Rosie displayed much more caution. This could be a difference in species behavior, it might be sex-related, with females naturally being more cautious; or it may just be an individual trait.

I know this is Rosie's story, but I couldn't help but notice differences between her and Squeak, and would like to share some of these observations. The comparisons are neither favorable nor unfavorable. There is no *right* way to bathe, for instance, but it is interesting to see how different individuals, as well as different species, react under similar circumstances or to similar experiences and daily needs.

Rosie was a much more aggressive hunter than Squeak. Except that Squeak displayed some sexual awakening, he seemed to be relatively oblivious to nature. Rosie, on the other hand, at least gave the impression that she was very attuned to what she *should* be doing.

Whereas Squeak spent a tremendous amount of time under the fluorescents, Rosie's time there became minimal and strictly for the purposes of visiting certain flowers such as *Mimulus* or to dry off after a shower. Squeak did much more preening than Rosie, but Rosie spent infinitely more time near water, showering or in the waterfall.

Johnsgard has indicated that there's not much tail movement and, for Western species, that may well be, but Rosie displayed much more tail movement than did Squeak. Rosie's tail constantly flapped up and under her and then back and up in the air as she moved in and out at the feeder. She also held her tail higher in relation to her body than did Squeak.

As far as I'm concerned, both were little darlings.

Prospects for the Future

Quite simply, there were two alternatives with respect to Rosie's future: either she'd stay or she'd go. I wanted to know which to expect. I remembered what I had learned about Charlie and his strong territorial instincts, and speculated about what had happened with Squeak and then tried to objectively apply it to my thoughts about Rosie's future. Neither of the former birds was out of an area where he would have occurred naturally, while Rosie was totally away from her range.

Rosie appears to have followed a natural spring pattern, including movements that might have been a substitute for regular migration. But one thing Rosie didn't do for this "pseudo-migration" was gain weight. I have seen fattening rubythroats preparing for their southward migrations, and have watched fattened hummers embark on their journeys (singly and in a pair on one occasion). So if she did gain weight the amount was so negligible as to be imperceptible. By the time Rosie would be released, she might be beyond a state of migration and ready to nest. Artificial lighting didn't appear to have interfered with normal spring behavior or to have extended the short periods of diurnal activity during winter for either bird. Regardless of the lights, Rosie appeared to be totally influenced by natural solar conditions and right on schedule. Her release time would coincide with the time she should have been at her destination.

I never worried about her becoming dependent upon me. This is not a concern because of the opportunistic nature of the hummingbird, which accepts, basically, whatever comes along. Nor was I concerned about Rosie continuing her interrupted southward fall migration when she was released; that was finished business. Her options, therefore, would be either a northwest migration back to her original breeding ground or setting up a nesting territory right here in the Mid-Hudson Valley. I would have expected her to migrate back to her original nesting territory if it had been possible to release her in February, March, or even April, but her release time here might just be too late to guarantee that in May, and secretion of the hormones that initiate migration might well be over. Because of the strong homing instinct, returning to her birthplace would still seem the most natural and logical outcome, except that this is a bird that had traveled across a continent and would have to travel back at least 1,850 miles. How much time would she need?

With the first option—returning to her birthplace— the most desirable of circumstances, she might very well return here next autumn, repeating her previously successful migration. On the other hand, were she to set up a nesting territory here, I would expect her fall migration to take her, perhaps, to the Southeast, with a return trip here in spring. For Rosie's sake, the perfect resolution would be that she go back to Alaska, Canada, or wherever else her breeding territory had been and follow her genetic map. Early during her stay I had wondered if it were possible she might correct her errant way and revert to her initial route. But Calder indicates that "migration terminates with *winter site fidelity* and seasonal residence"—that winter is not one of gradual wandering but established residence. Her body had given the signal that her migration was over in September, based perhaps on the distance or duration of her journey. And odd as it may seem, her fall migration to my yard had been a successful one. Also, rufous hummingbirds recaptured close to banding locations in Georgia and Alabama in subsequent winters indicate that such is the case. Calder reports that a juvenile female rufous banded in Metairie, Louisiana, in 1988 was recaptured each winter from 1990 to 1992. He recounts similar reports for Georgia, Alabama, and Florida. In Louisiana and Alabama, wintering rufous hummingbirds were captured four to six years after banding! It is likely that these birds enjoyed a normal nesting territory. So all that would favor a return to this yard either for the winter or on her return south. I would presume that genetic information with respect to at least the maiden migration is inherited and possibly relates to a parent's successful journey. If that were so, it could mean that Rosie is the progeny of one of those birds. It might also raise the question of whether at least some related birds winter in the same locality.

As the patch on Rosie's throat would change from red to scarlet, then amber, gold, and finally greenish, as her throat changed positions in relation to my line of sight, it would remind me of another unusual summer visitor to this garden. The visit occurred in mid-July 1987, when a new male hummingbird was noticed sitting on the clothesline. His gorget was quite an unusual color, glowing from a golden orange to rosy amber, depending upon the light. At first the very different coloration was attributed to the sun, but then other things were noticed about him as well. The unusual coloration didn't stop at the gorget; his green parts were extremely dark and quite different from any of the other hummers'. And he was large, at least one-half inch larger than the others. The bird stayed with us until mid-August and then was gone as abruptly as he had come. He did not return in 1988.

I've thought about that bird many times since then, and wondered how all of that may have come about, considering the possibility of genetic misfunction. However, there's one other possibility: the bird may have been a cross between a rubythroat and a rufous. Hummingbirds have been known to hybridize and certain described species have turned out to be naturally occurring hybrids. Although the breeding range of the two do not overlap, the westernmost portions of the

rubythroat's summering grounds are not that far from
the easternmost portions of the rufous's. Such hybridization might account not only for the unusual gorget
color but a darkened coloring overall. The larger size
may well have been the result of genes or the typical
result of intergeneric hybridization known as "hybrid
vigor." But these are chemical and genetic questions for
which I have no answers. Lynch and Ames describe
two male hummingbirds found at Sacramento County,
California, which later were determined to be a cross of
black-chinned and Allen's hummingbirds (*Archilochus
alexandri* and *Selasphorus sasin*), the same genera involved
here, and cite at least ten existing hummingbird crosses
as of 1970.[6] Typically, the eggs of such a mating are
infertile or, if fertile, the offspring are infertile. Dr.
Calder indicates that two hybrids allegedly involving
the rufous cannot be accepted for sure.

It must be emphasized that hybridization between
these two species is extremely unlikely. Not only is
intergeneric breeding uncommon, especially among
the hummingbirds inhabiting north temperate areas, it
is also unlikely on the basis of geographic distribution
and the fact that the rufous's habit of wandering is a
postnuptial one. Although it ends quite a bit earlier, the
rufous's breeding season occurs concurrently with that
of the rubythroat so it is possible that one of the parents of that bird may have been an off-course rufous

6. James F. Lynch and P. L. Ames, "A New Hummingbird, *Archilochus
alexandri* x *Selasphorus sasin*," Condor 72:(1970)209–212.

that developed a north-south migration up and down the East Coast.

Being the eternal optimist, and in spite of all considered, I hoped that Rosie would stick around, build a nest, and produce young—and continue her relationship with me.

Release

Eventually the long winter that everyone thought (and I hoped) would never end began to melt away. As spring came and winter released its icy grip on the Northeast, I began to envision heartbreak and another bittersweet good-bye.

On April 30 I put a couple of feeders out for the rubythroats, just in case. Although the first hummer arrived May 1 in the previous year, I wasn't expecting any for at least a week, as spring this year had been an average of seven to ten days late. The weeping cherry had just begun to bloom and the apricot blossoms were still on the tree—that is, the buds that weren't frozen during the horrendous winter. I glanced over at Rosie. She was staring out the window with that "incredulous" look about her, when she would swanishly crane her neck and pull her head back as close to her tail as it will go, as though she can't believe what she is seeing. I wondered what she had seen and looked out the window myself, but I saw nothing. A short while later, a beautiful male rubythroat appeared at one of the feeders. Could she also have seen that bird? Her behavior after that was different. She acted agitated and "antsy" for the rest of the day, and she became more vigorous about nesting materials again, with a brand-new round of gathering. She hovered under the chair and came out with a spider's web. Then she flew over to the frayed end of the self-tie that secures the cushion to the rattan, grasped it, and began pulling. Next she grabbed some more pieces of the fluff and went back to the basket to pull out some strands of the coconut-husk fiber. When she saw a hummingbird through the window, she would either lower her body and extend her neck and head as if she were going to give chase, or sail up to the window and flutter around, vocalizing, *chip-chip-chip*. She would then go to the different flowers in the sunroom, draining each of its nectar. At times she would just hang in the air with tail fanned, her version of a display. It was then that her throat patch would become particularly brilliant.

The first hummingbird to take shelter in my sunroom, voluntarily came in for the day during Hurricane Gloria in 1983. The door to the sunroom was deliberately left ajar. When the weather subsided, she stayed in for a while, and each time another hummer attempted to come in, she'd chase it and then patrol the inside of the room, flying from window to window around all three sides to make sure there were no other hummers there. When she saw one, she went straight to the door, flew out and chased the intruder, and then come back. She knew the boundaries of the room, and Rosie did too.

On May 2, I watched as Rosie earnestly gathered even more nesting material. First she looked for spiders' webs under the chair and brought one back to a branch and began to wrap it around. Next she went under a small wooden seat and, as she approached, opened her beak to an angle of about 20° and grabbed a piece about eight inches long. But it also had some dust on it, so she brought it over to another branch and just left it dangling there. Whenever she would get a piece of web, the feathers around her head and chin would stick up and then she would stiffen and arch her body as she wrapped the web around a twig. In the beginning I had systematically removed spiders' webs whenever I found them so she wouldn't get stuck in any, but now I was sorry. Afterward she went to the cotton sheeting and began tugging at pieces of the knap again and then grabbed some additional bits of coconut-husk fiber. Something was stirring up her nesting instincts and she seemed to be shifting into a higher gear.

I thought that I had been preparing myself for the inevitable all winter, but I was wrong. While it was off in the future, it was easy to think about her departure. But now I didn't want her to leave. I was her best friend, and she didn't even know it. I thought about how she'd follow me around chirping and demanding a treat, and how we'd practically collide as she'd dart over to meet me at the feeder or the door. I smiled about all aspects of her endearing personality and lamented the fact that she had never consented to sit on my finger. I remembered how she'd have the last little nightcap while sitting on her sleeping branch. And, oh, her shower, how she loved water!

I knew I'd miss her. She had captured my heart and I was totally under her spell. Each time she'd move to the closest branch and just look at me, I could feel that little tug at my heart. It was breaking. The day of reckoning was close. She had everything here: shower on demand; the waterfall; abundant and healthy food; flowers; insects; a warm, safe, dry place to sleep; and a human who catered to her every whim. She had everything but one—her freedom. But then I thought about the nesting material. She had something to do and it was time for her to get on with her life. She was ready, but she needed her freedom. Once again I would have to be prepared, like it or not, to say good-bye forever. In spite of prior experiences, I am the eternal optimist and I approached Rosie's release accordingly.

The final consideration was what day to release her. The picture in the garden would be significantly different from what had attracted her initially. All of the flowers that beckoned her in September, the *Salvias, Ipomopsis,* and *Lobelia* are flowers of very late spring, summer, and fall. Now there would be less abundance. Considering the brevity of the Northeast spring and the sweeping changes that can occur during the course of one week, a few extra days would make a remarkable difference. In order to give her the best possible chance, I decided that her release would be sometime during the week beginning May 8.

Just as the first time around, it was strongly suggested that I have Rosie banded, and I thought about it
right up to the end. It was a difficult decision; there was
such a good argument in favor of banding. Here was a
bird so very far off course; information gleaned from her
travels at some time in the future could make a valuable
contribution to knowledge about the migration of the
rufous. It almost seemed the responsible thing to do.
But Rosie was an individual, a free spirit on a little
detour in life, and I had become so very fond of her that
my heart said no. Could I rely on her not being captured just because she is a banded individual? Is there
any possibility that a band would be uncomfortable or
even get caught on something? I thought about a beautiful broad-billed hummingbird that I had pho-
tographed in Arizona's Ramsey Canyon. When I had
my film developed and pictures printed, the little guy
had a band on his leg! If that went unnoticed at a distance of four or five feet, Rosie's probably would as well.

Finally, I made an eleventh-hour-decision about
banding. This could definitely benefit the entire
species. For instance, if found next or some subsequent
winter in Mexico, it would tell plenty about the bird's
ability to correct its prior mistake. It was the responsible thing to do and so I called a couple of banders. The
first man contacted in Schenectady, New York, said no,
he only bands birds captured in nets on his own property. The second, a Sullivan County woman, could not
accommodate me because she had no small, humming-
bird-size bands. I scrapped the idea.

May 9 was a beautiful Monday morning—bright, calm, a tad cool, and relatively quiet, as are most weekdays. The forecast called for a high in the 70s and no rain. I knew it would be hard, but it had to be done. Rosie had things to do and, probably, places to go; the clock was ticking and it was time for her to leave. Ever mindful of the strong homing instinct, I had to be careful to allow sufficient time for her to complete her cycle. The rufous has a relatively brief nesting season and starts its southward fall migration earlier than other North American hummers. It was already May. Whereas every additional day she stayed improved her chances, the point would come when each additional day would be a detriment. The rest of May and all of June covers a period of sixty-three-days, nine short weeks. The nesting cycle—building through fledging—takes about six weeks and that leaves Rosie three weeks for travel. The distance from Saugerties, New York, to Cordova, Alaska, one of the farthest rufous nesting areas from here, is approximately 3,150 air miles. The closest point to Saugerties where the rufous might breed is roughly 1,850 miles. An average of those two distances—2,500 miles—would mean that Rosie would have to travel about 119 miles per day to be on schedule. In addition, there would be several days for refueling stops. In view of the time an ordinary migration takes, it doesn't seem likely that it can be done, but late egg and departure dates can run into July and September respectively in most breeding areas.

I removed the screen from the window, set it aside, and went outside where I could coax her out if needed, as I had done with Squeak. When she saw me on the other side, she came out without any trepidation, as nonchalantly as though she had been going in and out all along. She moved to the top of the overhang and pecked a couple of times at some of last year's dried-up leaves and then flew to the chokecherry tree about twelve feet away. The loud *chip-chip-chip* as she announced her presence immediately revealed her position. The whole thing was ending before my eyes. Fresh, vivid recollections of that emotional day when I released Squeak rushed into my mind and the five years since disappeared as I relived the heartbreak as though it had happened just the day before. However, as heart-breaking and sad as it was, I must admit to not only a feeling of happiness for her but a certain heartfelt relief to see her flying free.

Rosie left the tree and flew over to the still-brown rose-of-sharon, moving from branch to branch, in-specting everything and undoubtedly enjoying her regained freedom. Then it was back to the choke-cherry. After sitting a couple of minutes more in the tree, she moved to the catalpa and inspected emerging leaves at the branch tips, moving higher and higher in the tree as she did so. "Rosie," I called, "sip, sip," the same words I used when I would offer her a treat indoors. She cocked her head and looked at me. When I repeated the string, she moved to a closer position, cocked her head, looking at me some more, as if trying to decide. Again I tried and again she moved closer. Each time I called, she got closer still, one step at a time.

After several minutes, a male rubythroat flew over to use a feeder. I turned around to look at him for a second or two, and then turned back to Rosie. She was gone and I missed her departure. My heart sunk. After that I looked and called, but I neither saw any more of Rosie nor heard her loud and distinctive *chip-chip-chip*. I knew that she had left for her nesting territory.

The feeling is hard to convey. I suppose it is best to say it was bittersweet—happy, and grateful to have spent this brief interlude together, glad that she made it, satisfied that I was able to be of help, extremely sad at the prospect of her leaving, but full of optimism about an autumnal return.

Rosie, on her last day here, sits in her tree and surveys part of her garden—perhaps imprinting for next fall.

IN RETROSPECT

Many years ago I fantasized about a rubythroat spending a winter with me, never expecting it to become a reality. But then along came Squeak. Each time I read about an Eastern sighting of the rufous hummingbird, I wished one would pay a visit to my yard. Rosie, off course by practically the width of our continent, was my wish come true. Squeak appeared long after all the other rubythroats had migrated, right after frost claimed the flowers. Rosie appeared early but stayed. If her migration was based on the distance of her prior one, perhaps she had gone that distance. Nevertheless, and for whatever reason, Rosie did not plan to leave. I have but one little acre, more or less, in this world, and this is the second time in five years that such a visit has occurred. Who knows how many of these little birds fail to migrate or migrate to the wrong places? The numbers may be considerable.

Perhaps the most beautiful of the North American hummers, and a personal favorite, is the broad-billed hummingbird (*Cynanthus latirostris*). I read that one of these gems showed up at a feeder in North Carolina a couple of years back, and I recall thinking at the time, "I wish one would come to my yard." Well, if the past is any indication of the future, perhaps next I'll see that brilliant flash of turquoise at one of my feeders.

There were three things that Rosie loved—her flowers, her water, and her treat. I am pleased to have been able to provide her amply with what she liked best; I believe it made her stay here a positive one. At the very least, she has gotten a second chance. In his book, Dan True relates that a series of rufous hummingbirds at the San Diego Zoo all died within six months of being added to the zoo's collection, and he speculates that it is because the rufous is a "restless" bird with a need to be on the move.[7] From all outward appearances, Rosie has done exceedingly well here. If his theory is correct, then I would have to attribute Rosie's successful stay to a lack of boredom and the fact that she had been active.

7. *Hummingbirds of North America, Attracting, Feeding and Photographing*, University of New Mexico Press, 1993.

Rosie's initial visit and subsequent stay have provoked a lot of thought and I have entertained many possibilities for her future. Things may not work out as I would have it were I given the opportunity to write the script, but as long as things work out for Rosie, I'll be happy. In my heart I know there's an excellent chance she'll return in the fall, and evidence supports this feeling. But even if she doesn't, these experiences are truly what makes life rich and rewarding.

part **III**

HUMMINGBIRDS

My Winter Guests

There are many precious little hummingbirds
who get caught in life's snags.

This book is dedicated to them
and to those who help them.

INTRODUCTION

On September 20, 1995, the telephone rang. It was police dispatcher Kate Scheffel. "Is this Hummingbirds 911?" I smiled. "Yes, I suppose it is," I responded, but Kate wasn't being funny. She sounded a bit distraught as she asked me to take in an injured hummingbird that she had found.

Time and again her question has come back to mind . . . *Hummingbirds 911* . . . and each time it would rouse memories of the many injured or displaced hummingbirds in need of rescue that had taken refuge in my sunroom, from Squeak right up to the four spending the 1995/96 winter with me, each bird with its own unique story. Some have shown a remarkable will to survive after harrowing experiences. And thus, the nucleus of an idea for another hummingbird book was born.

Just as with the *Rosie* book, I hadn't been planning another on hummingbirds. Oh, perhaps something as noteworthy as a return visit from one of my former guests —or the highly unlikely event of a new species—but Kate's question and having had several hummingbirds winter here together have changed my plans. Perhaps I

shouldn't be so hasty in my thinking—hummingbirds are
so full of surprises that a pair and the offspring they produce may grace my sunroom and be the genesis of a future
hummingbird book.

Having more than one has added a new dimension to
my hummingbird experiences, surpassing by far all that I
had previously experienced. While it is easy to love and
enjoy each bird that stays, having more than one is just
plain fun—their antics, their behavior toward one another,
their surprises. The story of their time here begs to be told.

And, too, there is an insatiable curiosity about these
glittering little bundles of energy. So many people have
expressed a desire for me to write more about my adventures with hummingbirds. They have enjoyed becoming
acquainted with the individuals as much as I've enjoyed
working on these projects. And for me, these are journals
or diaries of my experiences, complete with pictures.
When I go back and read the books—as I do—I live these
wonderful experiences again through my memories, and
my enjoyment of these birds is extended. I've gotten what
I consider to be precious glimpses into the private life of
my favorite birds, the hummingbirds. I've gotten to know
some darling individuals on an intimate basis—experiences I wouldn't trade for anything. There are days when I
consider myself the luckiest person in the world, and sharing these experiences with other hummingbird fans has
opened up even more doors.

I've made so many new and wonderful friends, people

who have written to express their thoughts and share *their* interesting experiences. Hummingbird fans are the nicest people, sincere and so dedicated to their little feathered friends. While the response that I've gotten has been wonderful, I think the most gratifying aspect of my books—and one that I had never even considered—is that other people who find hummingbirds in need of help are less afraid to give it, whether that means contacting a rehabilitator, undertaking the elaborate measures that Geoff Dennis of Rhode Island did to winter over the state's first rufous hummingbird, or spending every waking hour Jim and Brian had to care for Rupert, a ruby-throated hummingbird. We do everything we can to attract these little gems, and when we do, we cater to their every whim to keep them coming back. Hummingbirds became quite popular a few years back, and I remember thinking, "What a wonderful fad." But I knew the truth; once we fall under the spell of the hummingbird, it is not a fad, it becomes a passion.

For most of my life, I must admit, I've hated winter. I don't like winter sports or being outside at all, for that matter. I don't like the cold. I guess I've always felt that the only good thing about winter is that it ends—eventually. But the most unlikely of all creatures—one practically synonymous with summer, the hummingbird—has finally, after all these years, given me something to look forward to during the dark side of the year.

I thought Squeak was a once-in-a-lifetime visit that just happened by chance. I was in the right place at the right time—or, rather, he was. Then, when Rosie arrived, I couldn't believe my eyes—it is a picture indelibly etched in my mind. I was astonished. Surely nothing like this could *ever* happen again, right? Wrong! It can, and it has. They seem to be so endlessly full of surprises.

Hummingbirds 911 . . . As each of their little faces drifts past my mind's eye, I think about how it all came about, and my imagination tells me that those little spirits of summer may pass along gossip and information to one another, as bees do. "If you're ever stuck in the Northeast, I know this great little bed and breakfast. . . ."

From Hummingbirds in My Garden to Hummingbirds in My House

Late May to early June is my favorite time of year—floral abundance; picture-perfect greenery, still with a hint of spring. The fragrance of lilac, viburnum, and mock orange fills the air. Birds, busy with nesting chores, greet each morning with their beautiful, cheery songs. And belligerent male hummingbirds establish and defend their territories. As our reward for January, June frequently gives us stellar days with superb weather; it is often perfect. Yet I remember one particular June 2—what now seems like ages ago—that wasn't quite so heavenly. It was my birthday and I was all alone, feeling a little sorry for myself. I probably didn't like my birthday gifts, or hadn't gotten them yet. I hadn't seen any hummingbirds—at least that day—and cleaning, changing, and hanging a feeder was beginning to look more and more like an exercise in futility. To add insult to injury, it was unseasonably cold, a rainy 45 degrees F., and I was using some precious vacation time to sit in misery. I guess nothing was going my way. Then, a female hummingbird appeared and visited the lilacs. When she finished, she flew to the feeder and took a sip. That drink was followed by one after another. And thus, with that little sip and after working so hard to attract them, my relationship with hummingbirds in my garden had begun.

Eventually, of course, other hummers followed and the numbers swelled—four, six, eight, many juveniles. I thrilled at seeing four young hummers using a feeder at one time. In some years, late in the season, there were as many as twenty-five or thirty, counting both adults and immatures. Essentially the rubythroat is a woodland bird, frequenting woodland and meadow edges, riparian areas, and other places rich in flowers and vegetation. Their numbers are greatest in such habitats, so for my area, which is a little more open, twenty-five is a staggering amount. In the beginning the only thing I knew about hummingbirds was that I liked them. For years I wasn't much different from anyone else: I admired and enjoyed them from a distance and was in absolute awe when they came closer. Nothing was planted in the garden unless the hummingbirds would use it. I added feeders to keep them close. I observed them constantly and learned to recognize identifiable individuals.

Before we put a screen on the door leading from the sunroom to the backyard, I'd make sure the ceiling fan was off and then just leave the door open for more fresh air. One day while I was working at one of the flower beds, my daughter informed me that a hummingbird had entered the sunroom and was flying around inside. Apparently one adult male had chased another right into the house. When I went inside, the bird flew past me to go back outside, but then another flew back into the sunroom from my kitchen! Since there is a short, not-too-bright hallway and a turn between the kitchen and sunroom, I had never considered turning that fan off, too. It was right after that incident that the screen went up.

Whenever I go out to the backyard from the sunroom, I open the door and first peer out to make sure there are no hummers at the feeder under the spruce tree a few feet from the door—I wouldn't want to startle them. One day I opened the screen door leading out, and as I opened it, two immature hummingbirds participating in one of their never-ending chases sailed past my head and entered the room, one in pursuit of the other. They flew around inside for a minute or so, and then over to the window and clung to a window screen. I picked them up, one in each hand, and brought them outside. I then opened my hands and

Squeak—he changed the course of my life forever

released them. Shiny, emerald-green-tipped feathers covering a three-gram body no larger than the tip of a thumb, they were so small that I was a bit afraid to touch them. Hold a dime in your hand and close your eyes—imagine a hummingbird! Those birds were born in a nest in the maple tree in front of my house, and after fledging were around my yard almost all the time. They entered the sunroom so often that eventually I took a window screen down and the sunroom became just another part of their territory. In the door, out the window, over and over, around and around. They never seemed to tire, and I never tired of watching them. I enjoyed their antics by the hour. I knew how empty the yard would seem without their twitters, squeaks, squeals, and chatters come fall, and I wished they'd decide not to leave but to winter right here with me.

Because of these birds' willingness to enter the sunroom, I felt comfortable offering it at other critical times, such as during Hurricane Gloria or other particularly strong storms, as well as during an early October freak, wet snowstorm. The thought of an unprotected hummingbird being pelted by hail or life-size raindrops won my sympathy. And thus began the transition from hummingbirds in my garden to hummingbirds in my house.

Then, many years later, another hummingbird entered the picture and changed the course of my life forever. That hummingbird was Squeak.

The end of summer is different for each person. For some it occurs with the geese flying south, with Labor Day, or when the children return to school; for some it is the first frost, the first freeze, or the advent of colder weather in general. For me, summer slips away with the hummingbirds, and the last day of summer is the day the last hummer departs—usually by the first week of October. Summer had been finished for weeks according to my criteria, and I had resigned myself to the fact that I wouldn't see any hummingbirds for months—always such a sad time for me. Then, when I went outside to feed the birds one morning in late October 1988, I found Squeak, searching for nectar among frozen flowers. I had no idea that my life was on the brink of its biggest changes ever, nor any idea that a few short years later I would be devoting myself to these marvelous little creatures on a full-time basis.

I recall how apprehensive I had been about my chances with Squeak, as I have been with each new venture into uncharted hummingbird waters. Who would ever have imagined, almost twenty years ago when I was so thrilled by that first visitor, that I would have them buzzing around my head in my own house?

There hasn't been one day that has gone by in the last several years that I haven't seen a hummingbird—most of them intimately. This winter I've had more hummers than humans residing at my home; maybe I should consider enlarging their sunroom. But even now, as incredible as it may seem, the hummingbirds still amaze and surprise me.

Squeak was *the* hummingbird in my house. Eventually, of course, others followed and the hummer numbers swelled—two, four . . . sound familiar?

RESCUED RUBYTHROATS

I wasn't expecting it. I hadn't even thought about it, but I suppose it was inevitable. Once the *Squeak* book was released, I would be called regarding other sick, injured, stranded, or otherwise misguided hummers caught in life's snags. When called upon for help, I *had* to give it. Although you know that some may not make it, you do what you can for all of them. Those birds that recover and go on to become healthy are so rewarding.

Hummingbirds are intelligent, resourceful, and adaptable within their niche. Some are hardy and well adapted to a range of conditions. They may be found living or nesting over a wide variety of habitats, from mountains to valleys, forests to deserts. Some make almost unbelievable migrations. The rubythroat crosses the Gulf of Mexico, a journey made possible by the storage of an extra 2½ to 3 grams of fat, the roughly 22½ to 27 calories necessary to make such a trip. The rufous migrates more than two thousand miles from its wintering to nesting area and crosses mountains 12,000 to 14,000 feet high on its return to Mexico. Some birds nest under harsh or extreme conditions, such as Costa's hummingbird of our Southwestern deserts. But in many ways, hummingbirds are delicate, finely tuned little specialists tied to a definite lifestyle. For them, ordinary problems may require very special solutions.

Some of the birds that have been brought here have stayed for just days. One that was knocked down by a cat's paw was unable to lift itself more than a couple of feet from the ground. He was able to fly, but couldn't gain any appreciable altitude. More likely than not, the difficulty was the result of a strained muscle. Three or four days of "R and R" remedied that and he was on his way.

For some, however, it is not that simple and the stay can be prolonged. The length is dictated by the nature of the injury—or when it occurs.

CHARLIE'S STORY

I was not surprised to receive a call early in the 1991 hummingbird season. A local woman's cat had captured an adult male rubythroat two days earlier. She had managed to get the bird away from the cat, but it was injured. The bird was fed some sugar-water with an eyedropper, but wasn't responding—what should she do? We discussed dietary requirements and the bird's absolute need for protein. I suggested that she visit a veterinarian specializing in birds and asked her to let me know of the bird's progress.

When I next spoke with the woman, I was disappointed to learn that no action had yet been taken. She asked if I would take the bird and arranged to deliver him to my office the following morning—five days after his encounter with the cat.

Upon his arrival he appeared generally unkempt, had missing feathers, behaved lethargically, and appeared to be underweight. An appointment was made to visit a veterinarian that afternoon and, more important, the bird was immediately put on a diet of NektarPlus. Charlie, as I had begun to call him, reacted almost instantly to his new diet. As he devoured it, he became much more alert than he had been. For the remainder of that first day Charlie rested on my desk, still in the shoebox in which he had been delivered. He was handfed the nectar every fifteen minutes or so, and at the end of the day, we visited the doctor.

The results of the examination were worse than what I had been expecting. Although the wing wasn't broken, a large piece of tissue was missing from the muscle used to elevate its wing—thus, the bird's inability to fly. Yet that might not be all. Owing to the extent of damage, the soft tissue might be irreparable and, moreover, the doctor was

Charlie

unable to determine whether any additional damage had been done to either the shoulder or the nerves. There was no clue to the bird's future. He suggested that I continue feeding and take a wait-and-see attitude; it might heal on its own. I could tell how badly the doctor felt about this tiniest of patients. He wished me luck and attempted to reassure me with "If anyone can do this, you can."

Charlie was compelled to spend his time in confinement. He was placed in an openwork basket instead of the box so he might have a view out. Since keeping him comfortable but quiet while he was incapacitated was my primary concern, the basket was positioned in such a way that he might have something to look at—a hummingbird feeder at the sunroom window or me at the office. For the first ten days, Charlie accompanied me to work and took the ten-mile ride each way in his stride—except when we'd hit a bump. With each day, he became more alert and active, and within three days of being entrusted to my care, he had regained some of his lost weight. As that first week progressed and Charlie's level of activity increased, he began to maneuver in his basket to reach the feeder secured in the corner on his own. When he wanted to be fed, his tongue would dart in and out and he would attempt to put his wings into motion. If I didn't respond quickly enough, he'd maneuver into position to help himself. It was evident that Charlie was making an effort to regain mobility.

Charlie made repeated attempts to lift himself from the substrate, but with power to only one wing, he could manage merely to go around in circles. When he rested in my hand, wings spread, I could feel a purr—the fluttering movements in his wings as he struggled to do what should ordinarily take no effort at all. Even with all the improvement that he had thus far shown, he would have so much further to go.

Charlie demonstrated a desire for self-maintenance by scraping his beak on a twig, paper towels, or the inside of the feeder tube to clean it, and by making an attempt to preen his right side. His ability to preen effectively had been diminished not only by the injury itself but by a deformity of his right foot, which may have been either a preexisting injury or a life-long deformity. With just a stab at preening, his feathers remained in a rather tousled and

scruffy condition and I knew he should have a bath.
Because of Squeak's fondness for bathing on a leaf, I tried
wetting a large hosta leaf and placing it next to him, hoping that he would use it voluntarily. He showed no interest, so he was helped. I cupped about one tablespoonful of
water in my hand and placed him in the little puddle, but
he didn't like that, either.

By the end of the second week, Charlie managed to
generate about two inches of lift and flew around the bottom of his basket. He engaged in this "flying" repeatedly,
and that evening he glided from the palm of my hand to
the window screen.

Charlie moved around quite a bit at night—it was too
warm and he was too well fed, with good energy reserves,
to become torpid. Conditions in the sunroom during the
summer season are not controlled, as they had been when
Squeak stayed with me, and the windows remained open
all day and night. Even when evening temperatures were
in the mid-forties, Charlie did not become torpid. He
never seemed ready to go to sleep at night and would
always wind up rather than down at sunset. Charlie's territory consisted of a small basket. To advertise it, he
engaged in head wagging, that side-to-side movement that
dominant males perform before retiring for the evening.

June 1, slightly more than two weeks after the incident,
was a big day for Charlie. First, he generated enough lift
to get himself out of his basket and was sitting on the floor
when I walked into the room. Once he became able to do

so, Charlie lifted himself out of the basket over and over again. Since he frequently landed on the floor, each time I walked into the sunroom, I had to stop and look around until I was able to locate him. Each time he was picked up and placed back in the basket. While there, Charlie was alert and interested in the hummingbird activity outside. He was sitting, as he frequently did, staring at a feeder, waiting for the arrival of the little female that had taken a fancy to that particular one. Then, when I approached to offer him some food, he started flying around the room!

Although he was interested in that female, he showed no interest in chasing her. He wasn't ready for that just yet. As a matter of fact, when she would look at him, perhaps instinctively knowing his limitations, he'd turn and look the other way.

At first Charlie was most cooperative about staying in his basket, but once he regained some independence, there was no holding him down. He was not willing to spend any time in it at all; instead, he wanted to perch on the skinny branch where Squeak had slept.

For his first night of semi-independence, I wondered where Charlie would be sleeping and whether he would be content to stay in the basket when he was placed there for the evening. Charlie made up his own mind by going to the basket on his own at retirement time, but that was his last night of such cooperation. The following night, he slept in his basket again, but only after I put him there. He really didn't want to stay and fidgeted and moved around for quite a while before finally giving in. That was the end of the basket.

When Charlie became more mobile, his feeder was moved from the basket to the shelf, and he was encouraged to fend for himself. Leading a relatively sedentary lifestyle during his recuperation, Charlie consumed approximately 32 milliliters of nectar each day, which consists of water and approximately 3.2 grams of food—roughly equivalent to his body weight, itself close to 3 grams.

In spite of his repeated attempts, the ability to hover independently remained elusive to Charlie for quite some time. Yet he repeatedly tried. When I fed him, he would put his wings into motion while grasping the branch and practice hovering by keeping his good left foot on the perch and raising everything else and spinning his wings. By June 5, he finally managed to hover for several seconds and with each passing day, proficiency increased. He had progressed from a slight purr of his wings to the actual movement of both wings while in a stationary position. This was just going to take time.

When hovering would permit him to visit a hanging feeder, Charlie used that one exclusively rather than the one placed where he might conveniently reach it. He loved his regained ability and hovered constantly. Each time he took a drink, he would fly back to his branch, do a little pirouette, and return for another drink; he frequently exercised his wings while perching.

In less than one month after Charlie's episode with the

cat, he was flying and hovering and vigorously exploring his surroundings, and it seemed appropriate to have familiar flowers around to alleviate any possible boredom. In addition to potted plants such as *Bouvardia ternifolia*, fuchsia, *Mimulus cardinalis* and *Hamelia patens*, fresh cuttings of bee balm (*Monarda* spp.), *Spigelia marilandica*, columbine (*Aquilegia* spp.), the beloved *Salvia coccinea* and trumpet vine flowers (*Campsis* spp.) were cut and brought to him daily. The avid interest that one might expect to be displayed over such scrumptious offerings was noticeably absent in Charlie—at least while I was present. When I entered the sunroom, Charlie would immediately engage in a swallowing action, and his tongue would dart in and out in anticipation and expectation of being fed. When he was alone in the sunroom, however, he visited his feeders at regular intervals and investigated all the flowers brought in for him. He may have been unwilling to do this in my presence, but the telltale dusting of pollen on his crown told another story: it was a dead giveaway to his activities. Basically, his private moments were held private, but some of that private activity was simply obvious. On a number of occasions when I entered the sunroom he was soaking wet and his head was loaded with pollen.

While he had been reluctant to bathe on a leaf or in my hand, and openly disliked being misted, he apparently had the desire to keep himself clean. The first time that he was noticeably soaking wet I realized that he had been secretly visiting the waterfall. Eventually, I was permitted to watch him bathe. First, he would approach the top pool, where the water flows from the hole in the lava rock and stand on its rim. After allowing the splashes from the running water to hit him for a few seconds, he hopped into the pool and stood in the shallow water, pecking at it. I waited to see if he would lower his body into the water to bathe, but then he continued across the pool and stood directly under the flow—that soaked him. He bathed that way by repeating that action and then abruptly left to dry off.

By June 18, Charlie's hovering had been perfected and the tautness that had been previously noticeable on the injured side was absent. Once physically fit, Charlie finally began showing some real interest in the other hummers, chattering rapidly during their fighting squeals. He wanted to participate, and I knew he was very close to being ready to leave. Not only had he begun chattering and attempting to chase all the other hummers away from the feeders near the windows, he even started to patrol the sunroom. He had truly made the change from total dependence to complete self-sufficiency. His tongue no longer darted in and out in anticipation of being fed when I walked into the room. Now he preferred to do it himself. Although he tolerated me, he wanted no one else on his territory. Charlie was released a few days later. Like Squeak before him, he stopped at the fuchsia and then took off. He followed that irrepressible urge to get back where he belonged—home. And in spite of the maze of directions he had traveled, that urge prevailed. Charlie was an identifiable hummingbird because of his deformed foot and was spotted back on territory, business as usual.

There were many differences between Charlie and Squeak, but the most noticeable was that, as Squeak's stay here progressed, he became more familiar with me and our relationship grew to include many different aspects, whereas as Charlie became more independent, our relationship lessened.

JUST A LITTLE ANGEL WAITING TO GET ITS WINGS

Hummingbirds truly are creatures of the air, and their wings figure prominently in almost all that they do. Because the wings are such an integral part of their very being, when one is injured it is particularly devastating. While other birds can hop from place to place with a pinned and healing wing, not so a hummingbird. These denizens of the air have spindly little feet and legs that are weak and serve little purpose other than for scratching and perching. To get from Point A to Point B, the wings are used.

I don't know the circumstances of this bird's injury. He was just "found" and brought to me after the woman who had found him had been caring for him for several weeks. The bird was alert and responsive, but as a result of an apparent shoulder injury, wing feathers—more so on the injured side—and the tips of most of the tail feathers had broken off. The bird was so tiny. I realized that hummingbirds truly defy the principles of distance and perception, for the closer one gets, the smaller they seem.

The minute I saw him, he peeped—not just once, but over and over again. So often that I said, "My, you're quite a little peeper." I never really gave him a name; as after that I would greet him by saying, "Hello, Little Peeper." But more often than not I referred to him as Munchkin, the Little Angel or, mostly, My Little Problem Child.

Their almost rudimentary feet and legs mean a special set of problems is created in caring for injured humming-birds. With broken wing feathers, this bird would be unable to fly and any attempt by him to do so could worsen his situation. For with just small bits of feather shafts remaining, the wing became vulnerable to direct damage that might make the wing unable to grow *any* feathers. He would have to be confined to a basket and kept as immobile as possible until his injury was healed and the broken wing feathers replaced during his first full molt, which might take at least until spring. Squeak never went through a complete molt, and I've always wondered about the photoperiod and what affect it may have on hor-mones that initiate feather replacement. This time it would be imperative that I do whatever necessary to encourage a molt, so I provided a maximum of only eleven hours of artificial lighting and allowed the sun to lengthen that time naturally as days became longer.

Being confined for so long could lead to boredom and frustration, and constant perching could create problems for Peeper's legs or feet. He was kept in a small basket lined on its insides with foam as a buffer to protect his wing. The bottom was covered with soft, six-ply paper toweling—soft enough to minimize damage to the wing should he fall but not so soft that his claws would get caught. A feeder was placed in the basket, as was a perch. The perch would have to be low enough for him to get up without using his beak as a "third foot," as they are inclined to do, but since hummingbirds perch best in a vertical position, it would have to be high enough for him to be comfortable.

Confinement and restriction were an absolute necessity if he were to heal and recover his flying abilities, but his problems were exacerbated by their remedy. Most solutions to his myriad problems seemed to fit into that "damned if you do, damned if you don't" category. For instance, any time I picked him up, unless it was an emergency, I scrupulously washed and thoroughly rinsed and dried my hands. Human skin has oils, acids, and other properties that might damage a hummingbird's feathers. Yet I *had* to pick him up. Gloves can't be used, no matter how thin, as you must be able to feel the claws from *both* feet before you lift. I would get my fingers underneath him and nudge a bit until he put his feet on me so as not to lift while they were clinging to something else. Since I picked him up roughly every fifteen minutes to change the padding in his basket, I tried to make that pleasant for him by also taking him to the window to look out or to some flowers for some real nectar.

For a tiny bird Peeper was quite a handful! He was his

Visiting flowers for real nectar

own worst enemy and not very patient with himself. He refused to accept his limitations and had quite a knack for getting himself into trouble. Occasionally his beak would penetrate the foam that lined his basket to about 1/64 inch, but he did not struggle to free himself—although he could have done so with ease. He was very cautious about that beak and wouldn't take any chances with it. Instead, he would sit as still as could be and wait for help. I was always nearby to pull the foam back. And each time he would get himself into trouble by falling off his perch, I would help him get back up so he wouldn't damage anything. Then, as soon as he would have both feet back on the perch and be in position to drink, he'd chirp as if to say, "I've got it."

But he wasn't doing that well. I couldn't keep him out of trouble no matter how hard I tried, and nothing I did seemed to help. It was as if we were always taking two steps forward and one step back or one step forward and two steps back. There were days full of tears of frustration over my inability to keep him immobile enough that he wouldn't hit his wing. And there were days when I questioned my own motives. I wasn't placing this burden only on myself; he was bearing the brunt of it. But when I talked to him, he "talked back" with his little peeps, or he'd stretch first one wing and then the other, enjoying my attention. He wasn't an unhappy bird, and I wanted to give him a chance. But there was something else that kept me going: when he would spin his wings, they showed the same pattern and range of motion as any normal hummingbird and I knew that when his right wing got new feathers, he'd fly.

All it takes is just one little thing to turn the tide. Finally, one day I found the key that began to unlock the secrets to a smooth recovery. The inherent nature of close confinement made the daily bath an absolute necessity. On sunny days when solar warmth promoted speedy drying, Peeper frequently had more than one bath. But even on dismal days it was very important to keep him clean. As a confined bird, the chance of getting soiled feathers or having food drip on him was much greater. So when weather conditions were not conducive to rapid, natural drying, I'd use the hairdryer, held far enough away and never directed near the eyes. But his feathers were gradually losing something and one day, in spite of the sun, he just wasn't drying quickly enough. Fearful that he might be susceptible to respiratory problems, I thought it best to intervene. "A little feather-fluffing will do it," I thought as I reached for a small makeup brush.

I have been very surprised by some of the things I've seen hummingbirds do—most notable of which was the strength exhibited by Rosie when she lifted an entire piece of material three or four inches from a chair by a single fiber. But nothing I had seen thus far had prepared me for what I would see next. If I hadn't seen it for myself, surely I would never have believed it. I've always had to pick this bird up to change the padding at the bottom of his basket. He didn't like it and would shrink from my hand, but I had no other choice. While it was heartrending to see him cringe from me, there was no other way—he and his surroundings *had* to be kept clean. This time I picked him up and held him against my abdomen with my hand cupped lightly around him. With the small makeup brush, I began to lift and fluff his throat feathers to dry them off. He seemed to enjoy what I was doing and lifted his head, making access easier. Lifting against the grain, I ran the brush up from his breast to under his beak. The more I did that, the more content he became. I fluffed his cheek feathers and he closed his eyes; I fluffed his neck and he lifted his head. I was getting all the places he couldn't scratch because of his balance difficulties.

Peeper enjoyed this scratching so much I decided to have these preening sessions more often. To start, he would lie against my abdomen while I kept my hand cupped around him as he rested his head on the inside of my thumb. I could even feel the warm, spent air from his nasal passage. Occasionally he'd rub his beak and the side of his face on my thumb, or he'd check out little pieces of cuticle or flaking skin too small for me to notice. He'd start by sitting erect, but once I began fluffing his chin, he would lean to his side a tad. Then as I preened his side, he would lift his wing and the next thing I knew, he really began to list. Before long, he would roll over on his back and totally enjoy having his undersides done. When I'd fluff under his wing, he'd raise it. When I preened the side of his face, he'd close his eyes. But it was when I preened his throat that he was in ecstacy. He'd stretch his neck and open and close his eyes the way a cat does when it feels such pleasure. The only thing he didn't do was purr. He enjoyed it so much that at times he appeared to drift off to sleep while I preened him. Since drying him this way proved to be so welcome, I reasoned that it might also be the best way to bathe him. Initially I'd make a cup with my palm and create a little puddle to stick him in—after all, it was the underparts primarily that needed the water—but with the brush I could concentrate on the feathers that needed it most. And so, his grooming sessions became two parts—wash and dry.

There were two brushes that I would use during grooming. The first was a sable artist's brush dipped in water to clean his feathers, particularly the ones around his face where there might be food residue; the second was the small makeup brush for fluffing and preening. And he knew the difference between them. He loved to rub his beak all over the wet bathing brush and liked me to lie it on my thumb so he could rub his chin and throat over it until he was so wet that he looked like a hatchling—perhaps one-half the size of a fluffed-out hummer. He was so small and cute in an ugly sort of way, scrawny looking, with his tiny head sitting on his skinny little neck. He reminded me of a chick just out of its egg. I tried to compare his tiny body to some other familiar object—all I could come up with was an almond.

Peeper would inspect the brush, sticking his beak through its bristles, and every once in a while he'd open his mouth and try to bite it. When he'd grab it, he'd invariably give it a shake or two in that side-to-side motion typical of a puppy. He'd bite it, grab it, pull it, and shake it. Then he'd rub his face on the brush and want to hold its tip with his foot while he made an attempt to rub it all over the rest of him. At least once during each session he would have to explore the brush, poking his beak in between the bristles and sticking out his tongue. With a $\frac{1}{16}$-inch-diameter, soft but strong and dense Kolinsky red sable brush, I could easily lift and fluff his tiniest feathers—the minuscule ones jutting out under the mandible—and even separate and fluff the downy feathers around his legs and his bottom. He loved it. After several minutes of preening, his feathers would suddenly become fluffy and he would look like a hummingbird again. His feathers were kept so soft and fluffy that his throat and breast looked like soft fur. What had started out as a way to make sure he was dry turned into a ritual. Hummingbirds don't engage in mutual preening, but I'll bet if they did, they would love it.

After that, when I would stick my hand in his basket to lift him out, he no longer cringed but practically jumped into my hand—that is, if he didn't explore my cuticle with his tongue instead. He expected me to preen him each time

The only thing he didn't do was purr

I lifted him out of the basket, so even when I was only changing his pad and hadn't planned to, I'd make it my business to brush him at least a little bit. Prior to that there was only one thing I could do that kept him happy and quiet: to have him sit in my hand and look out the window. He loved looking out, his little head would move this way and that, as he'd look up at the trees. He never squirmed or made any attempt to get away from me. He was truly content and seemed almost mesmerized by what was out there. His enjoyment of our newfound physical relationship made a tremendous difference in all aspects of his recovery, and now he wanted to be held all the time—either in my cupped hand or hanging on my T-shirt, where he would cling like a little woodpecker on a tree trunk. It kept him out of trouble, so that's what I did—I held him constantly.

As time passed, it became progressively more difficult to keep Peeper's feathers clean. They weren't drying rapidly because they were no longer *really* clean or protected by his preening oil. Food undoubtedly was the culprit. The NektarPlus is sticky, and it was difficult to keep it away from his feathers under such close circumstances. Water was no longer sufficient and as occasional slightly sticky feathers dried, they'd mat down on his skin here and there, probably pulling it. I had to think of something else. I found myself pondering the problem over and over in my mind. What could I clean him with? It is not only the feathers I would have to be concerned with—I didn't want to use anything that would irritate his skin. I was reluctant to try anything that hadn't been used on hummingbirds before, being unwilling to experiment. The only thing I could think of as a possibility was Dawn dish detergent. While I am unaware of its use on hummingbirds, I know it as the product used to clean birds caught in oil slicks. But first I would try to get an experienced opinion, if possible.

I called the Arizona-Sonora Desert Museum, as there is a hummingbird aviary there, and I hoped to speak with someone who could advise me whether or not to try this. Unfortunately I missed the return call. It was Friday and I didn't want to put it off for the weekend, so I went against conventional wisdom. After much soul-searching, I nervously made a bold decision to try it. I was afraid to use any more than just the smallest amount of detergent. I just touched it with my finger and then swished my finger around in a plastic film container of warm water. To test it, I took the brush and cleaned his uppertail coverts. These feathers don't lie directly on the skin and thus provided a good starting point. I could examine the result and determine whether it would be safe—or worth it—to continue. I then rinsed them well with warm water and dried them. The feathers were beautiful! It was working! When I saw how successful I had been, I was encouraged to be more thorough. I did all the feathers, section by section, stopping to rinse and check his skin. Then I absorbed what water I could with a paper towel and Q-Tips before proceeding to fluff him dry. We spent a couple of hours at this project, but when I was finished, his feathers looked great—green, shiny, and fluffy. I was so pleased and he was, too. With no feathers pulling at his skin, he was comfortable and happy. It was obvious that he felt better and he was beautiful. It was a success.

On Monday morning I received the call from a man at the museum. I told him what I had done and why. Ordinarily, he said, he wouldn't recommend it, but all things considered, I had probably done the best thing for him. Then he gave me one other bit of advice, something that might help with his molt. Because Peeper was a relatively inactive bird, he probably ate less than the others. I suppose that is true, although I had never measured food intake. When birds are active, they drink more frequently, converting sugars into quick energy that is burned during their constant comings and goings. NektarPlus contains 2.9 percent protein, which is stored. Constant feeding means more protein intake overall. Inactive birds need and drink less nectar and thus are taking in less total protein overall. But protein is needed for feather replacement, and an inactive bird consuming a diet formulated for active birds would need additional protein to compensate. He suggested that a pinch of high-protein flaked fish food be added to his feeder, which I promptly purchased. Analysis on the fish food container indicated 47 percent protein.

Once the preening sessions began and Peeper decided he liked sitting in my hand best of all places, I began holding him for extended periods to keep him happy and out of trouble. Almost immediately I noticed a remarkable improvement. He liked the warmth of my hand, he no longer hit his wing, his feet were no longer sore and in fact had regained their strength—he would clasp the skin of my hand with his prickly little claws and I could feel the difference. And after his feathers were cleaned with the Dawn, he became more comfortable and more active.

The consensus is that hummers shouldn't be held—it's too stressful for them. With this bird, however, the opposite proved to be his salvation. It changed his increasing problems into steady progress. He'd snuggle in my slightly cupped hand just the way a bird might sit on eggs in a nest, and he was content. He liked the warmth and, I believe, the texture of my skin. He'd exercise his wings while sitting in my hand just the way a juvenile in a nest might do, and he'd raise his body either by stretching his legs or pushing his beak into my palm while twirling his wings. He loved being preened and he loved looking out the window or lying in the sun when the rays hit him. He'd dip way over on his side so his skin could soak in the warmth. I could even see a difference when I took him to visit flowers. Now he actively bounced from one to the next. He felt well and he enjoyed life.

Peeper may have been feeling quite well, but he was nowhere near being out of the woods. We had managed to get him to the position where the wing was the only problem and then maintain the status quo, but our biggest challenge waited just around the corner. The wing feathers are sequentially replaced from the inside outward except that

the ninth is skipped and is replaced after the tenth.* This
would mean that as new wing feathers grew in, there would
be no old outer feathers to protect them. They would be
subject to direct damage. I figured that I might as well get
used to holding him because the better he felt, the more
active he would become. When his wing feathers started
to grow in, that activity might cause them to break off. But
we were on the right track and had finally hit just the right
combination of variables.

Having a more intimate relationship with this bird than
I've had with any other has opened much more to observation than I had previously and has revealed many new
glimpses into the private lives of hummingbirds that had
heretofore been secret—at least to me. For example,
Peeper drank frequently during the day, having many sips
before going to sleep, several of which he would take after
the lights went out but while there was still enough ambient light; at times he would drink so much that the swollen
crop stood out like a sore thumb. He urinated just as frequently but he never urinated overnight, and his pad,
which was changed for the last time each day just as the
lights went out, would be dry in the morning. Then, when
he did urinate in the morning, the concentration was especially strong. That tells me that overnight either his body

*Primary feathers are numbered 1 to 10, starting at the inside—closest to the
body—and working outward to the leading edge of the wing. There are ten tail
feathers (rectrices), or five pairs. The pairs are numbered from the center outward, the middle pair being the first and the outermost, the fifth.

used the water portion of the nectar in some other way or he lost it in some way other than urination—perhaps evaporation. What convinced me that the latter was the most likely was that he was noticeably lighter in the mornings. I didn't weigh him, but he felt like "nothing" in the morning, whereas during the afternoon I could feel a certain heaviness that seemed to be centered at his bottom.

When I tried to look at the tip of his wing through a magnifying glass, Peeper became extremely frightened as, from his perspective, my already large eyes became grotesque.

The uropygial gland is located at the base of the tail. This gland, also called the "preening gland," secretes an oil used to waterproof and maintain the feathers. On his "good days," while sitting in my hand, he would try to preen and I was able to get a bird's-eye view of the procedure. He would position his beak at the base of the gland (closest to his body), and with the little cone-shaped protuberance in between the upper and lower sections of his beak, he would squeeze his beak and pull it toward the tip. So instead of just touching his beak to the gland, he would squeeze the substance out. When I preened him, I would touch the brush to his preening gland, too. I hoped that would be beneficial to his feathers and an improvement over just the brush, but I don't know if it made any difference.

Peeper was the only hummingbird that has stayed with me to become torpid at night, and it only happened on a couple of occasions. But torpidity wasn't entered immediately, for he would move around in his basket during the evening—and had done so at least a couple of times on the nights before becoming torpid—but he was torpid in the morning. That indicates to me that hummingbirds can become torpid at any time if energy reserves dip below a certain point. It took him between ten and fifteen minutes in a warm hand to revive.

There probably has been no hummingbird in avian history that has been held, preened or pampered as much as Peeper. But he may have an insurmountable combination of problems and so I don't know if he'll make it. Certainly the deck seems stacked against him. But once I discovered the key to keeping him happy, clean, healthy, and injury free, his future began to look brighter. The rest is a matter of time. He is just a little angel, waiting to get his wings.

K-T—My Little Miracle Bird

While returning from lunch, Kate Scheffel, a dispatcher from the police department, found something lying on the ground in front of the bank's plate glass window. At first she thought it was a bug, then quickly realized that it was a hummingbird—but it appeared to be dead. When she took a second look, however, she could detect breathing and discovered that the bird was indeed alive. Apparently it had flown into the window and took a direct hit at full speed. Kate picked up the pitiful little body, returned to the desk, and called me. "Is this Hummingbirds 911?" As luck would have it, my husband George, a police officer, was on duty at the time and transported the bird to me posthaste.

George arrived with the bird within minutes, but it appeared that it might not have long to live. The base of the mandible was pushed quite far out at the left side and upper and lower portions of the beak were crisscrossed. In addition, the entire side and part of the top of its head was swollen and misshapen. And the bird was unconscious. Undoubtedly there was a severe concussion.

The sight of this poor broken and dying little bird was heartbreaking, and I had to decide what to do, as the injury looked as though it must be painful. First I placed a call to the veterinary college at Cornell, as one man there has done a little work with hummingbirds. I wanted an experienced opinion on whether there was *any* hope. I waited and waited for a call back. Finally, while I was waiting, the bird opened its eyes a bit—it was beginning to regain consciousness. All this time I had been holding the bird in my hand to keep it warm. Once the eyes opened, I tried to feed it. While it made no effort to eat, when some of the NektarPlus touched its tongue, the bird instinctively went through the motions. But the food just bubbled out the side of the beak where it was out of line, and the tongue flailed about wildly, since it was not following its normal "track." After several hours, the bird regained full consciousness and attempted to eat when fed, but the food still dripped out and down the side of its throat. The bird also began to move its wings but still looked absolutely

As K-T visits stachys, the injury to the healing beak is visible

K-T's throat was only very faintly streaked, a female characteristic

Leaves of zebra plant
(Aphelandra squarrosa) *are a good place to bathe . . .*

. . . and the flowers are a good source of nectar

awful. It couldn't keep its balance and flopped over when I tried to get it to sit up. When it was time to put the bird to sleep for the night, I placed a branch for grasping across the bottom of the bird's basket and circled the bird with rolled-up paper towel "bumpers," as it couldn't hold itself up. The basket was then placed side by side with Peeper's basket so they could sleep next to one another.

I waited all day for the veterinarian's call back, all the while worried that the bird might be suffering, but the call wouldn't come until the next day. Now I'm glad that it took so long, for the next morning I was surprised to see that the bird's beak had moved back into place just a bit —certainly not where it belonged, barely noticeable yet less pronounced. The food still dribbled out when it was fed, and I had to bathe the face with a sable watercolor brush frequently lest the feathers rot off its face. The bird had no trouble grasping a perch but continued to be unable to maintain its balance and couldn't keep itself upright unless the wings were in motion. If the bird tried to stop its wings, it would flop over until hanging upside down and then stay that way. But the minute progress that was evident by the next morning indicated there might be some hope.

There are several ways to determine the gender of immature rubythroats. Probably the most noticeable characteristics, at least in the field, are throat and tail patterns. Immature males tend to be darker overall and have throats (often with some iridescent red feathers) that are more or less heavily streaked. Females' throats are only faintly streaked, if streaked at all. Females have more white on the outer three tail feathers (Rectrices 3 to 5) than males, and often there is a small amount of white on Rectrix 2 (next to middle), as well.

Finally, when sexing a bird in hand, the shape of certain wing feathers are conclusive. While the inner six primaries are much narrower than the outer four, the sixth primary itself (fifth, counting from the outside) is much narrower on males. The tapered, outer web is virtually nonexistent in males, whereas it is at least 1 millimeter wide throughout in females.

The wings never stopped moving, so it was difficult to make an irrefutable identification based upon that character. However, the throat had no iridescent red feathers and was only very faintly streaked. In fact, the bird later replaced throat feathers with even whiter ones. The bird was a little dark around the edges, but based on the throat it seemed obvious that it was a female. Being more interested in the bird's condition than its gender, I made a snap mental identification and then forgot about it.

Later, quite by accident, I noticed that the sixth primary showed evidence of belonging to a male, but I still had that contradictory, snow-white throat staring me right in the face. What was going on here? Wear and tear might have shaved off an edge, but examination revealed that the right and left sides were alike. It appeared that bird was a male. Although that convinced me of the bird's sex, when the tail ultimately began its molt, I anticipated the final verifying word on gender. Then, once it began and just after the two middle pairs of tail feathers were pushed out, I noticed the tiniest, most minute iridescent red speck near the edge of the throat. Under advantageous lighting, it stood out just as though a tiny red sparkle had fallen off a Christmas card, landed on the bird, and burrowed down until it was nestled among the feathers of this otherwise snowy-white throat—ever so tiny but ever so present. The rubythroat was a male indeed and the wings didn't lie. Once I had made that initial determination, it just never occurred to me to verify gender later by examining the wings. The information was available to me—the signs were all there—but I neglected to use it. That was my mistake, and I think it goes without saying that I shall never make such a mistake again.

The bird would have to have a name and the *only* appropriate name for this lucky little bird would be some form of Katie—Kate Scheffel's namesake. But when I determined that Katie was a he, the name was changed. K-T was a good choice: first, the initials appropriately stand for King Tut, his very best behavioral trait and, of course, he would still be named after Kate.

To keep his feathers clean, especially when food dripped, K-T received a spray bath every day. But since he was not yet self-sufficient, I had to dry him with a hair-dryer, held away from his eyes and at a distance from his body. I just wanted enough warmish air to dry him off, not

dry him out. Each day K-T showed a little more improvement. I continued to hand-feed him and hold him periodically but frequently to give his wings a rest; if he became
tired and stopped, he still flopped. Eventually he was able
to stop his wings without flopping all the way over. He'd
sit up, sort of wrapped around the perch. Then, as he
became tired, the little semicircle of his body became
tighter and tighter as he tried to combat the slipping that
he apparently felt—until, when it reached its maximum I
suppose, his wings would go into motion, he'd straighten
himself up, and start again.

After several days, K-T was able to feed himself from
the feeder—and oh, what a voracious appetite he had! He
still dribbled a bit, still slept later than Little Peeper, and
still had a bit of a balance problem, but he was improving.
K-T had not vocalized at all and that, too, had been a concern to me. Could it be a sign of some other problem—not
external and therefore not visible? Finally, after he had
been here several days, I heard one weak chirp in the
morning. It wasn't a conversation, but it *was* a start. To help
with his balance, I made him a "donut"—a small semicircle
made from a pipe cleaner and attached at an upward angle
to his perch. This gave him something to brace himself
against and he had a double perch in front of the feeder to
serve the same purpose—they would stop him from flopping over as much. The device worked pretty well, but he
had to be watched constantly. After about a week, he was
able to perch while sleeping and, instead of being placed

K-T inspects water droplets before bathing

. . . then he wets his chin

. . . his breast

. . . and his abdomen

at the bottom of the basket surrounded by the bumpers, he slept normally. He still used the double perch and I checked him repeatedly. I was afraid that if he flopped over, he might land on his beak. And I no longer had to use a hair dryer after his bath.

Eventually K-T was graduated from the basket to a "halfway house," a small screened enclosure where he could practice limited flying, landing, and probing flowers. After a few days, when he appeared to be doing reasonably well, he was given free rein in the sunroom. He still had a bit of a balance problem; occasionally he would start to fall and then straighten up, and he still had difficulty lifting his foot to scratch without using his wings to maintain balance. It wouldn't be until November that he *would* be able to scratch. He still slept a wee bit later than the other hummer, and his face was still just a little screwed up, but all things considered, he was doing so well. I didn't know if his beak would ever be 100 percent, but he had begun to make a remarkable recovery and, while he was nowhere near strong enough to make a migration, I anticipated being able to release my little "miracle bird" in the spring.

There is a positive side to everything. If this had to happen to him at all, it occurred at the best possible of times, during his fall migration while he was carrying extra weight. K-T was more than chubby; he was fat and had gained weight in all the usual places—rump, back of neck, throat, and belly. This was helpful to him in two ways: the first and most obvious would be reserves to help him through a period of reduced food and possible body temperature inadequacies; the second was his speed, which may have been reduced by one-third to one-half of his average 27 to 30 mph, as a result of carrying that additional weight. Crashing at 15 or 20 mph instead of 30 probably saved his life. Although he lost some of the weight he carried with him upon his arrival, he still retained too much of it—he was obese for a hummingbird. He would be leading a sedentary lifestyle, particularly while recovering, so his obesity was a concern to me. I certainly couldn't put him on a diet. What he really needed was activity. He needed to burn off that extra weight.

Once K-T was released from the halfway house to the sunroom, his true personality began to emerge, and he turned out to be unlike any other hummer. Although I feel it is best to handle the birds as infrequently as possible, there are circumstances when that is not always an option —and so it was with K-T. Perhaps because I worked so closely with him, he had become accustomed to me. Maybe he was more trusting and friendly naturally; maybe he just liked me. But he treated me as no other hummer ever has, and he quickly wormed his way into my heart.

A 400-watt high-intensity grow lamp shielded by protective glass replaced the fluorescents of old in the sunroom. This was an improvement in efficiency and took up less space. It also generated more heat and the hummers are fond of that. When I would hold my hand under the

K-T positioned himself between me and the lemon flowers to drink nectar

The mother resumed the care of her chicks

Little One was an adorable little nestling—note the pollen on her beak

Flowers were Little One's learning tools—bee balm (Monarda)

light, K-T would fly up and sit on it and just bask in some beloved warmth. He was fearless. When I realized just how much he liked it, I knew it was incumbent upon me to provide something more permanent than my hand. A small bare branch stuck in a container of sand gave him a place to sit about eighteen inches below the light. But that wasn't enough. He might want to sit closer, so I rearranged some plants and dragged the trusty old honeysuckle over to where several either fresh or old branches would reach out at various levels under the light. Now he could be as close or far away as his fancy dictated. Of course, once I provided some natural sitting places, my hand was out of the picture. Sure, he was the typical little "user," but he obviously trusted me since he was willing to sit on my hand, crane his neck all the way to the side, open his wing, and give himself up completely to the light's warmth.

It was hard not to fall in love with K-T when he would do some of the things he did. Once I was on my hands and knees, picking up some dried-up blossoms, leaves, and dust with a small brush and dustpan when I heard someone hovering behind my head. All of a sudden he was in front of my eyes, looking as though to say, "What are you doing?" Next, I could feel him hovering over my head again, around and around, and then, finally, he sat on the top of my head in my hair. When I would do things at Peeper's basket, K-T would hover around my hands and inspect, touching my fingers with his tongue and exploring the folds in my skin where the fingers bend at the knuckles. He was outgoing and personable, nosy and brazen. When I changed the water in the waterfall, he would immediately come over to investigate. Even though he never chose to take advantage of the waterfall for bathing purposes, he could obviously relate it to bathing. The minute I would busy myself in his vicinity, K-T would inspect the gardenia leaves that I would wet down for him to bathe on. We—meaning K-T and I—had tried other places for bathing, such as the cattleya leaves, but they dried off too quickly. He liked both barleria leaves and those of the zebra plant (*Aphelandra squarrosa*), but the gardenia was his favorite—maybe because of the angle of the leaves, or maybe because there are so many more leaves altogether, or maybe no reason at all except that he just liked it. Since the gardenia was his obvious favorite, that was what he would have.

At the very least, K-T was insatiably curious about everything I did. He'd buzz around my head until I removed the feeder from where it was hung and hand-feed him. He preferred getting the food from me even though I only took his own feeder down to do it. I wondered why. When I would go over to the lemon tree to get a whiff of its fragrant flowers, K-T would immediately come over to inspect and then position himself between my nose and the blossom to drink the nectar—so brazen and absolutely adorable. One day he boldly hovered right up under my chin to get the embroidered flowers outlining the collar on my shirt. He was totally trusting and absolutely fearless, and I knew it would be extremely difficult to sever my relationship with him come spring.

LITTLE ONE

There are times when some advice and perhaps just a smidgen of help will do the trick. Take, for instance, the call that came regarding a rubythroat's nest built on a well-rotted oak branch that had blown down during a thunderstorm—with its occupants intact. The nest, still attached to its original anchor, was tied up in the same tree that had hosted it originally and was placed as closely as possible to its original location. After that, the wait began to see if the mother would return to resume the care of her chicks. By next morning, she had begun to care for them again and continued to do so until they fledged.

Some aren't that lucky. There are times when little nestlings just can't be put back. Take, for instance, the Little One. In late July I had a call from a woman who had found a baby hummingbird. The municipal highway department from a nearby town had been pruning some tree branches and while feeding the clippings into a chipper, discovered the chick on the ground. No one knows what happened to the nest or the other nestling; I make the assumption that the nest contained the standard two occupants. If left there, surely the chick would have died—the mother was nowhere in sight nor did she turn up later. The absolutely adorable nestling, still with a short and thick reddish-orange beak, short picket-fence tail, and small wings, all characteristic of a nestling, was brought to me for care until it would be ready to fledge.

Feeling right at home, Little One perched on my hand, drank some NektarPlus, and then cleaned her beak by wiping it back and forth across my finger. The bird sat outside with me each day and, growing at a remarkable rate, looked less like a nestling and more like a fledgling with each passing day. And the day quickly came that Little One, after having spent several days exercising her wings, raised herself up a couple of feet to a low branch of the spruce tree. After that, she stayed in the sunroom on a branch of the ficus that I borrowed from my Mom—now that the bird was moving about there would be no stopping her. When she showed signs of being on the road to self-sufficiency, her feeder was placed in the ficus and she was encouraged to use her own resources; she learned in no time flat. During this mock fledgling period, Little One should learn about flowers. Potted plants were bought for the garden—new salvia, bee balm, lobelia, spider flower, flowering tobacco. All would be planted outside ultimately, but for now they would be Little One's learning tools. I wanted to introduce her to favorite hummingbird flowers that she might encounter on her long, ultimate trip south. Before I released her I would introduce her to different feeders as well.

There's one thing I've learned about hummingbirds: as they move from one chapter in their lives to the next, they never look back. As usual, I was apprehensive about

releasing Little One—and hesitant. All the typical moth-
erly fears—outside, alone, overnight . . . maybe she'd like
to come back in for the night. I would have no trouble
should she come right over to me and perch on my finger.
Was she *really* ready? Would she stay around long enough
to show me that she truly was able to care for herself?
Concerns aside, it was time. Well, I did it—I brought her
out and released her. To my delight, she basically stayed
right near me all day. I continued to hand-feed her, and in
between she visited flowers close by or perches five or six
feet away. I finally released a hummingbird that didn't
leave me flat!

But "never looking back" means staying out all night,
whether I liked it or not. She was the last hummer to leave
that first evening—and each evening after. She slept in the
spruce tree, on a skinny branch two or three feet above the
overhang behind the sunroom. She looked so small, she
was all alone, and I felt sad. But I was relieved to know her
location. I was up before the sun the next morning and
before coffee or anything else, I went outside to see if she
was still there and check her condition. I was relieved
when I was able to detect her silhouette (only because I
had already known her location) and determine that she
had made it through the night. Being the closest to the
house, Little One was the first hummer to arrive at the
feeder the next morning. But she didn't visit an ordinary
feeder—she flew right over to me and hovered eye-to-
eye with me, buzzed around my hand, and then got right

back "in my face" and peeped. She was demanding some food. I loved it. I had her feeder in hand just in case and immediately gave her what she wanted. She expected me to be there, feeder in hand, at all times and when she wanted to be fed, she'd sail up to my eyes and insist.

For the next few days, Little One didn't venture more than ten or fifteen feet away from the fledging spot, just outside of the sunroom. She visited flowers, lobelia and cannas, but in between would sail over to my hand to be fed. When I wasn't holding the feeder, she'd be right up at my face, demanding.

Before long, Little One began to venture farther away and made forays to the different flower patches throughout the garden. And she'd sit on one of the hummingbird branches that I have scattered here and there and watch the other young hummingbirds. They moved quickly and obviously fascinated her. Before long she succumbed to a strong natural urge and began to chase them. She was brazen and totally fearless with the other hummers, and she seemed determined to let everyone, young and old, know that she had arrived on the scene.

Eventually, Little One became totally self-sufficient. She used all the feeders, explored all the hummingbird flowers, captured insects, and fit into the hummingbird community in that bratty hummingbird way. She had loads of personality. Everyone who met her fell in love with her instantly—the way she would fearlessly sail in, inspect the hand, fly up to the face, and peeping up a storm, demand some food. She made herself absolutely and totally irresistible. But as would be expected, that behavior was short-lived. Eventually she began sleeping elsewhere, and I wasn't privy to that location. And instead of begging me for food, I'd have to take the food over to where she sat and beg her to take it. I didn't want to lose that aspect of our relationship—it was special to me—but Little One didn't care about that because eventually she discontinued that, too. Oh, she'd sail up to my face and peep, but that was it. She'd sail up, peep, and then go off chasing something or using the "big" hummingbird feeders. She stayed around, eventually fattened up, and about mid-September left for parts unknown. She was born on the other side of the river, but she fledged from my sunroom. The mystery is: to which will she return in the spring—the birth or fledging site? Unfortunately, I won't recognize her unless she sails up to my face and peeps at me.

THE RUFOUS INVASION

My father spent a lot of time on the road during the 1930s. Depression-era America was a different time, a time when one could travel across this country or south as far as Panama, working a day or two here and there and then moving on, seeing everything in a way that just can't be done today, more than sixty years later. I can recall many of the interesting stories he had told me of his life on the road during that time, but the one that stands out most vividly is of one woman in Louisiana who had many beautiful flowers on her porch or balcony to attract humming-birds. "Look at the birds," she said to my father as she pointed out a number of hummers working the blossoms.

"And," my father remembered, "there were different kinds there—some were different colors; one was reddish." No doubt he had seen a rufous hummingbird.

This is obviously not something brand-new to the hospitable Southeast. A number of documented rufous hummingbirds regularly winter there. Some banded individuals practicing what is known as winter site fidelity have returned several years in a row. In fact, several species of hummingbird, none of which are considered eastern birds, now winter in the Gulf coastal area. The Northeast is quite another story.

RUFOUS PIONEERS

For years the rufous was considered strictly a western bird, but with a tendency to wander during its southward fall migration. The status of the rufous in the Southeast—particularly along the Gulf Coast—eventually graduated from casual (occurring infrequently in a geographic area) to vagrant (occurring outside its normal range usually during or following migration). Through banding efforts of people such as Nancy Newfield and Bob Sargent, we now know that the Southeast has become a major wintering ground for perhaps hundreds of rufous hummingbirds. So while the rufous became more recognized as a regular visitor (or migrant) to southeastern states, it was still considered accidental, or occurring infrequently farther north. Recently, however, there has been an explosion of rufous hummingbirds in the Northeast. Have they been around for a long time and we are just noticing them more now that we keep our feeders up longer in the fall? Or are we witnessing pioneers of this species expanding their range and settling in new places? Perhaps both are correct. There has probably been a range expansion effort in progress for quite a while, but it is really beginning to gather momentum. And being more hummingbird oriented, we are noticing them more now. This phenomenon may not be restricted to the rufous, but certainly that is the most common out-of-range species in the eastern United States. It has become our second most common Eastern hummingbird!

If a new or expanded wintering range is evolving, what about a correspondingly expanded breeding range? Did that already occur when the rufous moved into Alaska, or was Alaska just the start of what will ultimately include the Northeast as well? In *Netlines,* the Hummer/Bird Study Group newsletter,* Bob Sargent relates that rufous hummingbirds have been documented in every month of the year except June in the Southeast. Why—what is going on? Who knows. It is a nagging, thought-provoking question, and the possible answers are many. With thousands upon thousands of individual hummingbirds of many species either year-round residents of or wintering in Mexico, it is immediately obvious that competition would

*For more information, or for those interested in participating, contact Hummer/Bird Study Group, Inc., P.O. Box 250, Clay, Alabama 35048-0250. Another organization is The Hummingbird Society. Dedicated to hummingbird conservation and research, the organization has an impressive scientific advisory board and publishes a quarterly newsletter. For information about joining, call (800) 529-3699.

HUMMINGBIRDS: MY TINY TREASURES

be keener on traditional wintering grounds. Conditions in traditional wintering areas may have become—or are becoming—unfavorable. The balance between the number of competitors and the amount of available food may have changed—perhaps the result of habitat destruction not only on the wintering ground but also in nearby areas. That may have increased the concentration of residents, transients, and migrants into smaller areas. I certainly don't know; I can only speculate about the possibilities. The one thing I am sure of is that the status of the rufous hummingbird east of its purported range has changed. We can guess and speculate to our hearts' content, but there's so much that we just don't know. With each new bit of information, however, another piece of the puzzle drops into place, and one day maybe we *will* know.

As mentioned, this change may be occurring to compensate for added breeding areas to the north, a northward shift to cut down on travel time. Certainly the rufous spends a lot of time traveling, and for a great deal of its time it is en route somewhere. There are many people who never travel as far in their entire lifetime as the rufous travels on its migration—and they do it *twice* each year. Birds and other animals will expand or change their range in response to environmental pressures and other factors to better accommodate their needs. The basic needs for breeding and nonbreeding hummingbirds are flowers and insects. So the hospitality of, say, a Louisiana garden brimming with flowers and feeders means more time for the important stuff in life. The rufous breeds in some areas where the brevity of the flowering season restricts it to one brood per year. Perhaps this is part of an effort to extend the breeding season in some way so more offspring can be produced in additional broods.

Is this "explosion" a result of external factors, or is it internal? When weather patterns are examined, the increase in rufous sightings in the East is not any more or less common after an El Niño year, in drought years, in wet, hot, or cold years. It's hard to put a finger on any one common denominator. There is no parental guidance on a migration, but information about migrating has to span the bridge from one generation to the next. Maybe we need to look within, and that means genetic inheritance. But exactly what is passed on? It seems evident that if it were information on the exact winter site, we wouldn't be having all these "stranded" rufous in the Northeast; they'd all be going to a definite place. More likely it is general direction that is carried through generations. With this inherited information neatly tucked away in their little brains, the birds follow a guideline; the rest is experience. If they're successful, whether it's off the beaten path or not, they repeat it and pass it on to their offspring in an ever-widening genetic picture. In other words, birds that accidentally wind up in Louisiana, and then successfully winter there, pass on that information on Louisiana to the next generation. The burgeoning effect may eventually be a population of rufous hummingbirds even hardier than they already are—perhaps an Eastern race. Over the years, the dispersal of rufous hummingbirds to the East may give rise to a subspecies and we may be witnessing this evolution.

The biggest stumbling block for rufous pioneers—at least for now—may be that because their southbound movements occur so early, they settle in at some sites that ultimately are too far north and soon become inhospitable or totally unsuitable. Thus, many of these pioneers perish, casualties of their range expansion effort while those that survive at marginal latitudes create a strong gene pool for future hardiness. It may then be that food supply, not adaptability to weather, will be the limiting factor in new rufous wintering areas. Or future populations may begin the fall migration later and may not stop at Northeast locations at all. It might be suggested that intervention is not the best course of action on behalf of the species as a whole, that without the "weeding out" process of birds not strong enough to make the grade, long-term changes can't occur. Yet one must do what one's conscience will bear. Rather than sacrifice some birds for a possible long-term benefit for others, I follow my heart, giving concern to the individual first.

MY RUFOUS VISITORS

In September 1993, Rosie migrated to my garden. For years I had indulged my imagination with thoughts of a rufous sighting here, but when it really happened I was astonished. Not only did I glimpse this most sought-after visitor to the East, but she stayed—and stayed. Finally, in November, she was brought indoors to spend the winter in my sunroom. Rosie was my introduction to the rufous. Oh, I had seen them before, during their migration through Arizona. I marveled at one particular loud and pugnacious male that claimed everything in a Senoita garden, and I got the impression that the little bully would have fought with himself had there not been anyone else there to push around. But this was different. I got to know Rosie intimately. She charmed me almost instantly with her feisty, endearing personality, and she will always occupy a very special place in my heart. I learned much about the rufous hummingbird as she gave me so very much to observe—her hunting and bathing techniques, her interest in nesting

Rosie—my introduction to the rufous hummingbird

material, the chronology of her molt (except the tail), her behavior toward the rubythroats while she was in my garden, her floral preferences, her personality. When we parted company, I was happy for her and sad for me, but optimistically anticipated seeing her again some day.

When I released Rosie, I remember my husband, himself quite taken by the extraordinary experience, saying to me, "You'll probably never see another rufous." My response was, "Well, you never know."

In December 1994, I had a call from a man regarding an "off course" rufous in Minnesota. No hummingbird—not even our hardy little rufous—could ever make it through a rugged Minnesota winter. An airline company had agreed, as a public service gesture, to transport the bird to a warmer place. The man wanted suggestions about how to capture it. And there were an adult male at Cambridge, New York, and a juvenile in New Bedford, Massachusetts, for the same month. So when I received a call for help in December about a rufous that had taken up residence in an East Hartford, Connecticut, garden, I was not surprised, but I was concerned. The bird had been there since September. And while the weather had thus far not been too severe, the forecast was for a change to a more wintery trend. Again, the worry was not the cold per se, but sustained cold coupled with a lack of available protein and an inability to keep the nectar thawed in the feeders. The constant stream of birdwatchers adding this rufous to their life list had dwindled, but fortunately one of those visitors had given the bird's hostess some protein powder to add to the nectar, so the bird was doing well. Diet seems especially important, and protein may be even more important to these birds than nectar. Nectar gives quick energy, but most of these birds "stranded" in the Northeast aren't really very active—they need to keep warm and nourished. Sugar doesn't cut it. The Cambridge bird was brought here in December, after having lived on a steady diet of sugar-water. He was banded, weighed, and measured—and found to be obese. The bird lived only a few days, weakened, and died. I suppose that's bound to happen eventually—it's inevitable. But I always feel so personally responsible for a bird while it's here. Of course, I think of what I might have done differently. Perhaps that bird should have been weaned off the steady sugar-water diet and gradually introduced to a complete and proper diet. Under similar circumstances in the future, that is the way it will be handled. After examining all factors, the only thing we have been able to attribute his death to is diet. It may be that the bird reached a point where it just could not assimilate any food other than the sugar-water.

Days were getting shorter and colder. There was no way to predict the severity of the winter ahead, but one thing was certain: with the advent of colder weather, the nectar would freeze in the feeder and there wouldn't be anyone available to change it. My advice, based on the vagaries of a New England winter, was to harbor her until spring.

On December 11, I again called Jane, the bird's hostess.

Temperatures overnight would be zero to five above, and the next day would not rise above freezing. It seemed time to act. I got the capture cage ready, made a copy of my federal permit, and told her to call me as soon as she saw the bird the next morning. I was ready to go. Right from the start, this bird was different from Rosie—she was an early riser. I received the call at 6:55 A.M.—the bird had emerged from the cedar tree where it had been roosting and was active at the feeder. I was shocked. Although East Hartford is one hundred miles east of my area and might be a *tad* lighter, it was still dark outside.

When I arrived, Pixie, as the woman called the bird, was visiting the feeder and then immediately retiring to the sunniest spot to sit. It is said that hummers don't recognize individuals, but Pixie certainly knew her hostess. She was absolutely oblivious to Jane, who undoubtedly was an accepted part of the garden. I, on the other hand, was a total stranger invading her territory, an interloper, and she'd let me know just what she thought of the situation— and me. As I set up the cage to capture her, she sailed across the yard and hovered in front of my face, effectively scolding me with her chatter and attempting in her "David and Goliath" way to drive me out. I made an immediate assumption that this was an immature female when I saw four red feathers in the shape of a diamond on an other- wise immaculate-looking throat; indeed, as I was later told, the iridescent red feathers had only burst open within days of my visit. (By her release date in early May, that number had increased to fourteen and other new throat feathers were more or less outlined with buffy.)

Capturing a healthy hummingbird was a brand-new experience for me. I knew nothing about the use of mist nets and wasn't about to try anything that had the potential of harming her. My choice was a capture box. My husband made a soft screened box framed in cedar, with a door on one side. Her feeder was hung at the opposite end from the door. When she went inside to use the feeder, I'd close the door from a distance via the attached string. Sounds easy, right? Well it sounded easy to me, too, but Pixie had other ideas. She was a savvy little rufous who wasn't about to facilitate this capture by being cooperative. She was sharp-eyed and quick, and she could detect even the slightest motion in the string and was quite able to differentiate between movement caused by ordinary breezes and me. I had to be careful and would only try to get the door shut while she was sitting at the feeder, away from the door. But even when I sat hidden inside the house, she kept her eye on that string. After several freezing hours and many futile attempts, I was finally able to close the door when the bird entered the capture box. The way her capture was finally accomplished was quite simple. I threw a piece of camouflage netting over myself and sat next to the box with one hand on the door. She seemed to be completely unaware of my presence in that state and calmly passed just inches from my face as she entered the box. Just as calmly I closed the door behind her. Mission accomplished. She appeared

Pixie had much deeper, richer coloring

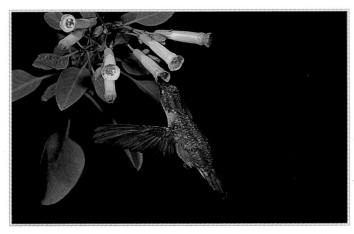

Pixie's outer three primaries were old and worn, and longer than the rest

Her undertail coverts were unspotted

The most notable difference was the lack of green on the outer tail feathers

Pixie sported her very own bracelet with her very own number

bright, healthy, and alert but she looked so small—and she didn't like being in that box. I put the cage on the back seat of the car, covered it with a sheet to keep her calm during the ride home, and proceeded on a circuitous route, adding at least thirty miles to the trip, to avoid the stop and go of traffic lights. Once in the sunroom, Pixie immediately left the cage, found her feeder of NektarPlus (she had been using the Perky canopy feeder exclusively, so that is the type that was provided), and settled down on a comfortable spot among some branches that had been placed around the sunroom for her.

The following morning I got my first good look at this beautiful young bird, and was promptly struck by how different from Rosie she appeared when viewed up close. She had much richer coloring, with more and deeper rufous throughout. The rufous coloring extended farther across the lower rump and her back appeared to have a coppery glow. The large amount of rufous at the base of each feather gave the appearance that specks of green floated over a bed of copper. Later, as molting replaced her head and facial feathers, she acquired much more color on her face, as well.

The wings were another source of dissimilarity between Rosie and the new bird. Immediately obvious was the warm brownish tone of her primaries, indicative of old, worn feathers. Indeed, as molting of the primaries occurred, the fresh replacement feathers were glossier, had more of a metallic sheen, and were darker in hue. The

outer three—Primaries 8, 9, and 10—on both sides, however, were never molted and revealed more than just color
differences. With both adult and immature feathers on
each wing, a basis for comparison existed that presented
visible evidence of the disparity between adult and immature wing length measurements. The smooth contour of
the wings was lost as the three remaining old outer feathers were noticeably longer than the rest. The oldest primaries also exhibited a great deal of wear and tear and
abrasion at the tips. And it's no wonder; unlike Rosie, who
never hit anything with her wings, this little one constantly sent small flowers flying via her wing tips while she
hovered and drank. So many differences. Even her soft,
undertail coverts were different from Rosie's—they were
unspotted.

The most notable difference between Pixie and her
predecessor was their tail feathers. There was no green on
Pixie's two outer pairs. Even with all the plumage variation
one might expect, this was not insignificant to me. Because
there wasn't the same green separating the rufous and
black on her outer tail feathers that I had seen on Rosie,
and not realizing just how much plumage variation there
can be in the rufous, I questioned her identity. Could she
be an Allen's hummingbird? It is unlikely but not impossible. The Allen's makes appearances in the Southeast,
although not with the same frequency as the rufous. She
didn't have those characteristic ribbon-thin outer tail
feathers, but the range of measurements for rufous and

Allen's can be very close and, in fact, overlap in almost all characteristics. Since I had these doubts, it was important to have her measured and banded. There are only a handful of people federally licensed to band hummingbirds in the United States, and I believe licenses aren't generally granted unless an apprenticeship has been served. Licensed bander Bob Yunick is not too far away and he graciously consented to come and do the job.

So, in late April, Bob arrived, scale, calipers, and notebook in hand, and he patiently waited while I got Pixie back into her capture box. Again, it took some time. I removed all the feeders except the one in the box, so she used the flowers instead. It was four months later and she was still uncooperative. Bob performed the task gently with a great deal of finesse, and it was interesting to watch the exacting procedure. The majority of her measurements fell within the range for a rufous and so identification of this bird is no longer in question. When he was finished, Pixie was no worse for the wear, but she now sported a little piece of jewelry—her very own bracelet with her very own number. I was able to observe Pixie over the next couple of weeks until she was released, and was happy to see that she didn't peck at it or pay any attention to it at all. In fact, she may have even been absolutely unaware of its presence.

Pixie was a real education to me. She taught me much about rufous plumage. She looked so different from Rosie that I questioned her identity and the more I questioned, the more I delved. And the more I delved, the more I learned about how variable that plumage can be.

Differences between Rosie and Pixie didn't stop at the physical level. The personalities of these two birds were as different as night and day—as were the conditions of their release. When I released Pixie, she stayed here quite a bit longer than Rosie had. After she left the sunroom, I saw her several times as she checked out everything. I'd lose sight of her and then she'd appear again, sitting on the clothes-line, at different flowers, at different feeders. Eventually that same morning I heard a hummer on the north side of the sunroom, and it was Pixie at a feeder. I got that one additional morning from her; after that she was gone.

Pixie's stay here was relatively uneventful, especially compared to Rosie's. Rosie made the most of her situation —she settled in here and became very comfortable with her surroundings and interacted with me in a positive way. Pixie, on the other hand, ignored me. She wasn't afraid of me, but she didn't want to make friends, either. I couldn't get her to eat from the hand-held feeder, no matter how hard I tried. The time of her molt wasn't too different from Rosie's. In December, she molted on the throat and acquired a large throat patch. By mid-January, molting of feathers occurred on her face and head; and by late January, replacement of her primaries had commenced. Unlike Rosie, however, molting of the primaries stopped at No. 7. And, finally, like Rosie before her, no tail feath-ers were replaced while she was here.

*The molt of her
wing feathers stopped at Primary 7*

When Bob Yunick banded Pixie, he asked about my
plans for the following year. I promptly said, "Next year I
want a pair," followed by "I want two rufous hummingbirds." As usual, I wasn't expecting it to happen, I was
reaching for the moon.

I left a feeder up late during the fall of 1995 in case Pixie
returned, just as I had unsuccessfully done the year before
for Rosie's return. By November I had calls from Colorado,
Illinois, and North Dakota regarding stranded rufous hummingbirds. Then, in mid-November, I received a call from
my publisher, Crown. Apparently the people at Duncraft
in Illinois had called them with a message for me from
Mary Lou Benedict of Bainbridge, New York (a suburb of

Crystal—a particularly beautiful bird

I identified Crystal as an adult female—Her tail provided some clues.

Binghamton), regarding a stranded hummer. When we spoke, she told me of her concern for a hummingbird that had shown up in her garden about one week earlier. She put a feeder outside for the bird, but the nectar kept freezing so she moved the feeder into her sunroom and kept the door opened so the bird could enter at will to drink. Later she thought it wise to close the door while the bird was inside and then get some help for the bird. My mind began to work. Experience told me that it was probably too late in the year for it to be a rubythroat. I suspected that it might be a rufous, but since the bird was green, she didn't think so. She called the bird Crystal, a name chosen by the grandchildren of her friend. Mary Lou had a small fuchsia plant with some small bare branches embedded in the soil. This is where Crystal liked to sleep, and in fact spent much of her down time on it, as well. I suggested that she put the fuchsia and a feeder in a cage and allow Crystal to go in and out as she saw fit. Then, when Mary Lou was ready to transport Crystal to me, it would be easy to just close the door while the bird slept. We made the arrangements and Crystal, together with her favorite fuchsia, was delivered to me that weekend. She would be spending her winter at this safe haven.

Crystal was a particularly beautiful and healthy-looking bird with rich, deep rufous coloring and clear, sparkling green, a very small throat patch and a beautiful tail with clear, unworn white spots. I identified Crystal as an adult female in her second year—her tail had adult characteristics and her wings had both mature and immature length feathers. All that told me that in the prior year she went through an extensive molt except for the outer primaries. Her feathers were in excellent condition, but the rufous edges had worn off, so they were not brand-new. While it's possible that her molt was completed, including the tail, prior to her arrival, that didn't seem likely, not only because her feathers didn't appear to be fresh but especially considering what the others had done here.

By the end of the month I received another stranded rufous call. The report was that an immature female was hanging around a Stuyvesant, New York, garden and causing concern because of the weather. But the bird disappeared before it could be captured and transported here.

Finally, in mid-December I had a call regarding yet another immature female, this one in the Little Compton area of Rhode Island (a state record for the species). She showed up during the second week in October and her host, Geoff Dennis, took her in just after Thanksgiving, when it became apparent that she wasn't planning to leave. Geoff literally built a greenhouse around this bird and devised a method to keep sugar-water in the feeders from freezing. Visits such as these stir up strong feelings of responsibility within us. Geoff, with that sense and feeling of responsibility, wasn't entirely comfortable about having the bird winter there. He called me and we made arrangements for me to take the bird in. He hadn't named her, so I suggested "Red." After all, what would be

Some of Red's feathers were emerald, some mint, and some chartreuse

more appropriate for Rhode Island? Geoff agreed, and Red it was.

Red had various degrees of color and iridescence across her back. Some of her feathers were emerald, some were mint-colored, and some chartreuse. Her tail feathers were on the narrow side and one of the middle ones was practically worn down to its shaft.

With the arrival of Red, I would be hosting my fourth rufous in three years. Just a couple of years ago they were accidental in the Northeast, and the first state records for the species began showing up only in the late 1980s. Four rufous, and it nearly was five.

SUNROOM SHENANIGANS

By mid-November, when the call came about the stranded bird in Bainbridge, K-T was on the road to recovery. There were telltale signs of a slight balance problem—occasionally he would have to set his wings into motion to straighten up or a swaying movement might be detected in the feeder as he drank—but all in all, he was doing quite well. The miracle of his progress is a testament to the hummingbird's endurance and remarkable will to survive in the face of adversity. His beak would probably never be perfect, but it would be functional and serve all its intended purposes. I had every reason to expect that a complete recovery would be in order. Of course mid-November was much too late to release K-T, so he would be staying until spring, and time would be beneficial to that complete recovery.

When Mary Lou arrived with Crystal, I could tell immediately that the bird was not a rubythroat but a rufous, an aggressive bird, and that might spell troubles for K-T. What if she were to chase him and he hit his beak again? I transferred Crystal from her cage to the capture box. She would have to stay there overnight until I made adjustments to the sunroom to accommodate a rubythroat with a disability and a pushy rufous. The first thing I did was tack soft screening tautly across the windows. While I have never had a bird hit one of the windows, it might be quite different if one bird were chasing another. With the screening tacked up, a little brightness was sacrificed, but that would be a small price to pay for the assurance that a hummingbird would bounce off screen instead of crashing into glass. The next thing I did was create "private" areas to drink and perch for both birds. A feeder was placed on the north side of the room, behind Crystal's fuchsia and out of sight of K-T. I hoped Crystal would want to continue using the fuchsia perch to which she had become accustomed, and she would follow up by using the feeder closest to it as well—and thus not chase K-T. Having more than one hummingbird would be a new experience for me. I know how mean they can be. I know the rufous's reputation and I didn't want to be responsible for one of them being hurt. The fuchsia, of course, would not really be enough. I could divide the room in half with screening or latticework if need be, but first I'd try natural dividers.

By then, K-T's remarkable little personality had already begun to blossom and he became nosier, more brazen, and certainly more lovable.

Placement of plants was dictated largely by what would best accommodate multiple birds rather than an individual. The honeysuckle would have made a nice natural divider, but that had been placed in such a way that branches hung under the light where K-T liked to sit, so that wouldn't be moved. Instead a large cestrum and the *Pachystachys* were used as dividers between K-T's and Crystal's feeders. I also brought in the "tree" that had been Rosie's and then Pixie's, and which, in between hummingbirds, graces the lath-house. K-T had been using the honeysuckle branches for resting and at times sleeping, but with an extra bird, some additional perching places would be in order.

I released Crystal from the cage, fully expecting her to claim the sunroom as her own. I was sure K-T would be no match for this larger, "aggressive" rufous. Apparently I underestimated K-T's tenacity and ability when it came to defending what he considered his personal territory. He immediately chased her and, surprise of surprises, Crystal didn't defend herself. Instead she retreated to her fuchsia. Apparently that wasn't good enough for K-T—he didn't want to see her at all. I felt sorry for her and tried to divert K-T's attention with a feeder, but he was blind to everything except this new hummingbird in his area. K-T, who had been so silent all along, now began to chatter.

In the beginning K-T chased Crystal to the northeast corner constantly, and eventually she learned to stay there, more or less. Occasionally she'd sit on one of the cestrum or bare tree branches out of K-T's view, but frequently she hid on a crossbrace at the back of the plant shelf. There she could look outside and be out of K-T's view at the same time. To make sure that Crystal got her fair share of food, I brought in another feeder and placed it behind the plant shelf, where only a bird sitting behind the shelf would notice it.

From Day One, Crystal wanted to bathe and went to the waterfall. But that is on the south end of the room and K-T didn't approve, so he would chase her relentlessly before she had a chance to get even one drop on her feathers. Neither would relent, so I then decided to offer some alternative bathing water on the side of the room to which K-T had banished Crystal. A large plastic sweater box, some small flat pieces of bluestone, and a recirculating pump were purchased. I planned to arrange them so water would spill onto flat rocks, drop to a lower level, and continue in that fashion to the bottom of the tray. Then on a trip to a local nursery, I found a lava rock waterfall structure with little plants that was very attractive and seemed appropriate for the hummers, and I bought that. It was already constructed; all I needed to do was add water and plug it in. The only one who ever inspected it, however, was K-T. Crystal still wanted the "big" waterfall.

Red's arrival here wasn't much different from Crystal's. The minute she was released into the sunroom, she was given the "set of rules"—the dos and don'ts of the house. Unfortunately for her, being third in line meant that she would have two bosses—first K-T, who was *everyone's* boss, and the quiet Miss Crystal.

PERSONALITIES

Each bird is different from all others; each has its own personality. K-T was the bossy one and quite the brat, but an underdog. He was also the nosiest and most daring, the most inquisitive, the first to try new flowers, and the one most brazen and curious about me. Crystal was the docile one—usually, the most laid back, the most reserved, and the one most interested in the outdoors. She was also the nicest looking and least active. Red was somewhere in between the other two as far as personality is concerned, certainly the most brazen of the two rufous hummingbirds. For the most part, they were too interested in one another to be interested in me—except, that is, for K-T.

K-T was the nosy one, the most curious. He kept himself involved in everything in the sunroom. No matter what was going on, he'd be right there being nosy. There was a pot of nasturtium hanging in a cool, bright spot. The pot had no saucer attached, so when I put too much water in it, some dripped through the bottom drainage holes. To catch the water, there was a plastic container on the floor strategically placed beneath the pot. Since the water would drop about four feet, it made noise—lots of it. Each time I would overwater and K-T heard that noisy drip, he would immediately investigate, going right over to inspect. He approached first from one side, then the other, hiding behind the honeysuckle leaves and watching it from above.

K-T was the first to rebound after a hawk scare, breaking up the quiet with his wings as he bathed or drank. Crystal and Red would not copy; they sat until they heard the outside birds.

Much of my time was spent in the sunroom tending to Peeper, and that gave K-T many opportunities to interact with me. He sat on my hand under the lights, landed on my head more than once, would zip under my lifted arm, rush up to my face and stare into my eyes, touch me with his tongue and stretch when I talked to him. Or he'd fly over to check out my cup and spoon. If only I knew in advance when he'd be doing these cute things. The red sable brush that I preened Peeper with had about one inch of orange coloring at its base. When K-T saw it moving back and forth as I brushed Peeper, he had to come over to investigate. When I'd sit on the loveseat on the north side of the sunroom writing my notes, K-T would come over and sit about eighteen inches above my head just looking at me, watching my every move. His back was to the south side where the other hummers were, but if he heard a squeal or chatter, he'd chime right in—without ever leaving the branch. Occasionally I'd be aware of a hovering shadow or a bit of a breeze as he'd lower himself to check my pad or my pencil, just as a cat tries to play with your pen while you write. As I sat in the sunroom taking notes on their comings and goings holding a pen with a red casing, I became aware of a shadowy figure checking it out. It was nosy K-T, hovering back and forth in front of the pen. He was another hummer that couldn't stay away from my eyes. No matter what I would do in the sunroom, he would immediately float around my head, peering into my eyes. And he enjoyed having me feed him. He didn't like it because it was a treat; I hadn't introduced him to that. He just loved drinking from the hand-held regular feeder. I wonder if he claimed me as part of his territory. I had to be very careful, for I never knew when he would be between my arm and waist, or my body and Peeper's basket—he was always just there. It would be very hard not to love him. He had no reservations about me at all, a possible result of having such close physical contact with me for so long. When I talked to K-T, he would puff up and shift his weight from one side to the other, back and forth, then stretch his wings back and puff up again. It was a little routine that he went through—and all the time he was doing that, he would stare at me.

Many was the time I laughed out loud over K-T's antics. He would look to see my location and then bear down in my direction, deliberately passing as closely as possible to the top of my head. He'd then make a circle, fly back up to the chain, and do it all over again. But first he would wait until I was looking at him. When I bent over and snaked around some plants to change the feeder tucked away under and behind the plant shelf, K-T approached from the other side of the feeder and hovered there, just waiting and looking at me, eye to eye, almost as if he were playing peek-a-boo with me. He surely had a way about him. In fact, whenever I sat down with Peeper, K-T would join us. And as I sat writing notes about this very behavior, someone appeared about two inches from my eyes and hovered there, looking at me. Guess who? K-T, just as though he had been reading my thoughts.

When I walked into the room holding Peeper, just carrying him around to keep him out of trouble, K-T would immediately fly over for a handout. After he finished drinking, he retreated to a twig on the bare tree about eighteen inches from my head. But that wasn't close enough, he had to move to a twig about three inches away and above my face and just look at me. No one could ever tell me that there isn't something special there. And no one could ever keep from falling hook, line, and sinker for this little brat. K-T would hover less than an inch from my glasses and peer into my eyes. What was he looking for? I'd love to know what went on in his mind.

Neither of the rufous were afraid of me—they would do exactly what they wanted to do even when only inches away. They looked at me a lot and I certainly seemed to catch their interest when I talked to them, but neither ever showed any inclination to be as friendly as K-T, Squeak, or Rosie had been, although they watched with great interest when K-T interacted with me.

They may not have been as outgoing toward me as K-T was, but I was trusted and well accepted, and they certainly were curious. For instance, one day as I sat in the sunroom catching up on some correspondence, I was aware of something moving around. When I looked, it was Red, investigating my knee. When we made eye contact, she looked at me for a split second and then slowly moved along. Another time she buzzed around at the top of my head as she tried to figure whether a floral hair tie offered anything she might like. At the very least they were extremely comfortable around me, and I could work two inches away from either one and they'd just sit there, looking.

I wonder what they thought of me. They'd freely chase one another around my head, using it to hide behind, and Red would buzz by, inches away from me as though no one was there. Or when she whizzed by the others—and it was methodical, designed to pass as closely as possible to each one's face—she included me. Was I just another part of the sunroom as were the loveseat, one of the chairs or another hummingbird?

For almost their entire stay here, the girls were dominated by bossy little K-T. Had either rufous been a male, however, things might have been quite a bit different. There's little doubt that a male rufous would have been much bossier than K-T.

One thing that the girls were afraid of was human activity *outside* the sunroom. If they saw anyone out there, they would immediately withdraw to the opposite side of the room, or fly back and forth from south to north and vice versa until the "coast was clear."

One day a large shadow passed overhead—it may have been either a crow or a hawk. There wasn't any avian activity in the garden, but there wasn't any sudden cessation of noise, either. Perhaps they had been quiet for a while and I hadn't noticed as the hummers were active. Crystal had just visited the waterfall. But their awareness of the shadow, even without the accompanying bluejay warning, or sudden quiet, was enough to stop them dead in their tracks. So we know that they take advantage of multiple danger signals.

BUSY MORNINGS—LAZY AFTERNOONS

Each morning before sunrise I'd tiptoe around in the semi-darkness of the sunroom, installing feeders with fresh food in all the favorite spots. I wanted everything to be ready and as they liked it to start their day. There was a basic daily routine that the birds followed: they'd wake up, use feeders, establish daily dominance, visit a few flowers, bathe, and, finally, fly around.

Peeper was the first to wake up almost every morning, and the first thing he would do, of course, was drink. Next, it was Red, and the first thing she would do was visit a feeder to drink. Then it was K-T. The first thing K-T would do is charge Red, then visit some flowers and finally a feeder. Consistently last to waken each morning was Crystal. But once she had wakened and visited a feeder,

After K-T charged Red, he'd visit flowers . . . here it is penstemon

. . . and here it is Salvia elegans

the chattering would begin. All of this within a span of just a few minutes.

Mornings buzzed with activity in the sunroom. Hummingbirds were everywhere—they didn't sit still. While one would repeatedly fly around in a large circle, another would lift six or eight inches from her perch each time the first passed by. Usually Red circled while Crystal lifted, at times making a counterclockwise vertical-oval about twelve inches high. While one was at a feeder, another would be at another feeder and the third would be taking a bath. Then they'd all be flying around. I would hear chips, chatters, squeaks and squeals, and wings, wings, wings all over the place, crisscrossing back and forth in front of one another—just like an airport. Or one might fly up to another, fan its tail in display, and the third would give chase to whichever of the first two had flown off. This was a typical morning scenario, and any of the birds might have been playing any part at any given time. When I would enter the sunroom in the mornings once they were awake, it was more likely than not that I would find K-T hot on the heels of one of the girls. He was such a troublemaker. Birds that had stayed with me in the past were docile by comparison to these. With no competition, they could leisurely stretch, preen, and scratch to their hearts' content. But this year was different and it was lots of fun.

Soon it would be time for a bath. K-T would sit on an elevated perch watching as I sprayed the gardenia leaves. And as soon as I would stop, he descended with feet down and apart, preparing immediately to drop to the water. In fact, if he heard the sprayer when I wetted the tillandsias, he would immediately descend to bathe, whether the gardenia leaves were wet or not. Of all the different places, he liked bathing on the gardenia leaves best. When he would see me at the basket—either bathing Peeper or changing the pad in his basket—he would immediately go to the gardenia to see if its leaves were wet. He would then select one with just the right amount of water and while hovering in front of it, rub his face and chin. He would then select another leaf to slosh around on and, while "doing paddles" to keep himself "leaf-borne," he would accomplish the next part of bathing—rubbing his underparts. Apparently he didn't worry much about bathing his back. He frequently checked the leaves for water with his tongue, one of his favorite ways to explore. When he would cling to one of the leaves to bathe on it, he appeared to be hugging it. But he would stop in an instant to chase a rufous and then immediately return to bathe some more. Afterward he'd retire to a low, horizontal branch on the honeysuckle to dry off. The birds liked that honeysuckle branch.

While K-T was busy bathing on the gardenia, the girls more often than not were vying for the pool at the top of the waterfall. One would sit at its edge—or in the middle of the water—while the other tried to annoy her into leaving. K-T, meanwhile, would continue to slosh around on the gardenia, leaving the plant from time to time to scold the girls—or just stop and hover in midair, looking around

*One would sit on the edge
or in the middle of the pool while the other annoyed her*

K-T would stop bathing to scold the girls

Crystal in the top pool

to see if anyone needed to be sent packing. K-T's bath usually took longest.

The waterfall makes such a nice trickling sound, so tropical or woodsy, and I enjoyed hearing it in the background of their constant chips, chatters, squeaks, and squeals. But every once in a while that trickling sound would come to a halt, making it immediately obvious to me that one of the girls had parked herself in the top pool and pressed herself right up to the stream of down-flowing water. Crystal and Red both bathed that way, facing the hole at the top pool and pushing their bodies right up against it to get soaked. Red even liked sticking her entire beak right into that hole. Neither Rosie nor Pixie had bathed that way, and I had to wonder if one of these girls mimicked the other.

When a freshly bathed Red found a spot to sit and dry off, and the spot was in K-T's line of view, he again stopped bathing to chase her away. As far as K-T was concerned, all the best spots—those under and near the light—were reserved for him and him alone, and should be unoccupied and available at all times. When Red finished bathing and parked herself on a lower branch of the lemon tree to dry off, K-T immediately stopped his bath to chase her away. She was too close, she should dry off elsewhere. Some mornings Crystal would get out of the waterfall and find a spot on the chain to dry off. For no good reason whatsoever, Red would fly over and give her the boot. Not to be outdone, Crystal then found it necessary to travel clear across the room to K-T and give him a little of the treatment she had just received. Usually, however, Crystal and Red would dry off together on the chain, six or eight inches apart, neither feeling in any way uncomfortable about or angered by the other's presence. Within the first fifteen or twenty minutes, everyone had had his or her first bath of the day.

Rosie was the champion bather. She bathed more frequently and in every way imaginable, in and out of the waterfall. Neither Crystal nor Red showed any desire to receive a shower or bathe on a leaf—strictly the waterfall, and only the original waterfall. K-T would occasionally deliberately fly right through the mist while I sprayed the gardenia leaves for him, but that was infrequent and he

really didn't want to experiment with the waterfall or anything else. Now, if I took too long to wet the gardenia, he
would fly to one or the other waterfall, as if examining
whether other water sources had anything to do with his
gardenia leaves becoming wet—but that was lip service
only; he never went in.

Eating, bathing, and a small bit of preening having been
completed, they now had time on their hands. And there
is no better way to pass that time than chasing or otherwise interacting with one another. They'd play a game
similar to musical chairs, although to them I'm sure it was
no game. I wondered how they signal one another and
how they think. They might be sitting quietly, looking out
the window or just doing nothing when, "like a bolt from
the blue," they'd start. K-T and Crystal would face one
another, fan their tails, and chatter. K-T would fan his tail
so wide that the outermost rectrices would be perpendicular to his body, forming a 90 degree angle on each side.
Crystal would take the perch under the light but K-T
would replace her. Red would then chase Crystal and the
next thing I knew, Red was sitting where K-T had last
been. And in that two or three seconds, they had all
just moved over one spot. Then all would be quiet for a
few minutes, only to start again once they'd moved
around a bit. K-T would be back under the light and
Crystal on a lower branch of the honeysuckle when
they'd both attempt to use the same feeder at the same
time. Chattering, tail-fanning, etc., would ensue, and

First Red sat at the pool's edge . . .

. . . then she entered the water . . .

she frequently stuck her beak in the hole

Crystal and Red dried off on the chain together

appropriately Red, not wanting to be left out, would have to participate in the activity as well. Then all of a sudden, another lull—a quick look around revealed K-T on the honeysuckle branch or under the light, Crystal on the *Aerides* root and Red a few inches from K-T under the light or a few inches from Crystal on a *Russelia* branch— and they'd all be preening. But their uncharacteristic quiet wouldn't fool me for one second. They were just getting ready to raise the devil again. It was neither never-ending nor vicious, and I do believe it was good for them, very good.

When I thought they were getting too rambunctious or too vigorous in their chasing—that is, if Crystal and Red were getting the best of K-T—I would whistle and they would all beat a hasty retreat to a spot where they could sit and decide if there was a danger about. Basically, I felt that Crystal and Red were able to take care of themselves quite well, but K-T was at a disadvantage. I was more inclined to worry about him holding his own, although that had hardly been a problem and K-T had not done badly for himself. Red felt that in order to be dominant, she had to sit wherever K-T was sitting—the branch under the light or the branch of the russelia—exactly the same place on the same stem.

One day Crystal was at the southwest corner of the sun- room, an area where she didn't usually sit. K-T looked all over for her, at the lantana and all the other places where she could usually be found. All the while he looked, he was chirping incessantly, hoping to flush her from hiding. They certainly kept very good tabs on one another.

Identical environmental conditions and opportunity to feed existed for all in the sunroom, but the two species behaved differently in the afternoon. The girls were very quiet in the afternoon while K-T was active. Looking out the window was an afternoon activity—mornings, of course, being reserved for annoying one another. Crystal devoted at least some significant amount of time each afternoon on the diagonal crossbrace of the plant shelf or a branch of the cestrum, just looking out the window. I wondered constantly, "What *does* she look at"? On many afternoons while K-T and Red were engrossed in chasing one another, Crystal would sit on a twig just looking out the window. From time to time her head would jerk quickly to the side as something interesting caught her eye, but for the most part she sat quietly—just looking out. If Red approached and Crystal didn't want her there, I'd hear *tzeept* or *tchu-tchu-tchu,* over and over in rapid succession as Crystal chased her off. What did she look at?

The hummingbirds that have stayed with me in the past have shown little reaction to the weather, each day being more or less just as the one before. These birds were different—on dismal days they were quiet, with each staking out a branch or twig and staying put, for the most part, throughout much of the morning and all of the afternoon. K-T was the least quiet.

For years I've watched hummingbirds retire to the same

spot nightly. That in and of itself is not proof-positive that
they *sleep* in the same spot each night, but it's a reasonable
assumption. Squeak seemed to give some weight to that
assumption as he slept every single night but one at the
exact same spot on the same skinny branch. Then along
came Rosie. Although she started out sleeping in her
"tree," over her six-month stay here she divided her time
between the *Aerides* root, cestrum, and shrimp plants. I
referred to her as fickle, saying that she was faithful to her
habits only while they lasted. But then along came these
three to shatter all preconceived notions and expectations
of what they would do about sleeping. They made Rosie
appear the epitome of habit.

For this winter I was careful not to upset the photoperiod the birds would receive on a traditional wintering
ground. I was particularly concerned about Peeper. To be
consistent with a normal day length, artificial lighting
turned on at 6:20 A.M. and off at 5:20 P.M., thus assuring
short days over winter. Days were then allowed to lengthen
in the morning and evening naturally with the rising and
setting sun. Just before the main light turned off, a small
lamp turned on via a second timer and remained on for
about one-half hour. This provided a period of dusk for the
birds to settle in, if they hadn't already done so. When the
main light turned off, Crystal and Red immediately retired
to sleeping places, but K-T and Peeper continued to feed.
K-T would visit each and every feeder before settling
down. By late February, the sun set later than 5:20 P.M. and

there was a period of natural dusk in the sunroom rather than the dusk created by the extra light. The birds liked that much better. As soon as the light turned off, the melee would begin—a whir of wings could be heard as they vied for the best sleeping position among their favorite places.

In the beginning K-T moved around frequently at night, owing for the most part to an inability to balance himself properly. He probably felt a bit insecure and would start to flop over, try to right himself, and then move to a different place. So it would not really be fair to compare his sleeping habits to any other. He would start out on the small branch under the light but would invariably move somewhere else—the honeysuckle, the bare branches of Rosie's tree, or usually on a link of one of the chains strung across the sunroom and used to hang plants.

For the first night that Crystal was here, K-T, who had been chasing her all day, felt that she should neither eat nor sleep in his sunroom, yet in spite of the elaborate measures I had taken to provide private places for them, he settled down about six inches away from her on the chain. I could see that K-T slept in a more vertical position than Crystal. I speculated that this was his way of keeping his eye on her. And he stayed put for the whole night!

After that, Crystal pretty much settled on a branch of the lantana at the southeast corner of the sunroom, still less than a foot from K-T, who continued to start out in one place but move to another. Red, who was prohibited

by K-T from sleeping near the other two her first night
here, found a place for herself on a petiole high up on the
Pachystachys plant on the opposite side of the room. So for
many days, that's how the hummers spent their evenings.
By January, K-T stayed put for the entire night.

FAVORITE PLACES—FAVORITE THINGS

THE LANTANA AND OTHER SLEEPING PLACES—The lantana
was unique, so it deserves special mention, not because of
its flowers, although they are quite attractive to hummingbirds, but because it played such a large part in their activity. Each fall I would bring in the lantana and hang it in
front of the window while it still had flowers of the past
season. But when the last flower faded, the plant would be
cut back somewhat severely and placed under the grow
light in the basement for new, compact growth and a fresh
crop of flowers. The birds had something else in mind. For
some reason it became *the* place to be, a favorite spot for
quiet afternoons, sleeping, or resting in between attacks.

Early during her stay, Crystal settled on the lantana as
her choice sleeping place. Needless to say, once she did,
it began to appeal to the others. There's nothing special
about the lantana, and in fact, it wasn't even Crystal's first
choice of a sleeping place, but everyone wanted it. Each
evening Red would try to take the lantana by retiring to it
before Crystal got there. One night she even stood firm
about taking the spot. When Crystal flew right up to her
to "annoy" her, in an attempt to encourage her to leave,

Red stayed anyway and opened her mouth in a threatening gesture to hold Crystal off. But Crystal was tenacious and eventually Red left. Even K-T had to get in on the act, claiming a lantana branch for his own sleeping purposes. It was a little lower on the plant and Crystal basically paid no attention to him. I had to wonder, what do they think they're missing when they don't have exactly what another has?

When Red couldn't claim the lantana as *her* sleeping spot, she settled on one of its branches as her choice resting spot in the afternoon instead. Then each night she would unsuccessfully attempt to claim it from Crystal. So they worked out an arrangement that basically gave Red the lantana in the afternoon until Crystal wanted to get ready to go to sleep. As soon as K-T saw Crystal and Red argue over the lantana, he had to start his shenanigans. Not only did K-T have to sleep on it too, he began to claim it at other times of the day, just to sit, as Red had been doing. K-T took it the next night, too, and on the third night he got there early just so he could claim it first. There are so many other choice places for little hummingbirds in the sunroom, but the grass always looks greener . . .

One day K-T was chasing Red all over the place because they both wanted to sleep on the lantana—an exercise in futility for both of them, I thought, as Crystal wasn't about to give it up anyway—and using me in the argument, chasing one another around and around my head. How wrong I was. K-T got the spot he wanted and

*Under the
light . . .*

Crystal attempts to annoy Red away from lantana . . .

. . . but Red threatens to hold her off

K-T claimed the lantana

Crystal took another. When I think of all the nights Red tried to get that spot but failed I had to laugh at little K-T —such a brat! He never ceased to amaze me. He meant business, he wanted that lantana spot—and he got it.

K-T would sit at Crystal's sleeping spot on the lantana and then almost as though in an act of total defiance, leave, buzz over to Crystal (who was just sitting there bothering no one), stay for a second, and then return to the lantana, almost as if to say, "What are you going to do about it?" At times while he sat there with his tongue sticking out about one-eighth of an inch, he would chirp repeatedly at one of the others, warning her—or them— to stay away.

For the first couple of nights that K-T managed to get a spot on the lantana, he edged Crystal to another spot but shared. Then finally he commandeered it. I'm happy to say that eventually Crystal was permitted to return and remain, but only because even though they were only six inches apart, they faced in opposite directions. By early March and at long last, the three birds slept in the lantana together. Do I need to say that K-T got the best spot (by their standards) while the other two were relegated to inferior positions?

K-T was the one that always remained active longest in the afternoon—probably a species trait—but would settle in first in order to get the best spot on the lantana—as if any one spot is really any better than the next. That same night I watched K-T hide on one of the branches of the passionflower vine—he was waiting to ambush Crystal going to the lantana. I've seen other males exhibit that sort of behavior on numerous occasions and have always marveled at what seems to be an ability to scheme. Certainly if the birds had had a contest to see who was most terrible, K-T would have won hands down.

Eventually Red gave up the lantana for sleeping entirely and moved instead to a horizontal bougainvillea branch. K-T had been successful in driving her away. But once K-T knew that taking the most desirable spot on the lantana was his uncontested right and Red no longer wanted it, K-T lost interest in it and began sleeping on a honeysuckle branch. Crystal stuck it out and stayed with the lantana for a while, but moved back to her favorite branch—the one that had been usurped by K-T. So Crystal wasn't willing to give up the lantana entirely, but did consent to move over, and Red was banished to the bougainvillea and thus the lantana lost its appeal. One night, that little urchin, K-T, showed some interest in Red's bougainvillea but lost interest just as fast when he realized that Red didn't care. Please don't dislike K-T for being such a brat—he was a cute brat and earned every privilege he had, or took. He started out with three strikes against him, one of which is that he is not a rufous, and if someone *had* to be boss, it's best that it was K-T.

In the beginning—when Red was still testing the waters and the other two were still attempting to drive her away, the introduction and adjustment period—she

Sunset over the lantana—K-T (above) got the best spot and Crystal (below) took another

The girls slept only inches from each other on the tree

K-T island-hopped from one tillandsia to the next

They frequently argued over the honey-suckle branch—Crystal and Red

Aloes took precedence over   *. . . Red with an aloe*
the feeders . . . K-T with an aloe

. . . Crystal visits an aloe

slept wherever she could stay without being harassed. At first it was a petiole of the *Pachystachys*—she was practically driven to it. Later it was the chain—after all, she *wanted* to be near the others. They were less than kind and tried driving her away from that side of the room, so she settled on a large S-hook that holds a feeder. That lasted a couple of weeks—just until she felt that she had been there long enough to assert some authority herself and try for the lantana. But just as quickly as the lantana gained status as *the* place to be, it fell into disfavor and the strangest thing happened: there was a mass exodus to the north side of the room and that became *the* place to be— K-T on a branch of "Crystal's" fuchsia, Crystal on "Red's" petiole, and poor little Red on a bare "tree" branch right near them, but all within two cubic feet of one another. When the leaf, with its petiole, fell from the *Pachystachys*, Crystal lost her chosen sleeping spot. The next night she slept, somewhat awkwardly, on the little stump that remained, but thereafter she chose a place on the "tree" about four inches away from Red, and that's where they slept until their new spring behavior. Why did they (the girls more so than K-T) constantly gravitate toward one another? Once they had adopted that new area and stayed there for more than a week, I seized the opportunity to remove their beloved lantana—they no longer used it anyway—and replaced it with a second, large honeysuckle vine. It had flowers, great places to sit—or sleep— and some juicy little aphids for them to gobble up.

THE SUN AND OTHER WARM PLACES—K-T had pretty much worked out a routine—where he liked to go and what he liked to do—early in his stay. He reveled in warmth and it figured heavily in his daily activities. From the time the light turned on in the morning until the southern sun hit the plants on the west side of the room, he sat under the light and soaked in the heat it emitted. Once the sun entered the room, he followed its path across the sunroom from east to west, until its last rays streamed into the southwest corner. First he sat on a piece of wire on an *Angraecum* orchid. Then he moved westward to a piece of cork bark hosting a tillandsia. From there it was an *Aerides* root midway across the south windows, and finally he moved from one piece of cork bark to the next, island-hopping from one tillandsia to another, accompanying the sun.

Once the girls joined us, K-T had to share the sun. Crystal liked that aerides root and Red liked the russelia branch just behind it, and of course they all liked the lantana at the southeast corner. When the lantana was replaced with a honeysuckle, that became a favorite afternoon perching place and whenever one sat there, another would try to take it away. The south side of the room, but especially the southeast corner, was the area where everyone wanted to be, except on dismal days, when the light's warmth was the hot spot. Another favorite spot—and one that they often argued over—was a spent, horizontal branch low down on the honeysuckle near the light. Why

Tillandsias were the second most popular . . .
Pixie scatters pollen at T. aeranthos

Red visits a tillandsia

it was so appealing, I do not know, except that it provided a clear view of the feeder hanging behind the shelf, as well as the ones on the south —the popular ones. It was the same branch that K-T liked to use to dry off after a bath. It got good sun in the afternoon and a bit of the warmth from the light. How did the honey-

Cestrum elegans *bloomed for the entire length of their stay—Crystal*

Marmalade plant (Streptosolen jamesonii)
flowered for the entire winter—K-T

suckle branch become a favorite spot? In the beginning, when K-T was the only hummer flying around, the branch was never used. Early in Crystal's stay she used it as a sneaky way to approach a feeder or flowers on the south end of the room. Eventually when K-T realized that Crystal used it frequently, it became appealing to him. Once Red arrived and created a place for herself, it became desirable simply because the other two used it.

FAVORITE FLOWERS—The question I am asked most frequently is whether any of my little friends have returned, and the second is about the flowers that I grow for the them. Of course, any discussion of hummingbirds is bound to include or at least touch on their favorite flowers.

With a limited amount of space available for gardening indoors, I'm always on the lookout for new and better plants to grow for my little guests, searching for flowers more attractive to them or hummingbird plants with longer flowering seasons. So the stock would change as I replaced some with other, more desirable offerings. To have just feeders in the sunroom seems far too clinical and not conducive to well-being. Flowers are, therefore, the backbone of the sunroom and are the primary ingredient —in my opinion—in keeping the hummers "happy" and in touch with the outside world. But for the most part, with multiple hummingbirds, they didn't participate as much in the leisurely enjoyment of flowers. The feeders were the most reliable and abundant source of nectar in the sunroom and with competitors to think about, the feeder became the most coveted and protected food source. This behavior was especially noticeable in late winter and early spring. There were some flowers, however, that stood right out for their ability to take precedence over feeders. First and foremost were the aloes, those honey-dripping tubes that hummers find absolutely irresistable. Second were tillandsias. They have consistently been extremely popular. They take up very little space and are very attractive and quite easy to care for. And the hummers love them, inside *or* out.

Now that it appears that I may be hosting hummingbirds every winter, flowers for that period are a big plus. *Cestrum elegans* and marmalade plant (*Streptostolen jamesonii*) have a long flowering period over the entire winter and into spring. Both are very attractive to hummers. The cestrum has proved to be a great winter flowering plant. Blooming began in late fall and continued for the entire time the birds were here, so it provided a constant source of nectar to them, as did tree tobacco (*Nicotiana glauca*)— almost eight months of bloom on a real top hummingbird attractor. Pentas has restrained growth with constant flowers attractive to hummingbirds, and Cape honeysuckle (*Tecomaria capensis*), sporadic for the entire season, is highly desirable.

Some flowers are tried and true and are always very popular with the hummers—*Mimulus cardinalis*, honeysuckle (*Lonicera sempervirens* is the one that I grow and is great under the new lights), tillandsias, *Bouvardia ternifolia*,

Pentas has
restrained
growth
with
constant
flowers
—Pixie

Teco-
maria
capensis
is highly
desirable
—K-T

Always
popular is
Mimulus
cardinalis
—Red

Bouvardia
ternifolia
—*Crystal*

*Ribes
is a rufous
favorite—
Pixie*

*Crystal
with ribes*

calliandra, penstemon, ribes, arctostaphylos, shrimp plant (*Beloperone guttata*), and columbine (*Aquilegia* spp.), as well as members of the acanthus and mint families. Columbine has continued to a big favorite except that the very beautiful, blue Rocky Mountain columbine (*A. caerulea*) had much less appeal. This, I believe, is because except when they are just opening, the flowers are upright rather than reflexed, and access to the nectar is from above rather than below. Fuchsias continued to be popular, but less so indoors than out.

New to the sunroom this year were the citrus trees (lemon and grapefruit). Citrus, of course, would offer abundant winter flowers and cover for the birds—although their use of these two for that purpose was limited—and delightful fragrance for *my* pleasure. Another new plant that proved very attractive to the birds was *Mimulus lewisii*. This plant is a bit more difficult, needing constant moisture but with good drainage. It was worth the effort—the flowers are a beautiful rose-colored version of *Mimulus cardinalis*—and they loved it!

There have been several new plants to grace the sunroom over the last couple of years that have passed the "hummingbird test." Bolivian sunset (*Gloxinia sylvatica*); Coromandels (*Asystasia gangetica*); *Clerodendrum splendens;* blueberry (*Vaccinum* spp.), with bunches and bunches of manzanita-type flowers (this is not a "house plant" and must be moved to the garden); *Justicia spicigera;* and *Anisacanthus wrightii*, which has been grown here for many years, primarily for its summer flowers. Now, instead of cutting it back, I've let it grow for some earlier flowers for the winter hummers. Once daylight increased in late winter, buds began to form. This plant may be light sensitive as I've had winter flowers only in years when I had "long" winter days via artificial lighting. Coral fountain plant (*Russelia equisetiformis*) is another favorite with a long flowering season. With the new lights, this sun lover now blooms in winter as well as summer.

I can't say enough about aloes. The hummers loved the spikes of its dense, hanging, tubular flowers, and it was a contest each morning to see who would get to them first during their winter blooming period. They'd hover from one to another, drink nectar, sit on the leaves or spikes, and even revisit flowers that apparently hadn't been drained during the first visit. The aloes were the first flowers to be visited in the morning, frequently even before visits to a feeder, and were probably the most favored of all that had bloomed while the birds were here. When K-T got them first, the girls respectfully left him alone, but when one of the others was first to visit an aloe and K-T decided that *he* wanted it, he'd chase her away. These flowers are so full of nectar that if they were not drained by one of the birds on a regular basis, the nectar would drip out on its own.

I was very surprised at the hummers' reaction to two orchids. *Dendrobium victoriae-reginae*, a cool grower from Luzon with blue, smallish flowers and a typical nectar-filled

Mints are very popular—K-T

Salvia chiapensis,
another mint—K-T

The up-facing Rocky Mountain columbine
had less appeal—Red

Fuchsia continued to be popular—Red

Less popular inside than out—K-T

The beautiful rose-colored Mimulus lewisii—*Red*

New to the sunroom was Clerodendrum splendens—*Crystal*

spur, was extremely popular with K-T and both girls, and
they visited the flowers very frequently. This was the first
of only a handful of flowers that the birds visited together.
Trichopilia suavis, a very lovely and fragrant species orchid
with a large, beautiful, frilly lip, was the second orchid that
gained favor with the hummers. Crystal paid no attention
to it, but K-T and Red liked it so much they wouldn't stay
away from it. It bloomed while both Rosie and Pixie were
here, but they never even inspected it once. On the other
hand, Red and K-T would even visit these flowers together,
drinking nectar only inches apart—without any arguments.
After the birds were released in spring, the orchid remained
indoors until the weather became much warmer. One day I
took it to the kitchen sink and watered it. When I put it
back on the hook and removed my hand, I found a rufous
primary stuck to my finger—a P.S. from Red.

Tiny Tyrants

While K-T and the Little Angel were confined to side-by-
side baskets, they paid little attention to one another.
Once K-T graduated, however, he became much more
interested in his "brother." But when the girls arrived, he
lost most of that interest and concentrated instead on the
ones that could fly.

Right from the start K-T felt that the whole sunroom
was his, at least the southern part since he had relinquished the northern half to Crystal. The girls more or less
accepted that, and held their own floating territories—

wherever they happened to be at the time, a perch, a feeder, a flowering plant, the lemon tree, or even bathing water. In other words, K-T protected everything, whereas the girls protected just what they were using. Later that behavior would become evident in another unusual way. And K-T was smart about defending his territory. For instance, he would sit and face away from the girls and listen for the hum of their wings, or fly right around my head, hovering behind me out of sight for a second or two, just waiting for the right time to launch an ambush attack. He'd get so close to me that I could feel the vibration of his wings in my ear.

Eventually K-T accepted their presence on the south side of the room and no longer behaved that way. He saved his energy by only chasing them away from anything *he* liked on that side. In other words, it was okay for them to sit there and use a feeder, but that was all. Once K-T had established dominance in the sunroom, he slacked off a tad but was always boss. After all, he was here first and this was his territory—as was everything in it, including me. We've all come to the conclusion that when K-T collided with that window at the bank, he must have been chasing his own reflection.

The things they did to show how mean and ferocious they can be bordered on the comic. When K-T would feel ornery, he'd approach one thing after another—whether it was one of the girls, the window, or a leaf—with his tail fanned as widely as possible, and hover in front of the

Blueberry has manzanita-type flowers . . . Pixie hangs to reach flowers

object of his aggression. They competed with one another for everything and chased one another constantly—that's an integral part of being a hummingbird. It might start with

Anisacanthus wrightii—*Red*

Aloes were the first flowers to be visited each morning—K-T

one chasing another, but then wind up with the chaser becoming the chased. Most often it seemed to be done for no reason at all except, I suppose, that it's S.O.P. for a

Coral fountain plant (Russelia equisetiformis)—*Pixie*

They'd sit on the spikes—Red

hummingbird. K-T was the aggressor most often. When a rufous was the aggressor, it was usually against the other rufous. Either way, when the third hummer would see a chase, it would feel the need to participate, except when Crystal was the third bird. She was the most laid back of the three, and she initiated the chase much less often than the other two. And of the three, she was the most likely to sit and watch without participating—or at best, restrict her involvement to vocalization only. Crystal was not without belligerence, she was just the most docile of the three. Whichever of the birds was doing something, that one was at a disadvantage and subject to being chased.

When K-T would see one of the girls feeding at flowers, he'd replace her—just charge in and drink from the flower or feeder as though she weren't there. At times the sunroom was so busy that K-T didn't seem to know whom to watch.

Two feeders on the south side of the sunroom were the favorites and alternated at being the most popular. Every once in a while K-T and Crystal would not let Red use either of them and would even make it difficult for her to use the others. If she approached the feeder closest to the light, Crystal would warn her with a loud *tzeeept*, whereupon Red would turn and leave without using it. K-T would emit a somewhat similar screech to stop her from using the feeder next to the lemon tree. If their warnings weren't effective, a chase would ensue. Once a chase started, the third hummer would invariably join in. No one ever minded his or her own business!

Red, too, had her aggressive moods—quite a few of them, actually—and the longer she was here, the more numerous they became. Occasionally she would chase K-T, but most often it was Crystal. Perhaps the primary concern for a rufous is to dominate a member of its own species or gender. I can't believe that either rufous would accept an inferior status just because K-T was here first and had established the sunroom as his territory. Perhaps it was because K-T was a male and so bossy. Whatever the reason, the girls deferred to K-T more often than not. I found that they were most tolerant of one another when there were more feeders in the room. But, ironically, feeders were just as frequently the source of an argument.

Everyone knows how bossy hummingbirds can be, how one can take over a garden. In fact, they can be and often are downright mean. Does that meanness really relate to food availability? Probably to some degree and at certain times, but it seems that for the hummingbird, being mean is, plainly and simply, just sheer fun.

As we know, K-T "owned" everything. It was comical to watch him keep Crystal away from the waterfall while trying to simultaneously keep Red away from the aloes. He was the most horrible when it came to the other hummingbirds. But likewise, he was the sweetest and most trusting when it came to me—perhaps because I handled him so much in the beginning. He always wanted to be close to or touch me—with his tongue while I worked at the basket, by sticking his beak in the creases between my

K-T replaced Crystal at a tillandsia

finger joints, by hovering in front of me and staring into my eyes. He constantly interacted with me or used me to hide behind and attack the others from ambush. K-T

K-T replaced Red at a columbine

When one was in the water, the other would attempt to annoy her

always made me feel that I was a definite part of his world. But how could anything so tiny, so beautiful, and so sweet be so mean?

Nothing special about this vine but everyone wanted it

The rufous hummingbird has the reputation of being the most aggressive of all North American hummers so, when Crystal arrived I was surprised that, irrespective of that reputation, K-T was such a little terror and bossed her around so—or rather, I was surprised that Crystal allowed K-T to get away with it. But I was flabbergasted when Red arrived and K-T continued the barrage of terror, now over both of them. I went through elaborate preparations to assure that each could hide from the others by placing trees in strategic places between feeders, yet all three birds spent more time than not sitting in the same cubic foot of air space with either one or both other birds. Did my little guests like one another after all?

While I never witnessed an act of violent physical aggression, there were plenty of threats and occasionally relentless chases. At times the birds were so loud, chattering and screeching as they chased one another around the sunroom, that I could hear them from my kitchen. Yet I can remember only one occasion when they really were angry. The "argument" was between Crystal and K-T, and it was over the feeder hanging from the back of the plant shelf—the one that had been placed there for Crystal's convenience. Apparently they had both decided to use it at the same time. They fanned their tails and flew here and there in unison, beaks perhaps one-quarter to one-half inch apart, for three or four minutes. After that Crystal sat and emitted one *chip* after another for about five minutes—every once in a while, the string of *chip*s became a chatter. Since Crystal was being so vocal and was sitting about six to eight inches away from the feeder, I presumed she had been victorious this time and was warning K-T to stay away. But when I looked up, K-T was at the feeder. They argued off and on for the rest of that afternoon—Valentine's Day, February 14! That was the one altercation in which Red did not get involved. Perhaps because they were serious, perhaps because Red was the quietest one in the afternoon anyway.

THE GRASS ALWAYS LOOKS GREENER—My little guests seemed to live by the saying, "the grass always looks greener . . ." and if they could have spoken one sentence, I'm sure that sentence would have been, "I want what you have."

There were six feeders in the sunroom for the three active birds, but invariably all three would want to use the same one, whichever one that happened to be at the moment. Likewise, there were three bathing places—counting K-T's gardenia—but both Crystal and Red would want to use the old waterfall—at the same time, of course. And when one was in the water, the other would attempt to annoy her into leaving. When K-T would see me lift Peeper and the feeder out of the basket, he would sail right over for his share. All this because, to a hummingbird, the grass always looks greener.

The desire to have what another uses can run from a favorite feeder to a small branch—for instance, the low, semicircular passionflower vine branch. Nothing special about that branch at all. It offered neither vantage point

Crystal's favorite honeysuckle branch

nor spectacular view of the sunroom or outdoors, yet each took a turn claiming that branch as though to convey superiority to the others. Red had used it in the beginning, but it was usurped by K-T. Eventually, when K-T commandeered another sitting place, Red took it back. Then when Crystal began feeling her oats, she took it away from Red. Each one was constantly tempted and motivated by what the others did or had.

The instant K-T passed Crystal on his way to a feeder, Crystal would emit a *tzeept*, followed by a number of *tchu-tchu-tchu-tchu-tchu* vocalizations. After all, Crystal was sitting on the horizontal honeysuckle branch that they frequently commandeered from one another. But K-T was oblivious and went instead to that dried-up piece of passionflower vine, that naked, curved branch at about mid-height—the place where Red had just been sitting. He took that over instead! Then a few minutes later, he sat on Crystal's favorite honeysuckle branch, as if sitting on these favorite spots obliterated the others' existence. Everything always looks so good when someone else is using it because for a hummingbird, the grass always looks greener.

There was no territory per se, it floated with the birds, except that K-T felt that he owned everything. With nothing clearly defined, their attitudes regarding territory may be summed up in one or two sentences. At times, it was, "This is my spot, you go away," or, "I want your spot; go away." They all, however, like the warmth of the light and worked out a nifty arrangement. To start with, the best spot—the horizontal branch under the center—was K-T's. Occasionally Red would take it, but she was usually replaced by K-T. To "replace" her, K-T basically acted as though no one was on the branch and just sat. Crystal took the mostly vertical twig right behind and above K-T, and, when she couldn't have K-T's, Red took the one closest to the light. Crystal was the most skittish of the three, and at times the thumping of her little heart could be seen when she sat under the light with the others.

BIRDS OF A FEATHER . . .

The Yucatán Peninsula to the Louisiana-Mississippi area is one of the major migratory routes taken by a staggering number of birds passing each spring from the Neotropics to North America—millions of them, some traveling in pairs, some in flocks, and some alone, including ruby-throated hummingbirds. Imagine being on a boat or ship on a body of water so vast that nothing but the sea is visible for miles around. Then, in the middle of this veritable "nothingness," a bird as small as a thumb flies out from nowhere and passes you by. A ship's captain told me of having seen rubythroats migrate across the Gulf of Mexico while he was en route from the Yucatán to Texas. One solitary migrant passed the ship, itself moving at about sixteen knots, in a northeasterly direction from the Yucatán on a course that would have it arrive at a destination somewhere between Mississippi and western Florida, if the bird were to continue in its direction. Quite a journey for such a tiny mite. Since the bird was moving along at a different rate of speed from the boat, it was difficult to determine exactly how fast it was traveling, but the captain reported that it was flying approximately fifty feet above the water.

That picture pretty much typifies the life of the hummingbird. They are notorious loners. Promiscuity is the rule. They form pairs strictly for the purpose of mating; incubating, brooding, and raising of chicks are all done exclusively by the female. Any interaction with other hummingbirds seems to be of a combative nature. When nesting season is over and migration begins, the birds—adult and immature alike—usually go it alone. In the interest of total accuracy, however, I must say that I have

watched many immature rubythroats leave on their migration, and it appears that going it alone is not absolutely
etched in stone. Occasionally juveniles migrate together,
or at least start out that way—a behavior that appears
more common in birds born later in the season. That may
also be true for rufous hummingbirds, and may account for
two birds appearing together out of the normal range,
which has been the case on many occasions. Immediately
coming to mind is the pair that appeared at Wave Hill in
Riverdale the year that Rosie visited me.

Some birds have such intricate relationships with one
another, but hummingbirds, with an energy-demanding
lifestyle, are so different. They are solitary little critters,
but is that always the case? That lifestyle, while convenient, may not be all that it is cracked up to be for a hummingbird. Maybe they *do* like one another. Maybe they *are*
kindred spirits. Keeping more than one bird together for
the winter has given me the opportunity to make some
observations regarding relationships between them, a
somewhat different aspect of their personalities. In spite of
the hummingbird's legendary "loneness," my birds gravi-
tated toward one another constantly, particularly Crystal
and Red. In the beginning it was obvious that they wanted
to sit near one another, but the rule of thumb for amicable
communal perching, at least when K-T was involved, was,
"we just won't look at one another at the same time." That
restriction was dropped as they became more relaxed in
one another's presence.

The two girls spent much time together

The three frequently sat in the same cubic foot of air space. More often than not, however, it was two of three, and the two most often to be together were the two rufous hummingbirds. I'm not sure if that was because they are the same gender and/or species, or whether it was just an individual thing. Perhaps they are, after all, kindred spirits. I'd guess that more than 75 percent of their down time—that is, time not at flowers, feeders, or a bath—was spent less than one foot away from the other.

The girls' behavior toward one another—their interaction—made me really stop and wonder. They stayed in the same vicinity as one another, dried off together after their baths, slept within inches of one another, occasionally visited flowers on the same plant at the same time, and frequently just sat around near one another. True, these birds were not living under natural conditions, but certainly the opportunity was there for them to stay away from one another, if they wanted to.

They didn't indulge in customary social behavior such as mutual preening, but they rather seemed to enjoy one another's company. It went beyond just wanting what the other one had. And they kept in touch. If the girls chattered or otherwise "talked" to one another, K-T had to get involved and chatter too—even when he was a distance away and unsure of what was going on.

One event convinced me that while they may be scrappy little sprites in their everyday dealings with one another, there's something between hummingbirds that transcends that feisty, ornery belligerence. Fear can produce the most unlikely of allies or the most unlikely of sleepmates. In late April, during a severe wind and thunderstorm, Crystal and Red proved that. As the storm cell approached, the room grew darker by the second and Crystal moved to the tree and sat there quietly. Within minutes, the rain started, the room became darker still and the wind picked up, causing the branches to sway vigorously on the spruce tree just outside the southeast corner of the sunroom. Red, deciding that it was time to lay low, also moved to the tree. However, instead of settling down on a branch a couple of inches from Crystal, as they had done when they slept there, she sought out the safety and

*Crystal and Red sought out the safety
and company of each other during a thunderstorm*

company of her "sister," and settled down as close as she
was able to get. I doubt whether a piece of paper could
have been slipped between them. Crystal didn't object—
she was frozen in position, waiting out the storm. That's
where they wanted to be. They stayed there, snuggled
together like two peas in a pod. When the storm cell
passed and the sky brightened, Red left to visit a feeder
and it was business as usual again.

And they copied from one another. For instance, there
was one lonely flower on the *Kalanchoe uniflora*—the first to
open, about two weeks earlier than the others. For the first
ten days or so, no one went near it. I even brought it over
to K-T in an attempt to rouse his interest, as he was fre-

quently the leader in trying new things. I tried it with the girls as well. No dice; they just weren't interested. Then, one day I noticed K-T draining some nectar—he had finally "discovered" it. Within minutes, Crystal visited the flower and then Red. I watched for the next ten or fifteen minutes as K-T and the girls took turns, like little ants going back and forth, first one then the other, until it apparently was empty. Surely they didn't all "discover" that flower. It's much more likely that they kept an eye on one another and then copied. In fact, each would constantly watch what the others were doing.

On several occasions I witnessed what I consider to be unusual behavior between Crystal and Red. While Red would be sitting, Crystal would fly over and hover just above and away from her with tail fanned in braking position and then touch beaks with her and fly off. She lowered herself slowly and gently to do this; it was not the usual dart and attack. Her action, which reminded me of a feeding action, appeared to be quite deliberate and not aggressive. Red seemed to sense that as well; hers was not a normal defense response, either. I've seen them do it a number of times, but I don't have a clue about what it means.

K-T and Little Peeper went back a long way together, starting out side by side in baskets, but he showed much more interest in Peep before Crystal and Red arrived. Of course, that didn't stop him from being interested in Peeper's feeder. Whenever K-T would see me hand-feeding

Peeper, K-T wanted some too. He would even lower himself almost all the way into the basket to get some.

K-T would come over for a drink from Peeper's feeder and then turn around, holler at everyone else with his chatter, come back, turn around, and scold some more. When I would bring Peep over to drink nectar from the flowers, K-T would immediately sail over to watch, but he never indicated that he wanted to chase him or otherwise behave aggressively toward him. Crystal watched Peeper a lot as well. Whenever I would sit on the loveseat and hold Peeper, I would notice Crystal sitting just a few feet away, watching. I've also seen her looking in the basket for him while I would be holding him out of her view. She was very interested and would watch intently. Red was totally oblivious to him, but Crystal knew there was a hummingbird involved. I don't think she knew just what to make of the situation, but she knew something.

When Peeper would cling to my shirt, Crystal would cock her head and look. While she may have even been slightly apprehensive, nosy K-T would come right over to see what was going on.

K-T frequently circled my head slowly while I sat on the loveseat tending to the Little Angel. Occasionally he would even lower himself to within inches of the bird to get a better look. Somehow, though, no one seemed to consider him a threat and that's probably because he didn't fly around with them.

Crystal was very interested in all that I did with Peeper and watched so intensely when I fed him that I held the feeder with an outstretched arm and offered Crystal some food too. When I stretched my arm in Crystal's direction, K-T got in front of the feeder and turned toward Crystal, chased her, and then came back to use the feeder himself.

K-T would come right over, beak-to-beak, to use the feeder when I was giving some nectar to Peeper. Then he'd hover about two inches away from the hand that was holding Peeper and just look. Often he would come even closer than that and inspect little snags of my cuticles—all the while spying on the bird in my hand. One day he attempted to put his beak in the feeder tube while Peeper was making use of it. Was he jealous?

Hummingbirds may be essentially solitary critters, but even with the constant chasing and occasional mean behavior, I really feel that having more than one made for a healthier, more natural, and—yes, happier—atmosphere, with no boredom.

PLACES TO GO, THINGS TO DO

One of my new and wonderful friends is Miriam Jenkins of Houston. A couple of years back Miriam had a pair of rufous hummingbirds winter in her garden. Sunny, the male, came and went so Miriam didn't see him on a regular basis, but the female, Sparkle, who favored her crape myrtle and loquat tree, was there practically all the time. Sunny migrated northward early in March, a couple of weeks earlier than Sparkle. March 28 was the last Miriam saw of Sparkle. March is the month that I always hear mentioned from other hummingbird fans from the south. It seems to be the preferred month for initiation of migration in birds that winter in the southern states.

Based upon what they've done here, the birds are quite a bit more tolerant of one another in the nonbreeding season and may even seek out one another's presence. But once the breeding season begins, all that changes. I would consider breeding season to begin once hormonal changes start on the wintering ground. And once those changes began, the camaraderie or tolerance that my hummers had exhibited flew out the window. Therefore it was no surprise that a whirlwind of changes, both physical and behavioral, began in March.

A FLURRY OF FEATHERS

There was some feather replacement activity on the throat of all the birds over the winter, but other than the throat, and contrary to what my earlier guests had done, there was a molting drought for the winter season. Once spring rolled around, however, that changed dramatically.

Feathers were everywhere, but it was easy for me to separate and identify the fallen ones. The color of K-T's primaries was a deeper, grayer, brown—a taupe—than that of either rufous, and the rubythroat's outer primaries are somewhat club-shaped and wider at the tip in relation to that of the rufous. Contour feathers for the rubythroat are a deeper green than rufous feathers (which are more to the yellow side of green), and of course, there is never any rufous at the bases or edges of rubythroat contour feathers. Tail feathers would have been the easiest to separate with different color, shape, and pattern for each of the two species.

Separating Crystal's from Red's feathers might be a bit more difficult, but there would be ways to do that, too. Again, the tail would be simple; the shape and pattern were different from each other. For the rest of the feathers, the birds mostly dropped them right where they sat. Additionally, Crystal's coloring was deeper and richer overall than Red's, who looked like a speckled bird with all her shades of green. It would have been a bit difficult but quite possible had Crystal molted at the same time as Red, but since she did not, that challenge never arose.

The only difference in the conditions of captivity for this year's birds, other than the number of birds being kept together, was lighting. When artificial lighting provided "long" days, as it had always done in the past, molting was early, but when winter consisted of "short" days that lengthened naturally with the sun, molting occurred much later and was basically concurrent with and of similar chronology for all three birds.

Word has it that the rubythroat often does not molt its wing feathers in captivity. Squeak hadn't, but his were as perfect the day he left as the day he got here, so it really didn't matter. Crystal's and Red's were in decent condition, so it didn't matter that much for them, either. But K-T's wing feathers had become extremely raggy—wear and tear, I'm sure, from being such an aggressive little bully and chasing the girls around all the time. Feathers can become so worn that a bird may be unable to fly. This was a concern and a factor to be considered with respect to the release of K-T. I wished he would molt those worn wing feathers—in the conventional manner, of course, one pair at a time in succession. Finally, by the end of March, K-T began molting his well-worn primaries. But instead of molting each pair in succession, from the inside out to the leading edge of the wing, as hummingbirds commonly do, K-T lost Primaries 4 through 7 on each side—a whopping eight of his wing feathers gone at one time!* That slowed him down a tad. Then, when those eight primaries were only partially grown in, K-T lost the next succeeding pair.

By early April, Primary 10 was gone, Primary 8 was partly grown in, Primaries 4 to 7 were almost grown in, and his other major primary, No. 9, was so raggy that it was practically useless. But that's not all. The four central tail feathers had come out as well, two of which were just starting to be replaced. I supposed that might impede his braking ability, although in mid-May of this year an extremely plump female arrived in the garden with no tail feathers at all, and she seemed to be totally unaffected by it. With half of his primaries either growing in or missing entirely, K-T's abilities were diminished and he had some difficulty achieving altitude and kept himself less active. Yet he *had* to participate somewhat, so he'd chatter a chorus of *tchews* when the girls chased one another and passed

*Primary feathers are numbered 1 to 10, starting at the inside—closest to the body—and working outward to the leading edge of the wing. There are ten tail feathers (rectrices), or five pairs. The pairs are numbered from the center outward, the middle pair being the first and the outermost, the fifth.

over him. K-T was no longer able to maneuver with the same agility and at times had all he could do to elevate himself to a perch. Indeed, on several occasions he had to make a large circle around the room to gradually gain altitude (similar to an airplane versus a helicopter) and I had to keep an eye on him constantly. When he couldn't achieve the speed necessary to elevate himself, he would land on something low and start again. At a time when he would need more protein, K-T became less active and took in less. Because he seemed to be compressing the molt of his flight feathers into a very short period, I thought it best to add the fish food protein to his diet as well.

K-T had started with the others so many times, and turnabout *is* fair play, but since he was at such a disadvantage, I often would stand guard so he could drink in peace.

All winter long K-T kept a snowy white throat. In fact, when I looked up at him while he sat on the chain, he reminded me of a tree swallow, such clean, white underparts and so streamlined from shoulder to tail. By early spring there still were no signs of growing up from K-T. He was a typical male hummingbird bully all right, but there was no "buzzing," as Squeak had done when he began to reach sexual maturity, nor any other masculine behavior or physical characteristics.

With the exception of her tail, Rosie went through a pretty extensive molt, adding to her throat patch and replacing her wing and many contour feathers variously over her body. When Pixie came, she had, within just a few days before her capture, acquired four iridescent red feathers on her throat in the shape of a diamond. By month's end, she had acquired many more red feathers in that area, and through February, molted her wing feathers through and including the seventh primary—and that was it; the outer three were never molted. They were a different color, lighter—evidence of wear, and a different length, evidence of the disparity in wing length measurements between adult and immature birds. At the time I considered that the molt may have been curtailed by being in captivity. But this suspension of or failure to molt the outermost primaries may be a common occurrence not relating in any way to captivity. Three of the four to have stayed here displayed some form of interference in the molt of the wings. Even Crystal, an adult probably in her second year, had both adult and immature primaries when she arrived in November. This appears to be evidence that for her first molt, she *also* stopped at the outer three while in the wild (unless, of course, she had lived in captivity somewhere else).

Somewhere along her way, Red had molted Primaries 1 through 7 before December. Geoff Dennis told me that she had some either missing or in growth while she was in Rhode Island. But when she got here, either feather replacement came to a halt or it had already stopped naturally to be resumed at another time. The molt of her primaries resumed by early spring, and by April 8, Primary 10 was missing—which made her wings appear so very tiny.

Feather replacement—Red

When the molt of the primaries was close to completion, she molted variously and extensively over her body, including her back and head. So many feathers were replaced that her little gray head looked like a little pincushion with feather sheaths sticking out all around. When she scratched, sheaths scattered and dropped and a powdery white "dust" filled the air around her head and fell like dandruff —we'll call that *angel dust.*

One of Red's middle rectrices was worn to a frazzle

After the feathers of her crown were replaced, the new ones were dull for days afterward. Fresh feathers on Red's rump showed characteristic rufous edgings.

A leopard may not be able to change its spots but can a hummer? Red appeared to change hers almost daily while she was molting on her throat. The pattern of her throat patch appeared to change—one day white was visible where red had been the day before, and vice versa for another day. In one or two places where there had been red, white feathers grew, but the red area expanded elsewhere. One day she seemed to have a solid patch, another day a Fu Manchu type, with white cutting up the center. But in the end, her throat patch changed little from the December explosion to the spring molt. She had only a few masculine type iridescent red feathers on the throat in December, but the number had increased early on and then remained the same until her complete-body, spring molt. Although her iridescent throat patch changed little, she acquired a necklace of bronzy-green spots on the lower throat.

Red would have done quite well with a new tail. One of her middle tail feathers was worn to a frazzle. It showed extreme wear and tear right from the start and by April, little more than the shaft remained. But that was not to be, at least not while she was here.

Crystal molted a little on the throat in December, with no change to her small, existing throat patch. Nothing until her uppertail coverts in March. Once Crystal lost her

The amount of primary growth in a 24-hour period—Red

The amount of primary growth in a 24-hour period—Crystal

uppertail coverts, her middle tail feathers were held slightly parted as she sat—Pixie had also done that and it made her tail appear as though a molt was imminent, but it never started. Crystal commenced an extensive molt late in April, a little later than Red, and very late in the season. When she did start, it was fast and furious with simultaneous head, body, and wing molt—very similar to Red but a bit more compressed.

One thing that I observed when Rosie was here was that she vibrated her tail. It was not something that she had always done—as a matter of fact, it didn't start until after she completed her molt. Since it came right on the heels of her body and wing molt, I remember attributing it to an attempt to dislodge tail feathers and complete the replacement of all her feathers. I have also observed this tail-vibrating behavior in both Crystal and Red. But the odd thing is, all did this in late winter and all started roughly the same time, so for Crystal and Red, it was *prior* to the wing molt. For Crystal, the behavior was often accompanied by sharp, high-pitched vocalizations—*chip-chip-chip*, vibrate, spin around, repeat. This behavior may relate to migration, breeding, or establishing a nesting territory. It has to have some significant meaning, and if anybody out there knows, I wish he or she would tell me.

When I took photos of Red two days in a row, I discovered that her primaries had grown in about one-quarter of the total length in a twenty-four-hour period. I later duplicated that finding when Crystal was molting her primaries.

Photos taken at the same interval revealed a similar rate of replacement for a primary.

Logic tells me that it would be *most* desirable to have the freshest feathers while on territory—after all, for the male, the gorget is likely his most potent symbol of masculinity and is used as a visible badge in his territorial defense or display to a female. It is the last area to molt. For the female, the tail may be her most attractive or potent physical defense attribute. Accordingly, it seems reasonable to expect those feathers to be replaced last; in fact, it is customary for hummingbirds to start tail feather replacement when the wing molt is nearly concluded. But not even one of the females to have spent the winter here has replaced her tail feathers. Even though we're talking about only four birds, that number represents 100 percent, and while four isn't enough to make any generalizations about the molting pattern, it is enough to ask the question: just when does the female rufous molt her tail?

For solitary critters such as hummingbirds, design of the molting process would have to favor continuity of their lifestyle. Carried out, it seems pretty obvious that the molt of K-T's wings could not have been of normal design. K-T also had not acquired any iridescent gorget feathers during the winter, as would be expected from an immature male. He waited instead until spring, long after other molting had begun. As always, I questioned why and wondered if it had anything to do with his accident. Could the damage to his head or the swelling thereafter have affected the glands

The hummers received gifts of fruit flies—K-T and a fruit fly

involved in giving the signals or secreting the hormones relating to feather replacement? If so, would it—could it—happen again next spring? I always have so many more questions than answers and more concerns than solutions.

NEW SPRING BEHAVIOR

ON SAFARI—Insects play a very important role in a hummingbird's life. While sugars in the nectar they drink keep their energetic little bodies on the go, the source of all the substantive properties without which they cannot live is protein. The hummingbird's primary source of protein is insects.

Conditions in the sunroom were more natural than ever

Crystal was an opportunist, snapping up whiteflies that flew by

before. First, the integrity of the photoperiod had not been compromised and a natural autumnal decrease and spring lengthening of days had occurred. Second, the level of activity came closer than ever before to duplicating what would be found on the traditional wintering ground than when a bird is kept alone over winter. Common sense tells me that active birds will eat more as a result of the extra activity. Of what they eat, the sugars are converted to quick energy, but they are also constantly taking in more protein with each sip that isn't burned off immediately. And so, with their protein needs more than adequately met through the NektarPlus, they were a bit lazy about hunting—or more picky.

The hummers received two gifts during their stay here; ironically, both were quite similar. First, my friends Jim and Brian brought them a large jar of fruit flies that they had started. Then later, Geoff Dennis sent a "grow-your-own" fruit fly kit. Great little gifts to give hummingbirds. But the fruit flies were rarely taken. All three preferred whiteflies and spiders—those were the favorites all winter long. A plus for lantana is that it never seems to be without whiteflies.

Even so, the birds didn't seem to exert much effort to catch anything. K-T seemed to like swarms. He would watch snow as though the flakes were a swarm of gnats and then inch his way around in front of the window, waiting for one to get close enough to grab it. One day I watched him sitting with his mouth open, trying to catch a whitefly as it passed by. But then, almost with a "what the heck" afterthought, he chased it and caught it. After that little hors d'oeuvre, he began moving around among the leaves to flush more of them out. He knew what brushing against the leaves would accomplish; he obviously planned this deliberate action—he wanted a swarm.

Crystal loved whiteflies, and while she would go after something that caught her eye, she was basically an opportunist and was most likely to sit on a branch and wait for something inviting to go by and then snap it up. She enjoyed sitting on that little dried-up lateral honeysuckle branch, and without exerting too much effort, would snatch whiteflies as they flitted around her. I rarely observed Red hunt—in fact, I hardly observed it at all until she began her molt and then she became a very active hunter. K-T was probably the most aggressive hunter and the only one, prior to the molting period, to go on safari, looking for insects. Red took the least amount of insects, making only occasional forays, but that would change.

I remember how active a hunter Rosie had been, patroling every inch of the sunroom in search of live food. Her insect consumption increased dramatically at the beginning of the year, and I suspected that there might be a physiological need for insects during molt or other pre-migratory hormonal changes. Now I am firmly convinced that protein is more important to them at certain times during the year than others and that increased insect intake is not the result of a lack of floral nectars during, say, the wet season, but a definite requirement when they undergo certain physical changes.

Once the birds began their molt, their attitude toward protein changed dramatically. Red, who waited to go through a major molt until early spring, also put off her hunting until then. But once her molt began, she suddenly became quite the explorer as she gathered nectar and hunted on safari, just as Rosie had. Quite the little hunter, she was all over—here and there, and everywhere—in search of insects. Blink an eye and she'd be in one place; blink an eye and she'd be somewhere else—on safari. She was obviously driven by an inner need. She had rarely hunted for her entire stay until she started her molt. She

would deliberately upset leaves and was very resourceful
with her tail. I watched on several occasions as she flicked
her lower body at some leaves to upset the whiteflies; that
same flick that might be used by someone closing a door
with his or her hip. She'd zip over, flick or snap her tail to
the side, catch a whitefly, do a little pirouette, zip back,
and catch another, flitting in and out, back and forth
almost as though she were doing a little dance—dancing
with whiteflies from dawn to dusk.

Red would watch as I replaced the lantana after having
stirred up and scattered the whiteflies in all directions for
her. Then, after seeing what I had been doing with the
plant, she decided to help herself. The lower half of her
body would move from one side to the other as she moved
up inch by inch. Her actions were intentional. She would
deliberately brush against leaves to stir up the whiteflies. I
remembered how Squeak would wait for me to do that for
him at the fuchsia and I marveled at Red's ability—and obvious forethought—to do that very same thing for herself.

Once, while K-T was sitting on the chain right above
an area where Red had been hunting, one of his feathers
floated down toward the floor, and Red darted over to
catch it. K-T just watched.

Crystal didn't go on safari until the very end, but when
she did and just as Red had done, she put her heart and soul
into it. Ironically, it coincided with the start of her molt.

Once they began to hunt energetically, the girls decided
that they liked fruit flies and would even go over to the

large opaque jar that held the fruit flies to capture them as they flew in and out. The girls were smart and treated the container as just another feeder as they flew back and forth to visit it each time they wanted some solid food. I had been wondering if I'd ever be able to get rid of all those fruit flies once the season ended, but once Red and Crystal went on safari, that concern was eliminated; anything that moved was fair game and they wiped me out.

PERSONALITY CHANGES—My foremost concern in keeping more than one hummingbird is fighting—one has only to watch them in the garden for ten or fifteen minutes to know how pugnacious they can be. I had to think of something to combat that tendency to meanness that they possess. My theory and method was to supply an over-abundance of food and, further, try to keep the feeders as much out of sight of one another as possible. Providing copious amounts of food would mean plenty for the bossi-est or most hoggish bird and ample left for the others. In taking clues from nature, birds should defend an area large enough to suit their needs only, anything beyond is a waste of energy. Even though hummingbirds don't always follow that rule, if the birds were to coexist in the sunroom peacefully for half a year, I'd have to provide plenty. Beside the generous amounts of food, a variety of flowers were offered, but it was the NektarPlus that ruled. For the most part, my method worked.

There were six feeders for the three active birds in the sunroom. Each afternoon I replaced all of them with fresh nectar in a second set of feeders. One day I had replaced five and taken the last one down on the south side of the room when the telephone rang. When I went back to finish the job, I noticed K-T, who was molting and not flying that well, chasing both Crystal and Red from one of the feeders on the south. The girls almost seemed to be working in tandem to get at the feeder he was protecting, each making an approach as K-T chased the other. In spite of his reduced flying ability, he managed to hold both of them off. Every once in a while one of them would use one of the three on the north side, but for the most part they were as determined to drink from one particular feeder on the south, as K-T was to keep them away. There was something else I noticed. When the missing feeder was replaced, Red became extremely mean, particularly toward Crystal. I might have just made a mental note of that and let it go except that the very same thing happened a second time—telephone call and same feeder—and then when it was replaced, Red became very mean toward Crystal again. On both occasions, her meanness lasted for the rest of the day and the next day, too.

The springtime change in personality was noticed first in Red. She became vicious toward Crystal, chasing her relentlessly. That mean behavior, while directed primarily at Crystal, was not confined to her totally. Although she wasn't *as* mean to K-T, she chased him as well. True, K-T had been a horrible little bully all winter, but he was never truly mean. Red was.

When Red's personality changed, the camaraderie she had shared with Crystal disappeared and made unlikely allies of K-T and Crystal. Crystal would hide behind the new honeysuckle in the corner to get out of Red's line of sight so I hid a feeder behind some branches and leaves there, in a place where she could sit quietly and drink in peace. The idea was to keep her wings quiet so Red wouldn't hear her. Within hours, however, the other two had discovered the secreted feeder and began using it for themselves, too. Crystal managed to retain it as her territory for a few more days, until K-T decided that if Crystal wanted it that much, it must be good. That honeysuckle quickly became *the* place to sit—and he might just as well use that feeder, too.

Red gave K-T a hard time about bathing, and I had to stand guard, positioning myself between them, so K-T could bathe. When he couldn't get to the gardenia without being harassed by Red, he went to the waterfall and pecked a bit, but could never work up the nerve to plop down right in the stream of water as Crystal and Red had done.

I've often been amazed at the way a hummingbird can fly right on the heels of another, duplicating every twist and turn as though the two were part of a kite string—as if the bird in the rear had prior knowledge of the pattern. While K-T was at his worst and flying with just partial power, the girls—actually, Red most of the time—seized the opportunity to give him a little of his own medicine. I don't know if they were deliberately using his disadvantage against him or were just more aggressive closer to nesting time. At any rate, K-T was slower, with diminished lifting and probably braking abilities. Red could easily have caught him and flown rings around him at any time. Yet when she did chase him, she paced herself to stay just behind him, at a drastically reduced speed, here and there and around and around the room, identical twists, turns and undulations. So obviously it was chasing for its own sake that appealed to Red—she was doing it just for the heck of it!

For a while everyone picked on poor Crystal. Red was being mean all the while she was molting and K-T was, perhaps, taking clues from Red. K-T would go looking for Crystal. He'd hover and then move forward, inch by inch, chattering and trying to flush her out. Once she moved, he would chase her. Then for several days Red was very mean to Crystal—and K-T joined in. They didn't want her to use any of the feeders and chased her constantly to the chain behind the light. Of course, I had to set up additional feeders and try to hide a couple where she could sit and eat in peace, as I had on the honeysuckle branch. As long as they didn't hear her wings, they weren't incited and were less likely to detect her presence. When she finally had enough of their bossiness, she gave it back a bit, but for the most part she was intimidated by them. Red seemed able to detect the unique sound of her own species' wing oscillations or knew the difference between the sound of Crystal's and K-T's wings. And why did Red target Crystal all the time? Perhaps because she was also *the* rival in the sunroom.

Once Red became mean, Crystal no longer wanted to sleep near her—no more communal roosting. She moved back to the south side of the room to the bougainvillea branch where Red once slept. K-T had already broken away and was only loosely part of the group anyway. For a while they slept apart. That coincided with the molt of K-T and Red, insect increase, and normal nesting season. I thought they were following the dictates of nature, but eventually Red followed and they all were back on the south. Just as with their migration to the north, K-T started, to be followed by one girl and then the other. Eventually they split up again. K-T slept on the honeysuckle, Crystal on the bougainvillea, and Red still on the bare tree. Toward the end of their stay here, Red spent much time sitting on low branches of K-T's gardenia—and after having spent much time watching K-T do it, she too began to leaf bathe.

"Sugar and spice and everything nice, that's what little girls are made of"—except when the girls are hummingbirds. That bossy stuff was too good to last for K-T, as by mid-March and coinciding with a time of more naturally agressive behavior, the girls became more feisty, defiant, and belligerent with K-T and would sometimes gang up on him. Red would chase him from a feeder on the south side, and when he got to the other side of the room, Crystal would chase him away from a branch. Even when he'd come over to me to be fed, they'd follow right after him and chase him away from me. I could see changes in the

girls. They became more aggressive—with K-T. I don't
know if it was a result of natural hormonal changes or if
they had just had enough of K-T's bossiness and now realized that they could get away with it. Once they started to
pick on him, he expected me to feed him all the time, but
always wanted to be situated on the side away from
"them." Occasionally he would stop, turn around, fan his
tail, and chatter. Once in a while they'd come over while
he was drinking to call his bluff, but usually they waited
for him to be finished and then chased him.

When Red started her molt, she increased her insect
intake and became very aggressive, particularly toward
Crystal. When Crystal began her molt, she also acquired a
voracious appetite for insects and became equally as
aggressive toward Red, in spite of the fact that she was
generally a more docile bird. Although I hadn't noticed
such behavior with their predecessors, Rosie and Pixie,
they didn't have another hummingbird to be aggressive
toward. For weeks, Red was "feeling her oats." She thought
she was hot stuff, chasing everyone for the sheer pleasure
of it—but I never thought Crystal had it in her.

In late April, Crystal molted those old, juvenile outer
wing feathers. When the molt began, her personality
changed as well. No longer the opportunist, Crystal also
began to go on safari for fruit flies, whiteflies, and spiders
—and she finally began chasing Red around quite a bit.
Crystal was slightly behind Red in both her physical and
behavioral changes. From the time she arrived in Novem-

ber, she allowed herself to be dominated first by K-T and later by Red. But that all turned upside down in late April. What really amazed me about Red's reign as Queen Bully is that she immediately relinquished that position the instant Crystal began to flex a little of her own muscle.

ANOTHER HARROWING EXPERIENCE FOR K-T

K-T's flying abilities had diminished as a result of his compressed molt, and occasionally he had to make a large loop around the sunroom to help generate some lift. At times he didn't make it and would land on a low branch and start again in an attempt to achieve his goal. Under the circumstances, it was incumbent upon me to monitor him frequently, and I did.

One evening I checked when I removed feeders from the room for the night and then, as it was still dusky outside, I checked again a few minutes later just to make sure they were all in a sound sleeping place. But that time there was no K-T. I looked on all the different branches and places where he had slept at other times, but still no K-T. I looked on the floor and at the flowerpot rims. Then I looked at the new waterfall. In the very dim light I noticed something floating in the water at the bottom—as a result of the movement of the water, it was bobbing up and down. It looked as though it might be a leaf but I scooped it out anyway. It was K-T.

I have no idea how he got there. The waterfall was not directly under where he had been roosting when I checked

him the first time. It was dusky and he ordinarily would
not have moved under such lighting conditions—not voluntarily, anyway. Perhaps he had lost his balance and
attempted to lift but couldn't generate the altitude. He was
wet, his eyes were closed, and he made no noise when I
lifted him—perhaps he had tired trying to free himself. I
immediately sucked his beak and nostrils in case any water
had gotten in. Then I held him upside down and rubbed
him. Finally he cried—a sound we humans rarely hear. I
then dried him off and placed him in a basket, at least for
overnight. He didn't like that one bit, and I was treated to
a barrage of chips and chatters, and his tirade continued
on and off for several minutes. No, he didn't like it at all,
but he would stay there for the next day, too, while I monitored him. He appeared to be just fine and so I released
him back to the sunroom. Everything had happened so
quickly the night before that I couldn't remember whether
his head was wet or not. All I knew was that K-T had thus
far been leading a charmed life. How many times can this
bird's life be saved? Soon he'd be on his own and I hoped
that he would stay out of trouble.

And what do you suppose K-T wanted to do first when
released back to the sunroom? Why take a bath, of course!
Obviously his life was not ruled by fear. "Didn't you have
enough water the other day?" was all I could say when he
inspected his gardenia leaves for bathing water. I knew
that I'd breathe a sigh of relief once those feathers were
completely grown in. As a precaution—and one which

shall remain permanent—I covered the bottom of the waterfall with some screening so no one else would ever fall into the water. And I "bird-proofed" the old waterfall as well by adding rocks to keep the water level up with less volume and then covering the entire bottom with some soft screening. After that, the girls placed a moratorium on its use. Neither would use it the following day—it was different. But the ban only lasted one day.

Regardless of how K-T wound up in that water, I was sure that the bottom line was his wings. He crashed into that glass and couldn't keep his balance; he almost drowned in the waterfall. I didn't want any more problems. So a few days later, I decided to place K-T back in the halfway house until his wings were up to snuff. He didn't like it at first, but he adjusted. The girls were just about ready to leave, but K-T wasn't. I'd keep him there until they left and then he could have the sunroom back and stay for as long afterward as need be.

FROM HUMMINGBIRDS
IN MY HOUSE TO
HUMMINGBIRDS IN MY GARDEN

Wondering when to release the western birds continued to bring me much consternation. The window of opportunity is small for the rufous, as they must be back on territory in time to produce offspring and then return either here or to more southerly wintering grounds before the snow flies again over the Rockies—frequently as early as August. Late March to early April is probably the ideal time to release; that would allow ample time for travel while keeping nesting duties within a traditional time frame. Northeast weather is not cooperative at that time of year, however, and April frequently gives up the most violent weather as arctic and tropical air battle to take control of the country east of the Rockies. The last of winter's cold is frequently well entrenched over the Northeast at that time.

As far as food availability—nectar and insects—is concerned, late April to early May seems to be the most appropriate time for release here in the Hudson Valley. But the best time here may find winter conditions still in existence over the Rockies, where they experience snow, reliably, well into May. The hummers must cross these mountains to get to their breeding areas. That they are a naturally hardier species is without doubt, but one must consider that migrating up the coast early in spring and down the Rockies in late summer is an advantage to the rufous that they can't experience when they winter in the Northeast. Their hardiness, coupled with that milder coastal climate, allows for an earlier spring return to the breeding ground from traditional wintering areas. Since temperatures become more amenable from south to north, birds from Southeast wintering areas probably cross peaks and summits of the Rockies at more southerly latitudes, under more benign conditions. Perhaps they may even make their way through West Coast mountain passes and canyons and then take a "normal" route northward. Whichever way they go, many have successfully returned to the Southeast during subsequent winters, so it is working for them.

There is no such thing around here as a tailwind from the southeast. It seems that whenever breezes come in off the ocean, they invariably carry it with them or wrap around a low pressure system moving up the East Coast and give us the dreaded Nor'easter. In late April there were heavy storms in the East, snow in Wisconsin and Iowa, some snow at the higher elevations of the Rockies—fast-moving systems coming out of Canada and traveling from west to east across the Plains and up into the Northeast, exactly opposite the direction the girls might take. Having the wind at their backs doesn't seem to be possible at these latitudes, but having them fly against the wind can be avoided by releasing them during a calm period. There is no way to assure clear sailing for such an extended voyage over such a long distance, but I wanted them to have at least a two- or three-day forecast of pleasant weather. It simply does not get any easier, but they had places to go and things to do.

RESUMING HUMMINGBIRD LIFE

My, my, how my life has changed. I remember when I'd rejoice at the arrival of spring—the robins, the tulips, even mud as the spring thaw would begin. I'd see signs as early as February—the cardinal's song, lengthening days, crocus breaking through the ground here and there by month's end—when there was no snow cover. But the greening of the earth that had always brought such joy to my heart now means something entirely different. When I see these signs, it reminds me that soon the end of a wonderful winter with my hummingbird friends will arrive. Of course, the end for me means new beginnings for them, with places to go and things to do as they resume hummingbird life.

As our time together drew to a close, I became sadder and sadder at the prospect of never seeing them again. They had brought so much joy—and laughter—to my winter, and I had become so attached. How would I ever bring myself to part with my little K-T? It certainly doesn't get any easier. The sunroom seems to be such a safe haven for hummingbirds during a long, cold winter—an eternal spring with an abundance of everything they need, a hummingbird heaven. But when spring arrives and conditions outdoors change, the sunroom suddenly seems too small for a hummingbird able to travel the entire length of the

Crystal retired to the bougainvillea branch

garden in the wink of an eye. And when what is available outside rivals or surpasses what is offered inside, the time is right.

On their last evening here, the girls made me laugh. It seemed their entire stay could be reduced to two or three minutes of interaction between Crystal and Red. Crystal retired as usual to her bougainvillea branch, but I had to get in there before they went to sleep to get the feeder from behind the honeysuckle. I'd never be able to reach it once she was tucked in—Red was on the *Nicotiana* branch about eight or ten inches away. I disturbed Crystal and she moved to the north side of the room. She returned to the bougainvillea a few minutes later, but while she was gone, Red gave her branch the eye and was just about to land on it when Crystal spied her and sailed over and landed on it first, before Red could take it for herself. No matter how many changes they had gone through, each still wanted what the other had.

That last night was the hardest for me. I watched as they finally settled in on their respective branches, waiting for darkness and sleep. They were so comfortable here. They knew where everything was located and life was easy, the weather great. I felt so sad. *Where will they be this time tomorrow?* I hoped together. I felt that uneasiness in my stomach as they watched me move feeders, and our eyes met.

FIRST, THE GIRLS—I opened one of the east windows to the north of the light. Red was the first to leave. It took her ten to fifteen minutes to realize that there was no longer a barrier there. Once she did, she just left. Crystal took considerably longer; she didn't even look at the window. But finally, she too noticed it and left.

Red flew northeast, but I lost sight of her almost immediately as I was still in the sunroom. Crystal stayed close for about fifteen or twenty minutes, catching insects and sitting here and there, high and low. She didn't try any feeders, but she stopped at a flower here and a flower there. Primarily, however, she was just flying in unbounded freedom, rejoicing. Such a freedom hadn't been available to her in months. It was almost as though she danced with delight as she flitted first from one place then to the next. Although she appeared to be dancing, she was actually hunting—she had developed that insatiable desire for protein since she began her molt, and this represented a new and abundant supply.

Finally Crystal moved to an area of old honeysuckle and lilac branches and approached and charged a hummingbird that had been sitting there—almost as though she were poking or jabbing it—then the two of them flew off. I'm quite sure it was Red, and I hoped they would travel together—that the incident was not just an ordinary hummingbird chase. I didn't see any more of them and by day's end I figured the book was closed on Crystal and Red. *Where were they? How far along had they gotten? Where were they sleeping? Were they together?* I hoped so.

There is no reason why they might not travel together. It is variously and repeatedly reported that hummingbirds migrate alone, even during their maiden migration. While I don't question the accuracy of such reports, I don't feel that this is set in stone, it's not *always* the case. I've seen rubythroats depart together on more than one occasion. I remember one year and one particular young pair that had spent a great deal of time in the garden, constantly chasing one another up and down and around and around the spruce tree trunk. On the morning of September 30, they appeared in the yard as usual, stopping to visit flowers in between chasing one another. Then suddenly they were quite high in the air, flying around one another, intertwining in a figure-eight pattern. They flew higher and higher, gaining an altitude that had not been noticed previously, and then they took off together, high in the sky and straight in a southerly direction. They hadn't been seen to go so far and in such a direction prior to that, and I was surprised at how far aloft they were. They kept going and I watched until they became tiny specks on the horizon. It was an interesting but strangely sad sight; and I've seen other, similar departures. And what about rufous sightings? Why would a pair of "off-course" rufous arrive together a couple of thousand miles out of range, such as the pair that appeared at Wave Hill in Riverdale? They *must* have been flying together.

About 5:45 the next morning, while outside to feed the birds, I approached the viburnum to enjoy its incomparable fragrance. I thought I heard a soft, but distinctive, *t-chip*. "I guess everything will sound like a rufous now," I thought.

Then I noticed a hummingbird at the apple blossom and I heard it again—*t-chip t-chip t-chip*. That *was* a rufous, it is unmistakable. I got closer to get a better look and saw the flash of her tail. It had to be one of the girls, but which one? I got closer still, and she moved to a bleeding heart and then over to a large flowering quince, visited a couple of its flowers, and then sat and watched a rubythroat already flitting around from flower to flower in the shrub. It was Crystal! I couldn't believe it. I hadn't seen her at all the day before after she sailed up to that other hummer and then took off with it. She sat there just looking at me. I wondered if she knew who I was. She wasn't the skittish bird Rosie had been while she was in my garden and allowed me to approach within a few feet. I was so excited and immediately conjured up visions of hybrid hummers —and why not? I've learned that they are so full of sur- prises—mostly delightful—that nothing should be ruled out. More NektarPlus was made and the door and window opened again in case Crystal wanted to come home. She spent most of the day at the quince, either drinking from its flowers or sitting on its branches.

Crystal surprised me by remaining in the garden after having been released. I had become accustomed to imme- diate—or almost immediate—departures. I think what surprised me even more is that she didn't take over any feeders. Instead she claimed the flowering quince, perhaps eight feet high with at least an equal spread and thousands of flowers. She'd sit comfortably on one of its myriad

branches somewhere at the lower center of the shrub, surrounded by a staggering number of beautiful, apple blossom–colored flowers. This was something she hadn't
experienced for a long time. There were flowers in the
sunroom, but it was never like this—they were all around
her. She shared the bush with scores of bees from large to
small, but paid little attention to them except to charge at
one every once in a while.

I wondered if she would fatten up and move on in a couple of days—or after the quince finished flowering. I wondered if she'd stay and perhaps claim something else. But
most of all, I wondered and hoped that she would nest here.

Orioles like flowering quince too, and they frequently
visit the shrub to take nectar, and perhaps pollen. I have
watched as many as seven males and two females descend
upon the shrub together for a feast. When a beautiful male
decided to partake of what was now Crystal's quince, she
sailed right over to confront him—the nerve of that bird!
She didn't chase him, but I'm sure she wanted him to leave.
But the next time the oriole had the nerve to visit the
quince flowers, Crystal gave him a piece of her mind, *t-chip
t-chip t-chip*, until he departed. After that, Crystal began
guarding the quince from a little branch. Similarly, when
the fisticuffs of several sparrows' squabbling led them to
the quince, Crystal appeared immediately to see what they
were doing on "her" territory.

Crystal seemed to be settling in and making herself
quite comfortable, and I hoped she would stay. A couple of

Outside, Crystal was surrounded by a staggering number of quince flowers

times a male rubythroat buzzed her—that short, whisking display motion that they commonly make to a potential mate—but she wasn't at all intimidated by it, as the female rubythroats are. She shrugged him off, conveying that "go 'way kid, you bother me" attitude. She couldn't care less about the pendulum display, either—perhaps it's the pitch; maybe it just didn't *sound* right to her.

Finally, a few days after her release, on a lightly rainy morning when nectar production in the quince might not be that copious, Crystal used one of the feeders. And then, before I knew it, she was trying every type of feeder around, even those right near the sunroom, and mastering each one in turn as though she had taken the course, Feeders II—the rufous is such a smart bird.

About midway back on my mother's property line,

which abuts mine to the south, is an old, long, and low outbuilding. On my property, and immediately to the north of the building, are several ten- to twelve-foot lilacs, an immature maple tree perhaps eighteen feet tall, and several densely twiggy bush honeysuckles and several wild raspberry and blackberry bushes—this is the area that Crystal retired to between her lengthy visits to the quince and this is the same area to which Rosie had retired when she was in the garden. It would make an excellent cover area for a nest.

For the first two days after the release of Crystal and Red, while K-T was still confined, I left the door open to the sunroom, but Crystal never showed any interest. But on that first rainy day when the quince was less productive and Crystal had begun using the feeders, she finally approached the door to look in. The screen was then shut as K-T had regained freedom in the room as he became ready to be released. Perhaps Crystal wanted to use the waterfall or chase K-T. Perhaps she saw the familiar NektarPlus feeder or saw some flowers. I wish I had been able to open it so that she might come and go, but I couldn't risk K-T's escaping until I was sure that he was fully able to take care of himself. Soon he would be, and Crystal, of course, would be welcomed—extremely welcomed.

When she couldn't get in, she sat on an old, needleless branch on the spruce and looked around. I called, "Miss Crystal," but she wouldn't even look my way. Then a male

rubythroat instantly appeared and began displaying to her
—back and forth, back and forth. I wonder if her reaction
confused him. She wasn't ready for mating, but she didn't
fly away either. She just looked at him—obviously not
impressed—while he kept it up, displaying from in front
of her, from behind her, from above and below her. Finally,
she darted right up to his face and then took off. I'm sure
Crystal's reaction to his amorous intention was a brand-
new one for him, but that didn't stop him from taking right
off after her. I sat about six feet away, watching this most
unusual picture and kicked myself all the while for not
having my camera with me.

More rain the next day and Crystal was at the sunroom
windows again. While she sat at the large Perky feeder just
outside of the north windows of the sunroom—the same
feeder she had watched so intently from inside—a bluejay
gave a warning call. She instantly spun around and dashed
into the forsythia about twelve to fifteen feet away. I've
seen rubythroats carry on boldly in the face of such dangers on many occasions, but not Crystal. She heeded the
warning just as seriously outside as she had while indoors.
That feeder was her favorite for a while and each time she
used it she'd stop and peer into the sunroom.

Over that night, there was a heavy rain with thunder
and lightning. I remembered how frightened she and Red
had been during a similar thunderstorm and thought about
her all night. I felt very relieved to see her bright and early

the next morning. On sunny days she still spent much time at the quince, but evenings and dismal or rainy days were reserved for the feeders.

I saw her frequently that day, but there was no indication that she was working on building a nest. If she were to stay longer than two weeks, I'd feel hopeful that she would. By the end of the day we had another severe thunderstorm as a cold front passed through. Once it passed and conditions calmed, Crystal made an appearance and drank from the feeders right along with all the others. She certainly fit right in. The next day was markedly colder than it had thus far been, and Crystal moved to the area under the spruce tree, designated it her territory, and "guarded" this spot. That was the most sheltered feeder spot in the garden and it was close to the sunroom door. She spent much time near the feeders among the spruce branches, but occasionally she'd leave to chase a rubythroat.

By Day 7, Crystal had taken over the spruce tree and I was privileged to witness the evolution of her territory. The tree has thousands of twigs and branchlets hidden from view where a highly territorial and enterprising hummingbird can sit unnoticed while guarding her possession. The spruce became Crystal's headquarters. From there she was a one-girl army, chasing all who would *dare* to use any feeder in its vicinity. If another hummer entered her territory, she warned it first with her *tchu-tchu-tchu*. If that wasn't effective, she'd leave her perch and chase the bird.

Usually she would sit somewhere at the lower portion

The spruce became Crystal's headquarters

of the tree, but when there were intruders to chase, she frequently moved to the upper portion. It was all very sneaky on her part. The others entered her web with much trepidation and would then relax when she wasn't seen. That's when she would descend. I believe she was attempting to scare the birds into not coming back. But I didn't want to watch her guard that tree, I wanted to see her bring some nesting material to it and start a nest.

While outside, I watched a male rubythroat sit on the clothesline near the spruce, and deep within its branches I could hear that unmistakeable music to my ears, *chu-tchip chu-tchip tchu-tchu-tchu.* Ignoring her warning, the male left the line and moved to a feeder hanging from a spruce branch. In a nanosecond, he was out and flying off. I wonder why? What part do you suppose Crystal played in that little scenario? Now it was Crystal's turn to be a tyrant. She didn't go out looking for trouble, but heaven help anybody who invaded her space.

I'm not really sure I know what its appeal is, but the spruce tree has consistently been a hot spot for humming-birds. There are feeders hanging on some of the lower branches, but there are feeders in other out-of-the-way places on my property as well. Yet they all seem to find it irresistible. Immatures chase one another around and around its trunk, spiraling up and down the tree. Each year there is at least one male rubythroat that constantly hides in it or the adjacent lathhouse, just waiting to launch an ambush. One spring, and for a very short time, the return-ing females held it from the males as a segregated area. And as many others before her had, Crystal found the spruce to her liking. When cold and rain put the kibosh on the quince, Crystal branched out to the feeders and ulti-mately settled on the ones under the spruce. By and by, the spruce became her territory and she defended it vigorously. She sat here and there, watching all sides. She could easily see out, but the hummers on the outside didn't have even a smidgeon of the advantage she had. The branches close to the trunk are bare and needles are clustered toward the source of light—the outside. She would move from side to side, looking out from behind the needles. From this little fortress, Crystal put the run on anyone who dared to enter the territory she had mapped out for herself.

Over the years I've discovered that the female rubythroats tend to prefer the quiet seclusion of the lathhouse. They like to slip in and have a drink in between nesting duties, without being bothered by amorous or combative males. A Droll Yankee Happy-8 feeder takes center stage in the lathhouse to accommodate them. Until juveniles start to appear in early July, the lathhouse is out of the war zone. There are sunny spots, shady spots, fuchsias and other flowers, and hundreds of places for a hummer to sit and take a break. Crystal expanded her territory and claimed the lathhouse as well as the spruce tree. With this new acquisition, she now had control of four feeders. But I could see her either in the lathhouse or tucked away on an obscure spruce branch, and her behavior mirrored that of the autumn rubythroat lazily sitting around and getting fat, just waiting until that increasing weight reaches a certain point, and that "get going" bell rings. Her ever-burgeoning territory was now extended to include the adjacent lath-house. Yesterday the spruce tree, today the lathhouse, tomorrow the world! It kept her busy, especially during cold spells when many hummingbirds used the feeders.

There was a tremendous amount of activity in the gar-den, and right in the middle of it was one tough little gal who managed to keep them all away from her stuff. Crystal had been so docile for most of the winter that I didn't think she had it in her.

A brazen male sailed up and entered Crystal's fortress. *Tzeept* and then he hightailed it out faster than he had gone in. A couple of *chip*'s after he left and Crystal settled down again to await the next intruder. She'd never get a boyfriend acting that way. If the other hummers drank from the feeders on the periphery of her "territory," she wouldn't bother them, so her tyranny was not automatically directed at any hummingbird that she saw, only those that entered the space she had mapped out for herself. Unfortunately for Crystal, day after day of cold and/or rainy weather kept the fifteen to twenty hummingbirds that were launching their nesting season from this garden right around the house vying for the feeders or squabbling just for the heck of it. They kept Crystal busy, especially the males.

Crystal was extra aggressive toward male hummingbirds. I might be inclined to wonder if this light camaraderie between Crystal and other female hummingbirds constitutes aberrant behavior, were it not for the fact that Red seemed to have fit the same mold. Even so, there was one hummer who was shown quite a bit of tolerance—a female with no tail feathers. She seemed to react differently toward females in general; she chased them, too, but was quiet and not nearly as aggressive about it. For some reason, however, she allowed the "tailless" female to eat first before she chased her, *if* she did. Frequently she would vocalize and not chase her at all. The tail is obviously an important part of female display, and Crystal may have considered that bird less of a threat since she had none. She was so lenient toward that female, allowing her to enter the lathhouse and use the Happy-8 feeder. Did it remind her of a fledgling? Did she not see any display mechanism and thus not feel threatened? There are so many of their secrets that I would love to know.

After Crystal would chase another hummer from her territory, she would follow it to the outside of the spruce, just far enough to make her point—as if to say "and stay out." A favorite spot to sit while guarding was on one of the little bare twigs of a large branch that hangs over and practically rests on the top of the lathhouse. From this little hideaway she could see it all in absolute secrecy. It would make a wonderful place for a nest—if only she would. By Day 9, when I watched her at a feeder under the spruce, I could see that she had become quite a little butterball and I didn't have to wait for an answer. She was fattening up and would probably migrate back to her breeding territory. Unfortunately, the longer she stayed, the more difficult it would be to complete nesting chores in time to migrate south under suitable weather conditions. I wished her the best whether she stayed or left, but continued to hope for the former.

That afternoon, Crystal started something new. I was sitting on one of the patio chairs just outside the sunroom. Rajah, my fifteen-year-old Abyssinian, was sleeping on the other, and Crystal was under the spruce, in the lathhouse, and here and there. She seemed to be looking for something. She looked all around the sunroom door and window, on the ground, on low twigs, near the back porch light and back on the ground some more. Then she moved in our direction and stopped just above the sleeping Rajah. She lowered herself until she was about six or seven inches above his head. Could she have been looking for nesting materials? The next morning I put out some cat fur (taken from the cat's brush and not the cat).

Day 11 was the first day in many that was not cold and/or rainy. There was less hummingbird activity in general as they took advantage of a pleasant day to map out available flowers or perhaps start building or refurbishing nests. Crystal spent less time under the spruce and when she was there, she spent much time poking around. I hoped, of course, that she was looking for nesting material.

Crystal continued to be less aggressive toward members of her own gender, and especially lenient toward that female with no tail feathers, but began to spend more time away from the spruce in between feedings. Eventually, long leaves of absence were sprinkled with periodic appearances as she spent considerable time away. I hoped that she might be building a nest, but her ever-widening girth told another story. Deep down I knew it was only a matter of time.

From the time I first discovered that Crystal had remained in the garden, I thought that if she crossed that two-week mark, she might stay and nest. That's exactly how long she stayed. On her fifteenth day here, Crystal was at the spruce bright and early. She sat and looked at me while I changed feeders, totally relaxed in my presence. She then had a long drink and disappeared. A little while later I saw her again but that was the last time. I looked for her all day, but I knew she was gone. That evening, a female rubythroat sat and rested at the spruce between sips. It was final. Crystal was gone.

AND FINALLY, K-T—When Crystal and Red were released, the last of K-T's primaries were coming in, his gorget was almost complete, and he was still molting on the face, crown, and back. Everything was coming together for K-T. He was in the sunroom and progressing quite well, but would have to stay with me a bit longer. It would be best to wait until the molt, at least of his primaries, was finished before releasing him.

When Squeak stayed with me, he showed signs of reaching sexual maturity—he buzzed constantly, "stiffening" the feathers on what should have been his gorget to show them off to their best advantage and utmost brilliance —displaying to, and even mounting, little egg-shaped

Everything was coming together for K-T

flower buds. He even became vicious toward them, stabbing them repeatedly each time he passed. Except that he was a little bully with an impudent personality, K-T never showed any masculine behavioral traits. K-T never gave any indication that he was becoming sexually mature—no buzzing nor displaying to the girls. K-T continued to do very well and his flying abilities seemed to be back to normal. Once he was released back to the sunroom, he showed a great deal of interest in the outdoors, flying to the window and back and forth when another male came to drink from the feeder, but he wasn't chomping at the bit to get out and he still was not displaying.

Then, several days before K-T left, a woman called and told me that her cat had captured a female rubythroat at her Virginia bluebells. She was able to get the bird away from the cat but it couldn't fly—could I take her? Enter Chloe.

Chloe was a pretty little bird and extremely friendly. Her wings appeared to be perfectly normal, and I suspected that a few days of "R and R" might be all that she would need. It was so early in the season, it is doubtful that any nesting had begun. She started out in a very small screened cage where she could perch and eat. As she began to regain some of her ability, she would graduate to the capture cage and eventually the sunroom. Then she'd be on her way.

K-T was extremely interested in Chloe and his behavior toward her was much different from the behavior exhibited toward Crystal and Red. This wasn't just another hummingbird competitor; this was a female rubythroat and he knew it. All of a sudden K-T began to display—to Chloe in her cage, to tiny tips of broken branches that just hung by a thread, to flowers; to anything and everything. When he wasn't "buzzing" or flying back and forth above her cage, he sat on a branch just above and closest to it, almost as though he were guarding her. K-T was interested and was now more demonstrative to the other rubythroats that visited the feeder at the north window. He lost all interest in me except when I sprayed his gardenia. K-T had grown up! And finally, after so *many* months and so many experiences that other hummers would never know, K-T was ready to be on his own again.

I opened the north window just near that feeder that he had watched so intently. He was free to leave. After fifteen minutes of flying around the sunroom, he finally flew over to the open window. Instead of leaving right away, he inspected the small thumbtack hole in the window's molding from where the screening had been tacked up. Then he went out the open window to inspect the "other side" of the molding and was just about to fly back inside, but stopped as though thinking twice about it . . . "hey, what am I doing?" He turned around, lifted up over the sunroom, and took the usual rubythroat route. My little K-T was gone.

After a couple of hours, a hummingbird sailed right up, looked at me and proceeded to drink quickly from the NektarPlus feeder and then from the flowers of the

Enter Chloe, a pretty and friendly female

K-T was ready to be on his own again

marmalade plant. It was my precious little K-T. In an instant, another male darted over to confront him. K-T turned to chase the other bird, but this was not like Crystal or Red; this hummingbird was serious. For a second or two, they flew back and forth, each trying to gain an advantageous position to be the chaser. Then K-T turned around to leave, but the other bird was hot on his heels and K-T landed in the *Caragana* shrub instead, spun to a face-down position and stayed there—similar to the way a paper plane might just nosedive. *Oh, no,* I thought as I jumped up and ran to see how he was. He wasn't stuck, he was just holding on that way—possibly a deliberately inferior position so the other bird wouldn't hurt him. And as I approached, he left, again with the other bird in hot pursuit. *Will there be no end to the trouble that bird gets himself into?*

A while later, a male was sitting on a catalpa branch with his back to me. I needed to see that face and those pin feather sheaths to know if it was K-T. Then, with the aid of my binoculars, I could see his beak. It was K-T and I was relieved. Still later, I was sitting behind the sunroom on a patio chair, my feet up, when a hummingbird appeared, flew to within three inches of my legs, and hovered there, looking for a feeder in my hand. It was K-T again. He stayed and drank for a minute and then moved over and sat on a honeysuckle branch just a couple of inches from my toes. I saw no more of K-T after that, and I have to assume that he, too, had places to go and things to do.

I think I will miss him most of all. I am constantly asked,

"Which has been your favorite?" My response has always been that I have no favorites—each and every one takes its turn. But K-T *was* special.

As one repeatedly faces the bittersweet inevitability of releasing these birds, it should become a bit easier, but it doesn't. Yet releasing the birds is what makes the whole thing a success. You think about it, plan it, and work up the nerve—but saying goodbye still leaves a lump in the throat. In the beginning I had hummingbirds in my garden all summer, and in the fall I wished they might stay in my house. Now I have them in my house all winter, and when spring comes I wish they might stay in my garden. I suppose everything has come full circle.

One day any one of these birds or one of the others before them will sail into another person's garden to visit some flowers or use a feeder. And that person will stop whatever he or she is doing to admire the beautiful hummingbird for as long as it consents to stay—without ever having a clue about what adventures or secrets that tiny mite has under its wing.

So if you see a little male ruby-throated hummingbird with a slight indentation on the left side of his head just above the eye, a slightly twisted beak, and a tongue that frequently sticks out just a tad, you'll know it's K-T. If you see him, blow him a kiss and let me know.